T5-AVO-042

The New World Fiscal Order

C. EUGENE STEUERLE and
MASAHIRO KAWAI
Editors

THE NEW WORLD FISCAL ORDER

Implications for Industrialized Nations

THE URBAN INSTITUTE PRESS
Washington, D.C.

THE URBAN INSTITUTE PRESS
2100 M Street, N.W.
Washington, D.C. 20037

Library of Congress Cataloging in Publication Data

The New World Fiscal Order: Implications for Industrialized Nations / C. Eugene Steuerle and Masahiro Kawai, editors.

1. Fiscal policy. 2. Competition, international. 3. International economic relations 4. Aged— economic conditions. 5. Economic history— . 1900– . I. Steuerle, C. Eugene, 1946– . II. Kawai, Masahiro, 1947– .

HJ141.N48 1996 95-26645
337—dc20 CIP

ISBN 0-87766-641-5 (paper, alk. paper)
ISBN 0-87766-640-7 (cloth, alk. paper)

Printed in the United States of America.

Distributed in North America by
University Press of America
4720 Boston Way
Lanham, MD 20706

THE URBAN INSTITUTE is a nonprofit policy research and educational organization established in Washington, D.C., in 1968. Its staff investigates the social and economic problems confronting the nation and public and private means to alleviate them. The Institute disseminates significant findings of its research through the publications program of its Press. The goals of the Institute are to sharpen thinking about societal problems and efforts to solve them, improve government decisions and performance, and increase citizen awareness of important policy choices.

Through work that ranges from broad conceptual studies to administrative and technical assistance, Institute researchers contribute to the stock of knowledge available to guide decision making in the public interest.

Conclusions or opinions expressed in Institute publications are those of the authors and do not necessarily reflect the views of staff members, officers or trustees of the Institute, advisory groups, or any organizations that provide financial support to the Institute.

ACKNOWLEDGMENTS

We would like to thank the many individuals from around the world who contributed to examining important fiscal conditions facing industrial countries in the modern era. Many served with important national and international institutions, universities, and research organizations, and were able to provide both a depth of wisdom and a breadth of knowledge that derived from many different, although related, perspectives. The project itself was coordinated by both the Urban Institute in Washington, D.C. and the Institute for Social Science at the University of Tokyo. Two conferences were held: the first in Washington, D.C., and the second in Tokyo with the generous cosponsorship of the Japanese Ministry of Finance. Many individuals in all these institutions helped in the planning of the conferences that led up to this volume; to them we are deeply indebted. Special thanks go to Kyna Rubin, who not only edited the volume flawlessly, but helped handle many other details of the project. Ann Guillot worked tirelessly, as always, to ensure that everything was coordinated to perfection, while Makiko Ueno was always available to provide invaluable counsel. Deborah Chien and Gordon Mermin provided invaluable research assistance.

Much of the funding for the project was provided through the generosity of the Center for Global Partnership of the Japan Foundation, while publication was supported by the Suntory Foundation.

Urban Institute
Washington, D.C.

Institute for Social Science
University of Tokyo

CONTENTS

PART THREE FISCAL POLICY AND WORLDWIDE SAVING AND INVESTMENT

Tables

Figures

FOREWORD

One of the disturbing trends to be observed as we end the 20th century is the increasing loss of fiscal control among the industrial democracies of the world. Country after country is finding its spending obligations outstripping its revenues, the interest payments on its national debt further constraining spending choices, and its public dissaving outdistancing private saving. Economic growth depends on the rate of investment and investment is strongly influenced by government budgets. Although particular countries may be able to borrow from abroad to finance their savings shortfalls in the short run, for the world as a whole investment cannot exceed saving. With the internationalization of financial markets, these fiscal problems, if unresolved, will inevitably slow the overall rate of economic growth and threaten the increases in living standards that we have come to expect.

In the belief that an international perspective could provide insight into the causes of and potential solutions to these fiscal problems, the Urban Institute solicited the wisdom of a wide range of budget, treasury, and financial officials; analysts from international organizations; and academics from the United States, Europe, and Japan. The general picture that emerges, which is captured in this book, shows a consistency across countries that is remarkable given the wide range of cultural contexts represented.

Populations in the industrial world are aging, increasing the number of dependents per worker, and slanting public expenditures away from investment expenditures on the young towards essentially consumption expenditures on the elderly. This spending burden is exacerbated by past legislative promises that have resulted in predetermined spending commitments so large that at best they leave little to meet new needs and at worst even exceed future revenue growth.

Population aging, obviously, is largely an external force. But the fiscal weakness that currently afflicts most industrial democracies is largely of their own making—reflecting their unwillingness to recognize the implications of past commitments, finance present commitments, or save to fund future commitments. These problems are solvable if the political will is there. But, as the volume editors put it, "the longer the industrial world fails to grapple fully with them—indeed, to recognize the commonality of the problems—the longer are its members likely to witness slower rates of growth into the future, and the less likely are they to find themselves capable of meeting new and pressing needs."

It is my hope that this book can stimulate further thinking about and understanding of these issues, and contribute to the ability and resolve of industrial democracies to learn from the insights and the experience of each other.

William Gorham
President

Chapter One

THE NEW WORLD FISCAL ORDER: INTRODUCTION

C. Eugene Steuerle and Masahiro Kawai

Despite widespread and significant deficit reduction legislation in recent years, the nations of the industrial world have not gained control over their long-term fiscal policy. The papers and comments in this volume concentrate on three common and powerful forces that shape this fiscal order: (1) the aging of populations, (2) the determination of current spending based on decisions made in the past—what we call the "yoke of prior commitments"—rather than on a current assessment of needs, and (3) unsustainable rates of growth in industrial country government debt, which eat up a substantial portion of worldwide net saving.

The combined influence of these three factors has led to the loss of control over fiscal policy. Most industrial countries are finding that their spending obligations arise more and more from the past, that they are not raising the revenues to meet those obligations, and that interest payments on government debt further exacerbate their future budget problems. A commonly recognized indicator of this loss of control is the deficit, but it is vital to understand that the deficit is a symptom, not a cause. It is the residual from all the other spending and tax decisions. A government cannot regain fiscal control simply by enacting continual deficit reduction efforts, nor does good expenditure and tax policy come into being when the focus remains largely on this residual.

Governments that do not exercise adequate control over fiscal policy soon find themselves incapable of generating the resources necessary to meet new needs or emergencies, either domestic or international. And therein lies perhaps the greatest long-term threat to the finance ministries and treasury departments around the globe. If the governments of the industrial world seem to be at bay, these common fiscal problems, more than almost any other factors, have put them there.

Past deficit reduction efforts have not been sufficient to override the usurpation of private saving through large public dissaving. Even recent deficit reduction efforts, such as in the United States in 1995, do not deal with most longer term pressures, in particular, the very large demographic pressures of an aging population. Without greater attention, the common fiscal problems addressed in this volume will likely slow the rate of economic growth of all or almost all industrialized countries. The rate of growth, after all, is dependent in no small part both on investment in physical and human capital and on supplying current wants in an efficient manner. Unfortunately, most industrialized countries have been decreasing the supply of saving that might be available for physical capital investment, increasingly allocating expenditures more and more to support consumption and leisure, and adopting budgets that are less and less based on current assessments of needs.

In the new international order these problems are shared, even by countries that may view their current deficits as temporarily under control. Each country's domestic fiscal policy cannot help but have ramifications extending far beyond its own geographic borders. When a country borrows today, it often draws upon saving generated in other countries. Whatever the openness of each individual country and its ability, at least temporarily, to save more or less than it invests, the world itself is a closed market where total saving is equal to total investment.

The internationalization of financial markets is not the only reason these problems are shared. Often countries march in some unison because they borrow ideas from one another and because they face similar shocks and problems. If nations have moved together to aggravate their fiscal problems, however, the flip side is that they could easily begin to move together to achieve some solution.

This reflection led us to conclude that fiscal policy required examination from an international perspective. This project, as shown in the chapters and comments in this volume, was fortunate enough to benefit from the input of a wide range of top budget, treasury, and finance officials, analysts from international organizations, and academics from around the globe. The fiscal issues identified here offer to policymakers of different countries a way to seek mutually beneficial cooperation, at a time when other common ground may be elusive. It is our hope that the common, long-term fiscal issues outlined in this book receive the prominence they deserve in discussions among the leaders of industrialized countries.

Before presenting the major conclusions of the contributing authors, we should also state what this volume does not do. It does not deal with fiscal policy as a tool of short-run countercyclical policy, that is, whether taxes might be lowered in a recession and raised in an upturn. It maintains a common focus on major, long-term fiscal problems but does not seek—or obtain—unity of authors about the most effective policy solutions. The deliberate concentration on major and common fiscal problems also means that the reader should not expect definitive discussion of certain debates in the economic theory literature, such as the relationship between interest rates and deficits. It is also clear from the contributions to this volume that long-term projections of the fiscal impacts implied by current law—and the extent to which there is a perceived moral commitment to future beneficiaries because of current law—are much more important to the policy debate in some countries than in others. For this reason alone, the contributors differ in how they couch their discussions of the future.

Despite such differences, what remains remarkable is that so many countries with very different cultural bases are experiencing such similar problems, often deriving from similar social contracts, and that so many authors from different backgrounds reach such similar conclusions.

THE FISCAL IMPLICATIONS OF CHANGING DEMOGRAPHICS

Increased life expectancies in developed nations have brought about a significant rise in the number of elderly relative to workers. People also have tended to retire increasingly earlier, defining themselves as "elderly" at younger ages. The combined effect has been large increases in the portion of people's lives spent outside the workforce. Industrialized countries face the additional problem caused by past declines in birth rates. Many countries experienced a temporary baby boom in the years immediately following World War II, followed by a drop in birth rates. In many cases, birth rates fell to levels well below those necessary to replace the population from one generation to the next, while some countries had an accompanying decline in population due to net emigration. Now, years later, many industrial countries face a significant rise in the ratio of elderly to total population, while others confront further dramatic increases just around the corner.

The drop in the number of younger dependents per worker somewhat offsets the total burden on working-age populations, but this offers little consolation. Spending on children is much more likely to involve private rather than public funds. Therefore, the impact of the elderly on fiscal budgets is not really balanced by a decline in spending on children. Moreover, spending on children is more likely to involve an investment in the future, especially when education is involved, while spending on the elderly usually involves straightforward transfers for consumption. The net shift away from spending on investment toward spending on current consumption itself is likely to contribute to a slowdown in economic growth.

In the United States, population aging has been delayed slightly relative to many European countries and Japan (Steuerle, chapter 2). U.S. data, nonetheless, are among the most comprehensive anywhere for projecting long-term trends. In the United States, as elsewhere, the costs of supporting the elderly and near elderly have been growing continually for decades. People live longer and retire earlier. For a couple retiring at age 62 in 1995, annuity payments can be expected on average to last for 25 years, until both spouses have died.

A significant decline in U.S. birth rates in the mid-1960s followed a baby boom expansion of the early post-World War II period. The baby boomers themselves will begin to retire on Social Security, at least under current law, as early as 2008. As a result, by the year 2030 the number of beneficiaries per every 100 workers is expected to rise to 43 from 27 in 1990. Other demographic trends offer little reprieve: Social Security has already garnered significant increases in taxes, with little change in benefits, due to the influx of women into the workplace. That is, the new benefits women earned through their tax payments mainly offset the spousal benefits they had already been promised. And despite a relatively liberal policy toward immigration, even large changes in immigration rates in the United States would moderate the forthcoming fiscal demands only slightly. Under current law, higher economic growth would translate into higher retirement and health benefits, thus offering little relief for the Social Security trust funds, the deficit, and the nation's ability to devote government budgets to other important needs.

Under current law, Social Security cash benefits and Medicare expenses are expected to rise from about 6.8 percent of GDP today to 13.5 percent by 2030. If tax rates were to remain constant, spending on all other federal government functions—defense, federal aid to education, the environment, interest on the debt, and so forth—would have to be squeezed from 15.4 percent of GDP in 1994 to 5.5 percent of GDP in 2030 to produce a balanced budget. This squeeze means that the federal government would be helping finance retirement, health, disability, and little else. These categories already rose from less than 10 percent of the total federal budget in 1950 to almost half by 1994. And efforts in 1995 to slow the growth of Medicare spending, while possibly moderating these numbers, do not even begin to confront the demographic changes.

Obviously policy adjustments are required. Steuerle favors increasing and indexing the age of retirement, further restricting growth in health care costs, expanding the Social Security tax base, and slowing down the rate of growth of cash benefits. None of these suggestions is without controversy. Starting soon is important, for it allows gradual adjustment to changes such as an increase in the retirement age and/or slower rates of growth in benefits. Unfortunately, the near term stability of the retiree-to-worker ratio hides the problem in the budget accounts, which do not take into consideration future liabilities. This tends to prevent American policymakers from taking adequate action, even though the potent demographic challenge looms right around the corner.

Naohiro Yashiro (chapter 3) notes in Japan that fertility rates have fallen so much that the working-age population is now beginning to decline in absolute size. Some modest reprieve might be provided by expanded female labor force participation. Perhaps of more interest to countries that have already benefited from increased numbers of working women is the fact that the labor force participation of Japan's older workers, a rate that is already higher than that of most other countries, has begun to rise. Between 1987 and 1993, for example, the share of working-age males age 65 and above rose from 35.6 to 37.9 percent.

After considering a number of different economic forces, Yashiro predicts a decline in household saving in Japan, in part because the elderly are more likely than younger cohorts to be dissavers. This, in turn, would lead to a decline in capital investment. It is possible, he suggests, that labor-saving technology may slow down the rate of decline in investment, which, in turn, could reduce Japan's external current account balances and net investment abroad. But this, of course, is speculative. Because Japan's elderly ratios are only now beginning to rise at a rapid pace, he finds that Japan's size of government may be understated by looking only at current spending. Based on current policies, Japan's expenditures could rise significantly as its elderly ratio in the near future moves ahead of that of other OECD countries. Public pension premiums would need to double between now and 2020 under current promises, and various increases in the statutory age of pension eligibility have been debated or enacted recently. Yashiro also notes that though Japan has managed to keep health expenses as a percentage of national income relatively constant in recent years, the elderly's share of those expenses has been rising.

This implies, of course, that declining percentages of national income are spent on the health care of the nonelderly.

Japan offers other interesting lessons for fellow OECD countries. Traditional family altruism has helped greatly to meet the needs of the elderly: approximately 57 percent of the elderly live with relatives, compared to only 7 percent of the elderly in the United States. Elderly people, however, are increasingly unlikely to be living with their children, so Japan may be less able to depend on this source of support in the future. At the same time, the elderly may also begin to make fewer intergenerational transfers than in the past, for instance, if they turn toward "reverse" mortgages rather than leave housing wealth to children. Yashiro sees much hope in the willingness of older Japanese to work later in life, although he also anticipates that increases in consumption taxes and other premium charges will be necessary to make retirees, as well as current workers, pay for a greater share of the benefits they will eventually receive.

Peter Scherer (chapter 4) offers a cross-country perspective on the problems of aging populations. His data reflect not what current policies promise for the future (as does Steuerle's discussion), but how differences in elderly ratios across countries have already played out in terms of public sector activity. Scherer's reference to the "myth" of the demographic imperative is well designed to call attention to the point he wants to emphasize—namely that much of the pressure brought about by population aging is the result of deliberate public choices and the way they play out in fiscal impacts. This, of course, is a major reason for the book and the conference on which it is based—to trace through the impacts of current law in plenty of time to be able to change policy directions carefully, gradually, and in full understanding of the implications of change.

Across 21 countries examined, he finds that each percentage point increase in the elderly population is associated with an increase in public social protection transfers of slightly more than two percentage points of GDP. Transfers to the elderly account for about half the overall relationship between total transfers and proportion of population that is elderly. Thus, there is still a strong relationship between increases in the elderly and increases in public transfers for social protection. Interestingly, he finds little relationship between health spending and aging by country.

If projections are made solely on the basis of today's cross-country comparisons, the proportion of elderly eventually in OECD countries would increase to the high levels now applying in Sweden, and transfers to the elderly would increase by about 5 percentage points of GDP.

Scherer's point is that, though a considerable sum, even this amount is less than that often obtained by projecting forward current promises and rates of pension expenditure per elderly person.

Scherer finds the threat to fiscal balance not so much in the ability to pay or modify pension and traditional health care benefits for the elderly, as in two related areas. His first concern is with early retirement, which has reduced the size of the labor force able to contribute to the truly elderly. There is, of course, an interactive effect, as the decline has been facilitated by the growing availability of pension wealth, both public and private. Individuals have been able to convert pension saving for later years into support for leisure in earlier years. Public systems, in turn, have been especially generous toward those losing their jobs in their later working years, thus reducing incentives for them to return to the workforce. Echoing in part Steuerle's and Yashiro's conclusions regarding later retirement ages, Scherer finds that a revival in total employment rates would do much to relieve fiscal pressures.

A second area of concern is with the growing demand for support of the elderly in long-term care institutions. These costs are growing rapidly relative to more traditional hospital and doctor care. To a large extent, they are also financed by the working-age population.

THE YOKE OF PRIOR COMMITMENTS

As Scherer notes, many of the projections of future fiscal problems accompanying an aging population are due to mechanical extrapolations of what is required under current law. Unfortunately, when current law places so many requirements on future spending, legislators and voters often feel that they have little control over spending patterns in their countries. In almost all industrialized nations a few decades ago, revenues expanded along with growth in economies, even in the absence of newly legislated tax increases. Democracies then voted on how to spend those new revenues. Today, however, promises made by past legislators predetermine how those revenues will be spent. Often the promises are so large that they exceed future growth in revenues.

These growing promises create not only a problem of government red ink, but an uneven playing field in determining the most important current needs to be met within these democracies. Established growth needs no new legislation. New areas of growth not only require new appropriations, but also require some source of funds—either new revenues or a cutback in other expenditures. Old priorities, therefore, are strongly favored over new ones. As a political matter, legislators and voters find that increases in spending due to prior commitments are sufficient by themselves to create future deficits. Legislative activity then turns to identifying losers, through either increases in taxes or cuts in expenditures, at least away from their previously legislated growth path. This type of legislation represents a formidable political task, especially when the media sensationalize the newly legislated "losers" while ignoring the extent to which past legislation tends to add new "winners" from year to year.

In the 1980s and 1990s, according to Joseph Cordes (chapter 5), American legislators became ever more aware of the limits that confront fiscal policymaking. Before that time, fiscal slack was made possible by both fewer claims on added revenue and a willingness of voters to devote a larger share of national income to public uses when the share was perceived to be low. The decline—often elimination—of fiscal slack has been a major factor behind a growth in deficit spending that has become more permanent or structural. As resistance to deficit financing mounted, pressures increased for budget-neutral financing of new initiatives. The story is not entirely a negative one. Although difficult politically, the removal of fiscal slack had the salutary effect of forcing policymakers to consider more directly serious trade-offs among programs.

Cordes notes three types of expansions of prior commitments, a typology that really applies across all countries: to spend for particular purposes, such as income support programs; to set aside tax revenue for specific purposes; and to index income taxes and spending (to maintain the real tax burden and the real value of benefits). Each of these may tie legislators' hands in different ways.

Budget accounting in the United States reveals the nature of some of these commitments by dividing spending into two large categories, excluding interest on the debt. *Discretionary spending* is determined every year through an appropriation process. *Entitlement and other mandatory spending* involves payments to any person, business, or unit of government that seeks payments and meets criteria set by laws enacted in the past. In the latter case, moreover, legal rights to the payments are often established. In 1965, about 65 percent of U.S. spending was discretionary; by 1993, about 65 percent represented entitlements and interest on the debt. Comparing similar breakdowns elsewhere would be valuable to put the U.S. experience into a wider perspective. Unfortunately, such a breakdown is not available for other countries. However, their increased level of commitment to areas such as retirement and health indicates that similar patterns are likely to apply across the board.

This yoke of prior commitments is expected to become even more burdensome in the United States in future years, in large part because of the interaction between the aging of the population and the large share of entitlements devoted to the elderly. Accordingly, increased attention is being paid to the distribution of burdens across generations. Cordes suggests that possible directions for future policy include reducing the costs of meeting promises currently enacted into the law. He cautions, however, that many changes should be made prospectively—again using the example of increasing the retirement age suggested by many authors in this volume. He also recommends re-examining indexing rules and carefully scrutinizing future obligations that may accompany current legislation. Some of his suggestions seem to have been reflected in the 1995 legislative efforts of the U.S. Congress.

By way of comparison, Toshihiro Ihori (chapter 6) explains that Japan's level of prior commitment is somewhat smaller than those of some other industrial countries, although Japan has also witnessed large increases in debt relative to GDP. By tradition, a strong Ministry of Finance has been an important factor in maintaining more moderate levels of prior commitments.

In the early 1970s, nonetheless, Japan's prior commitments began to increase substantially with the introduction of new social security and welfare programs. By the end of that decade, deficits also began to increase because of slower economic growth and increased spending on public investment—partly in response to the urging of many Western countries that Japan and Germany become "locomotives" for the rest of the world through stimulative fiscal policies.

The Ministry of Finance first responded to rising deficits by trying to adopt a value-added tax (VAT); then it turned to limits on increases in spending for each government ministry and agency. In the early 1980s, an Ad Hoc Council on Administrative Reform (Rincho) recommended reforms to reduce the deficit by trimming spending on public works, restraining social security benefits, and cutting the number of government employees. Spending constraints were eventually followed by tax reforms and the adoption of a VAT in 1989. Indeed, over the 1980s Japan witnessed a reduction in spending as a share of GDP and a rise in the tax share. The latter, however, was a bit misleading: Japan experienced a "bubble economy" at the end of that decade, with significant rates of economic growth and large increases in values of stock and land, both of which generated large tax revenues in the form of corporate, security transaction, and capital gains taxes. The bubble economy then burst in the early 1990s, accompanied by a rapid evaporation of tax revenues and a widening of the budget deficit.

Reflecting Yashiro's comments about the misleading nature of Japan's aging process, Ihori notes that Japan's social security system is soon expected to generate fairly massive income transfers between generations. In his view, one that appears consistent with some recent efforts by the Ministry of Finance, Japan should continue efforts to convert social security more into a funded system (as opposed to a pay-as-you-go system with no real saving), raise consumption taxes while reducing income taxes (to shift tax burdens from the young to the old), and create another Rincho to restrain the level of prior commitments in all programs. At a more controversial level, he also suggests that maintaining a very high bequest tax may actually deter transfers to the young and increase consumption by the old.

Paul Posner and Barbara Bovbjerg (chapter 7) indicate that many lessons about deficit reduction can be learned by examining the experience of different nations. They studied six countries: Canada, Mexico, Australia, Germany, Japan, and the United Kingdom. Although experiences differed in many ways, and success at deficit reduction depended upon time and place, certain common themes emerged, causes of deficits were similar, and methods to control those deficits were often related. The Posner and Bovbjerg discussion confirms yet again that there is often common movement among countries in both their social and fiscal policy.

In all these countries, fiscal deficits of the 1980s were rooted in decisions in the 1960s and 1970s to create and expand public programs based on expectations of future economic growth. The sudden rise of oil prices in the 1970s precipitated recessions and contributed to a slowdown in economic growth. Most governments then undertook deficit reduction during subsequent periods of slow economic growth or recession, despite macroeconomic thought favoring expansionary fiscal policy.

By way of contrast, as the economy improved in these countries, it became much more difficult to maintain fiscal discipline. Indeed, in many nations successful deficit reduction in the early to mid-1980s was followed by relatively lax fiscal discipline during later economic upswings. When recessions hit in the 1990s, these nations found that their fiscal situation had deteriorated considerably once more, this time on a structural, not just cyclical, basis. Thus, this historic round of fiscal discipline provides lessons not simply on the capability for action, but on the consequences of inadequate action.

Some countries reduced deficits through relatively incremental cuts in spending, modification of benefit indexation schemes, and deferral of capital spending. Others resorted to more fundamental reforms, such as privatization of government assets and means testing of some entitlements. Short-term fixes such as shifting political responsibility to states and private entities, as well as reducing capital spending, often only temporarily deferred spending pressures. Few governments reduced deficits through direct legislation of easily identifiable tax increases. Revenues did grow significantly in some cases, however, primarily because laws providing for indexing of income taxes were nonexistent, suspended, or modified so that average tax rates could increase over time.

All governments tried to use some form of spending "limit" or "target" to control aggregate spending. Social spending was constrained through various targets, conversions from grants to loans, and movement away from universality of benefits. Pension plans were adjusted by delaying payment of benefit increases, indexing to prices rather than wages, and applying some limited means testing. Management and budget reforms were often integrated into the process.

An important aspect of the political strategy was to turn fiscal austerity into a seemingly unassailable political virtue. This led to not just bipartisan cooperation but actual competition over how to achieve the common goal. Governments were sometimes able to convince the public that deficit reduction would bring gains in lower inflation and improved prospects for financing future commitments. A variety of strategies was used to defer or obscure the political pain of deficit reduction, including gradual implementation of cutbacks and calls for equal sacrifice from all groups. While large deficits returned in many cases by the 1990s, the lessons from the past still offer guidance on strategies that work, and on the limitations of changes that are not more permanent or structural in nature.

FISCAL POLICY AND WORLDWIDE SAVING AND INVESTMENT

When a government runs a fiscal deficit, it must borrow in capital markets that today are international in scope. In a world economy, therefore, public borrowing takes up a share of global saving. While each country may be relatively open and may invest more or less than it saves, this is not true for the world economy. In that wider universe, saving must equal investment, so that fiscal deficits may decrease worldwide investment even if an individual country does not reduce its investment as much as its saving. Deficits may also have an impact on interest rates, both in the country of deficit and on a worldwide basis.

Masahiro Kawai and Yusuke Onitsuka (chapter 8) examine data from 19 OECD countries for the period 1980 to 1993 to ascertain key relationships between various fiscal and macroeconomic variables. Despite international markets, they find that net national saving and net capital formation are closely related within each country. They also find a negative correlation between the excess of saving over investment in the government sector, i.e., the fiscal balance, and a similar measure in the private sector. There is ongoing controversy in the economic literature about how this correlation should be interpreted. Regardless of how this debate is resolved, the negative correlation indicates that an increase in one government's deficit tends to be financed partly through reductions in private domestic saving that would otherwise be used for private domestic investment.

Higher growth rates of real GDP are also found by Kawai and Onitsuka to be correlated with smaller government, as measured by current receipts, outlays, or transfers to individuals relative to GDP. The rate of inflation and the rate of unemployment also tend to be lower when deficits are lower. Real interest rates within each country rise slightly with government size, but do not seem to be affected much by deficits per se (however, see our discussion of chapter 10, below, on the effect of *worldwide* deficits on *worldwide* interest rates). Nonetheless, countries with high real interest rates do tend to have low investment and saving.

Kawai and Onitsuka trace changes in government size (as measured by outlays relative to GDP) and deficits in recent decades within the industrial world. While governments have tended to grow, especially in the European OECD nations, there has been no clear tendency for deficits to rise since the mid-1970s—confirming for a broader range of countries the types of patterns noted by Posner and Bovbjerg. Kawai and Onitsuka also confirm Ihori's conclusion that the Ministry of Finance's strong hand helped to keep Japan's deficits somewhat more under control.

Where slower growth occurs in OECD countries, saving rates may be likely to decline. Theoretically, private saving rates could go in either direction when growth rates change, but the Kawai and Onitsuka interpretation of the empirical evidence suggests that a permanent slowdown of real output growth reduces private saving rates, or at least that consumption growth declines more slowly than does a fall in economic growth. Added to this general experience is the impact of an aging population, which simultaneously increases consumption by the population and puts demands on governments that might be met by deficit finance. Interestingly, a shortage of saving relative to investment in the industrial countries has been complemented in recent years by the actions of the newly industrializing economies of East Asia, which have been transferring saving to finance investment in the rest of the world. However, economies in transition need foreign savings for their economic restructuring, reorganization, and development. These factors lead Kawai and Onitsuka to favor trimming unproductive and inefficient government spending and reducing structural deficits, both to promote capital accumulation on a global scale and to enhance prospects for better macroeconomic performance.

Can fiscal deterioration be met by adjustments on the tax side of government ledgers? Estimates of promised growth in expenditures are so large that it is extremely doubtful that tax rates can continually be raised to meet those growing promises. Historical examination of fiscal deterioration also reveals that taxes have tended to rise relative to income among the industrial countries as a whole, but not as fast as expenditures, including the interest necessary to pay for higher levels of public debt. All this implies that revenue increases will not solve the problem, and that expenditures per se must be brought under control.

Suppose, however, that taxes are changed, not to raise revenues but to encourage saving. Might saving incentives cause private saving to rise enough to finance both higher levels of private investment and large public deficits? Mark Robson (chapter 9) reviews a wide range of empirical studies that generally find little evidence that tax incentives for saving actually boost the national saving rate. Even the studies that do find a positive relationship between tax rates and saving find only a very modest link.

When considering tax effects on the *composition* of saving, however, the evidence is striking. Taxes do exert strong influence on portfolio composition. The effect of taxes seems to be stronger on the decision to hold or not hold a particular type of asset than on how much to invest in each particular asset, once held. Robson also notes that pensions and housing assets dominate household portfolios, and that the rates of tax on these assets already are low or, in some cases, negative.

There may be a variety of reasons not treated in this volume to change the taxation of saving, even to reduce that tax to zero. Reducing differentials in taxation of different types of saving, for instance, may promote efficiency. And some tax reforms, such as conversion to a consumption tax, might also be desirable for reasons of simplicity. Robson also notes how international flows of capital affect nations' ability to tax capital income. Nonetheless, the clearest and most direct route to attacking the problem of deficits and government dissaving is to reduce those deficits. Implementing lower or zero rates of tax on capital income will result, at best, in only a modest increase in private saving, and will require that lost revenue be raised from somewhere else, thus increasing other tax distortions. The bottom line is that whatever the potential merit of tax incentives and consumption taxes, these types of changes would not induce a large enough rise in saving to mitigate the effects of fiscal policy inadequately attuned to long-run issues.

Despite widespread concern over deficits, there are few, if any, measures of their combined scope within industrialized countries. Vito Tanzi and Domenico Fanizza (chapter 10) provide perhaps the most complete and up-to-date measures of these fiscal data ever assembled. They use four different measures of deficits: normal deficits, structural deficits (removing the effect of business cycles), inflation-adjusted deficits, and primary deficits (removing interest payments altogether). Each measure is useful for different purposes. Their data confirm what has been suggested for individual countries: that a serious deterioration of the fiscal situation in industrialized nations began to occur in the mid-1970s and continued until the mid-1980s. Improving economies tended to reduce the normal measure of the deficit more than the structural deficit. After 1989, all four measures of fiscal deficits began to deteriorate and, by 1993, the gains made between 1983 and 1989 were lost.

No country seems to have escaped some fiscal deterioration, although some countries did far worse than others. Fiscal virtue was not very popular during the period since 1970. The worst year of inflation-adjusted deficits for both the G–7 and the industrialized countries combined was 1993, and the highest normal deficits occurred in 1975, 1982–1983, and 1993. Gross private saving also declined somewhat from the 1970s to the 1990s, even while the share of that saving absorbed by the general government deficit of the G–7 countries rose considerably in the 1970s and 1980s—reaching its highest level in 1993, when 21 percent of the G–7 countries' total private saving went to finance fiscal deficits. More importantly, the deficit absorbed much larger shares (often 30 percent or more) of *net* private saving. A peak of 46.5 percent was reached in the recession year of 1992 (the most recent data available), although 1993 is likely to have been as bad if not worse.

These high deficits added to debt owed to the public, and debt rose faster than incomes. The debt/GDP ratio was roughly the same in 1970 and 1980 for the G–7 countries, but after that rose from about 42 percent to 71 percent by 1994. Various consequences may result, including a crowding out of both physical and human capital investment, an increase in public spending simply to pay the additional interest costs, a redistribution of income to bondholders (often older individuals who consume more and save less), and an increased threat of potential financial instability. Interest costs in the G–7 countries have risen from 2 percent of GDP in the early 1970s to 5 percent by 1994.

Tanzi and Fanizza also examine a related but more controversial issue in the theoretical and empirical literature—the relationship between real interest rates and fiscal variables. They find that the increase in the worldwide debt/GDP ratio between 1980 and 1993 could have increased worldwide real interest rates by more than 1.5 percentage points. Note that if international capital markets tend to cause real rates of interest to move toward equality across countries, the effect of deficits on interest rates cannot be determined on a country-specific basis, but requires the type of international analysis provided by Tanzi and Fanizza.

TOWARD THE FUTURE

The long-term fiscal problems documented in this volume are primarily structural. Whatever their merits, deficit reduction agreements will always be inadequate as long as they ignore the nature and built-in growth of longer term commitments and the full implications of an aging population. It is worth reminding ourselves, however, that these problems are practically all self-induced and amenable to change through sound fiscal policy. Unlike many problems, fiscal weakness is not a condition that is imposed from without but from within. It reflects the way governments have evolved in recent years, the commitments they have made, and their unwillingness to finance present commitments or to put aside saving to fund future commitments. Longer lives, for instance, are a blessing; only human foibles can turn them into a budgetary curse.

That these fiscal problems are solvable and tractable is the good news. The bad news is that the longer the industrial world fails to grapple fully with them—indeed, to recognize the commonality of the problems—the longer are its members likely to witness slower rates of growth into the future, and the less likely are they to find themselves capable of meeting new and pressing needs. These are the demands confronting industrial nations in the new world fiscal order.

* * *

The chapters in this volume are divided into three parts that mirror the structure of this introductory discussion—Part One: The Fiscal Implications of Changing Demographics; Part Two: The Yoke of Prior Commitments; and Part Three: Fiscal Policy and Worldwide Saving and Investment. Each part ends with comments from discussants who, like the chapter authors, are scholars, research analysts, and government officials from the United States, Japan, and Europe.

Part One

THE FISCAL IMPLICATIONS OF CHANGING DEMOGRAPHICS

Chapter Two

FISCAL POLICY AND THE AGING OF THE U.S. POPULATION[1]

C. Eugene Steuerle

Like most developed countries, the United States faces significant fiscal pressure from the aging of its population. Since this source of fiscal pressure is more current or imminent elsewhere, it might be argued that the U.S. is lucky in that it can learn by watching the actions of other governments. On the other hand, Americans are probably more tempted to deceive themselves—living off of the output of a fairly large middle-age cohort while preparing inadequately for that cohort's retirement and replacement by a smaller cohort of workers.

Although many policymakers decry the political difficulties of reducing fiscal deficits, as an economic matter fiscal responsibility will almost never be easier to attain than in the current period. Unlike the recent past, the U.S. is not engaged in any major international or domestic crisis. Its recent economic recessions have been relatively mild in both frequency and intensity. Its defense budget is in decline. Finally, the number of individuals entering the elderly population will remain relatively small until about 2010.

DEMOGRAPHIC TRENDS

In this paper, I focus my examination of the fiscal demands of an aging population on the Social Security system, including its system of cash assistance (Old-Age and Survivors Insurance—OASI, and medical care—Medicare). The fiscal balance within Social Security has been affected strongly by demographic trends. Longer lifespans and changing birth rates, in particular, have had a dramatic impact on who is retired, how many years of retirement are supported, and how many people in the workforce provide the funds necessary to support the retirement system.

Longer Lifespans and Earlier Retirement

Largely because of improvements in health care and standards of living, the portion of the population that survives its adult years and reaches old age has increased dramatically since Social Security was first adopted (see table 2.1). Only about 54 percent of men and 61 percent of women born in 1875 would survive from age 21 to age 65 in 1940, the first year in which Social Security benefits were available. In contrast, approximately 72 percent of men and 84 percent of women who were born in 1925 and survived to age 21 lived to see age 65 in 1990. According to estimates by the Social Security Administration, these figures will increase to 80 percent for males and 89 percent for females among those born in 1965 and turning 65 in 2030.[2] As a result, a larger proportion of those who contribute to the Social Security system will actually live long enough to receive benefits.

Those who do survive to age 65 can now expect to have many more years ahead of them than was once the case. As shown in table 2.1, for those turning 65 in 1940 the average remaining life expectancy was 12.7 years for males and 14.7 years for females. By 1990, life expectancy at age 65 had jumped by 2.6 years for males and 4.9 years for females, to 15.3 years and 19.6 years, respectively. Mostly because of advances in medical science, life expectancy will almost surely

Table 2.1 HISTORICAL AND PROJECTED IMPROVEMENTS IN LIFE EXPECTANCY

Year Cohort Turns 65	Percentage of Population Surviving from Age 21 to Age 65		Average Remaining Life Expectancy for Those Surviving to Age 65	
	Male	Female	Male	Female
1940	53.9	60.6	12.7	14.7
1950	56.2	65.5	13.1	16.2
1960	60.1	71.3	13.2	17.4
1970	63.7	76.9	13.8	18.6
1980	67.8	80.9	14.6	19.1
1990	72.3	83.6	15.3	19.6
2000	76.0	85.5	15.8	20.1
2010	78.4	87.1	16.3	20.5
2020	79.3	88.1	16.8	21.0
2030	80.4	88.8	17.2	21.5
2040	81.8	89.5	17.6	22.0
2050	82.7	90.0	18.0	22.4

Source: Mortality data undelying the 1992 Social Security Board of Trustees reports, from U.S. Social Security Administration (1992b and unpublished tables).
Note: Figures are specific to each cohort, i.e., a group of people born in the same year.

increase in the future. The Social Security Administration (SSA) estimates that life expectancy at age 65 for both males and females will increase by about two additional years over the next four decades, although some recent research suggests that expected lifespans could be extended even beyond these numbers.[3]

In the meantime, retirement has become much more common, and people have been retiring at increasingly earlier ages. Between 1950 and 1991, the civilian labor force participation rate for males age 65 and over fell from 45.8 percent to only 15.8 percent (table 2.2). For men age 55 to 64, it dropped from 86.9 percent to 66.9 percent. During this same period, the rate for females 65 and over declined from an already low 9.7 percent to just 8.6 percent, despite large increases in labor force participation among younger women (U.S. Bureau of Labor Statistics 1989, pp. 25–27 and 1992; Fullerton 1991, p. 36).

The average age at first receipt of Social Security retirement benefits for male workers remained above 68 until the late 1950s. As shown in table 2.2, it has dropped precipitously since then, to 63.7 in 1991, in part because an early retirement option for men was made available in Social Security beginning in 1962. The trend for female workers was similar; their average age at first receipt fell from 68.1 in 1940 to 63.5 in 1991 (U.S. Social Security Administration 1993, p. 247).

As a result of longer life expectancies and earlier retirements, the average number of years a retired worker will collect OASI benefits is now approaching two decades. Indeed, it is in excess of two decades for females. The average duration of an OASI benefit going to a married couple is even longer. Consider a worker retiring at age 62 with a spouse of the same age. Social Security provides annuity payments

Table 2.2 THE TREND TOWARD EARLIER RETIREMENT

	Civilian Labor Force Participation Rate of People Age 65 or Over		Average Age at Which Workers Begin Receiving OASI Retirement Benefits	
Year	Male	Female	Male	Female
1940	*	*	68.8	68.1
1950	45.8	9.7	68.7	68.0
1960	33.1	10.8	66.8	65.2
1970	26.8	9.7	64.4	63.9
1980	19.0	8.1	63.9	63.5
1991	15.8	8.6	63.7	63.5

Source: U.S. Social Security Administration (1993, p. 247); and U.S. Bureau of Labor Statistics (1989 and 1992).
*Not available.

that will last until both spouses are deceased. Payments can be expected to last an average of 25 years, or one-quarter of a century.[4]

Longer lifespans and earlier retirement ages have been among the most important factors contributing to the growing costs of the Social Security system.[5] Had retirement ages in Social Security been "indexed" for life expectancy—for instance, if the average number of years of support in retirement had been kept constant since first enactment—the cost of old-age insurance benefits could be significantly smaller than it is today, without any decline in real annual benefit levels provided to those receiving payments.

In 1983, Social Security legislation for the first time acknowledged some of the problems associated with providing more and more years of retirement assistance. The legislation scheduled an increase in the Normal Retirement Age (the age at which unreduced OASI benefits are first available), from age 65 to age 67, to be phased in gradually for workers turning 65 between 2003 and 2025. The two-year increase is roughly equal to the growth in average life expectancy at age 65, projected to occur over the four decades between enactment of the bill (in 1983) and when full implementation is achieved. No adjustment, however, was made for past growth in number of retirement years nor for future growth beyond 2025. The earliest age at which one can receive reduced OASI benefits, moreover, was scheduled to remain constant at 62, while the age at which all persons become eligible for Medicare was left at 65.

The SSA projects that this increase in the Normal Retirement Age will have only a modest impact on decisions concerning age of retirement, although future trends in this area are difficult to predict. Many people are expected to accept reduced benefit levels rather than delay retirement. Thus, the tendency of the system to support more and more years in retirement is likely to continue. For those retiring at age 62 in the year 2027, for instance, a Social Security pension can be expected to last on average about 19 years for a male, 23 years for a female, and 27 years for a couple (that is, until both are deceased).[6]

Lower Birth Rates

The birth rate is a second major demographic factor that strongly affects both benefits and taxes within Social Security. Demographers usually illustrate changing birth rate patterns by referring to the "total fertility rate," which is a measure of the average number of children that would be born to a woman in her lifetime if she were to experience the birth rates prevailing in a selected year.

The simple story, as illustrated in figure 2.1, is "baby bust" during the Great Depression and World War II, "baby boom" from about 1947 to 1964, and "baby bust" thereafter. The current cashflow situation of Social Security is especially misleading, as a small baby bust population of retirees now depends on an exceptionally large baby boom working population. In the not too distant future, those baby boomers will retire and be dependent upon a succeeding baby bust population. The impact of these birth rate patterns is softened only modestly by two other demographic factors—fewer dependent children and immigration—as described below.

Fewer Children: A Reduction in Fiscal Pressure? Future low to moderate birth rates mean that there will be fewer children to support. This can be expected to slow the growth in an overall dependency ratio—a measure of the number of dependent non-workers per worker. There is considerable danger, however, in taking this comparison too far. Except for educational expenses, children are supported more out

Figure 2.1 TOTAL FERTILITY RATES, 1920–2020

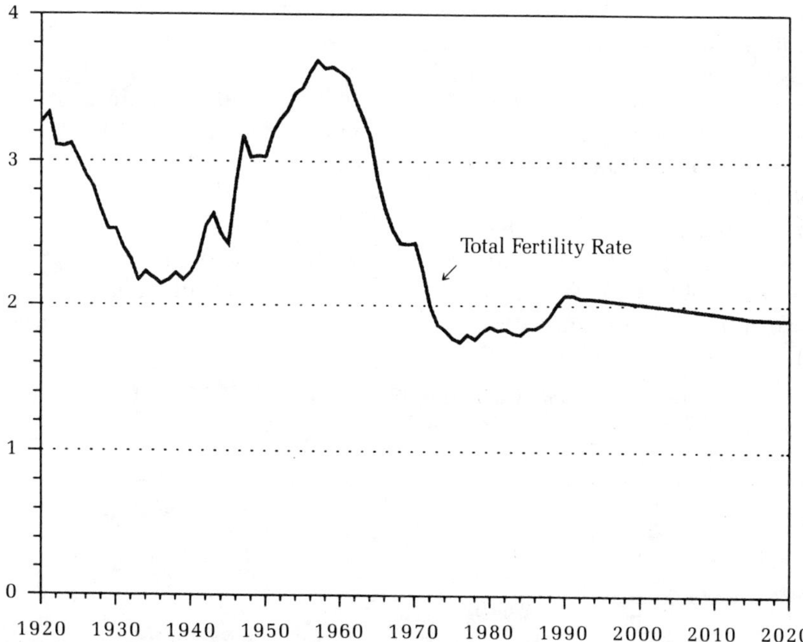

Source: U.S. Social Security Administration (1992a), and intermediate projections from the U.S. Board of Trustees of the OASDI Trust Funds (1994).

of private funds while the elderly are supported out of public funds. Thus, the fiscal pressures on the public sector are not eased significantly. Spending on children rather than on the elderly also may be more likely to result in future productivity increases. Finally, even if the demands of children on society decrease, there is no inherent reason why any savings or surplus generated should be predetermined to be spent on the elderly. Other needs of society may cry out for greater attention.

Will Immigration Help? A second factor that may help mitigate the decline in the number of workers per retiree is immigration. SSA immigration projections, however, already build in an immigration rate much higher than most other industrialized countries and foresee an increase in the net immigration rate in the future. An even larger than expected influx of immigrants over the next few decades might improve the demographic picture for Social Security slightly, since most immigrants are relatively young. Even significant increases in the immigration rate, however, have only a modest impact on the financial balance in Social Security.[7]

More Working Women

In some countries, increased labor supply by women might provide some reprieve against rising Social Security costs per worker. In the United States, however, many of these gains have already been largely achieved.

Table 2.3 shows how the overall civilian labor force participation rate rose from 59.2 percent in 1950 to 66.3 percent in 1992. Partly because of the increasing popularity of earlier retirement, labor force participation rates among males actually declined significantly over

Table 2.3 CIVILIAN LABOR FORCE PARTICIPATION RATE OF THE TOTAL POPULATION AGE 16 OR OVER

Year	Total	Male	Female
1950	59.2	86.4	33.9
1960	59.4	83.3	37.7
1970	60.4	79.7	43.3
1980	63.8	77.4	51.5
1992	66.3	75.6	57.8
2005	69.0	75.4	63.0

Source: U.S. Bureau of Labor Statistics (1989 and 1993). The projections for 2005 are from Fullerton (1991).

that time span, from 86.4 percent to 75.6 percent. Growth in overall participation, therefore, was due entirely to a rapid increase among women. Between 1950 and 1992, female labor force participation jumped dramatically from 33.9 percent to 57.8 percent (U.S. Bureau of Labor Statistics 1989, pp. 25–27; and Fullerton 1991, p. 36). Despite paying substantial taxes, however, these women saw little increase in Social Security benefits: their workers' benefits were often smaller or only slightly larger than spousal or survivors' benefits they would have received anyway. Given the large catch up that has already occurred, some believe that female participation rates will increase only moderately if at all during the next century, while the overall participation rate is likely to stagnate.[8]

More Retirees Per Worker

One consequence of the demographic trends described above is that the number of Social Security beneficiaries has grown much faster than the working population that supports them. When the post–World War II baby boom generation begins to retire early next century, the problem will begin to intensify considerably. By 2030, about a fifth of the population is expected to be receiving OASI benefits.

In 1950, OASI beneficiaries represented just 1.8 percent of the total U.S. population (table 2.4). Only 8 percent of the population was age 65 or over, many people worked beyond age 65, and only a fraction of the elderly had contributed to OASI long enough to be eligible for benefits. The share of the population receiving OASI benefits jumped to 10.5 percent by 1970, and to 13.6 percent by 1990. After remaining

Table 2.4 GROWTH IN THE ELDERLY POPULATION AND ITS IMPACT ON THE SOCIAL SECURITY SYSTEM

Year	Persons Age 65 or Over as a Percentage of the Total Population	OASI Beneficiaries as a Percentage of the Total Population	OASI Beneficiaries per 100 Covered Workers
1950	8.0	1.8	6.1
1970	9.7	10.5	24.3
1990	12.3	13.6	26.6
2010	13.1	14.5	28.2
2030	20.1	20.5	42.7
2050	21.0	21.5	45.4

Source: U.S. Board of Trustees of the OASDI Trust Funds (1994), historical data, and intermediate projections.

fairly stable for the next two decades, this figure is expected to skyrocket, reaching 20.5 percent by 2030. Thereafter, the proportion is projected to continue growing, albeit at a reduced pace.[9]

A summary measure of the effect of demographic trends on the burden of the Social Security system is the ratio of OASI beneficiaries to workers in employment covered by Social Security. In 1990, the ratio stood at 27 beneficiaries for every 100 workers. By 2030, it is expected to rise to 43 beneficiaries for every 100 workers. In other words, the number of OASI beneficiaries per taxpayer is expected to increase by about 60 percent over the next four decades (U.S. Board of Trustees of the OASDI Trust Funds 1994, p. 119).[10]

FISCAL IMBALANCE

The potential for fiscal imbalance in the Social Security system is easy to understand given the demographic trends just noted. It is also not surprising, given a system where cash benefits are designed to increase at the same rate as average wages for each successive cohort of beneficiaries,[11] and a health care system whose spending tends to grow at a much faster rate than the economy.[12]

Social Security Deficits and the Trust Funds

Recent reforms of the Social Security system—in particular, amendments enacted in 1983 (mentioned above) and, to a lesser extent, in 1977—were intended to deal with some of the fiscal imbalance that otherwise could be caused by these longer term demographic trends. When Social Security reform efforts have taken place, they have focused on putting the Social Security trust funds in an actuarial balance for 75 years—the maximum number of years for which benefit and cost estimates are prepared by the Social Security actuaries.

One part of the solution adopted in 1977 and reinforced in 1983 was to move to a combined tax rate for the Old-Age, Survivors, and Disability Insurance (OASDI) programs that would be constant for 1990 and thereafter, and would be sufficient to cover the 75-year cost of the system. Because of the irregular effect of the baby bust/baby boom/baby bust cycle, the system would move beyond what is often called a pay-as-you-go system—one that collects just enough taxes each year to pay out benefits that year and keep a small reserve. The combined employer and employee tax rate for the OASDI portion of

Social Security was set at a level rate of 12.4 percent for 1990 and thereafter. Temporary surpluses were to be deposited in the "trust funds" and "saved" until the baby boom retires. Eventually, rising costs would force the Social Security system to use the accumulated principal and interest to help finance benefit payments.

Since the enactment of the 1977 and 1983 reforms, projections of the long-run financial health of the system have worsened, partly because assumptions for the future have been revised in a less optimistic direction. As is apparent from figure 2.2, OASDI is expected to start running deficits around 2012, and spending will exceed income by an ever-increasing margin thereafter. OASDI deficits are projected to reach about 4.1 percent of taxable payroll by 2030, and 4.4 percent by 2050. The cumulated reserves and interest within the trust funds are expected to be sufficient to cover these deficits until about

Figure 2.2 OASDI TAX REVENUES AND SPENDING AS A PERCENTAGE OF TAXABLE PAYROLL

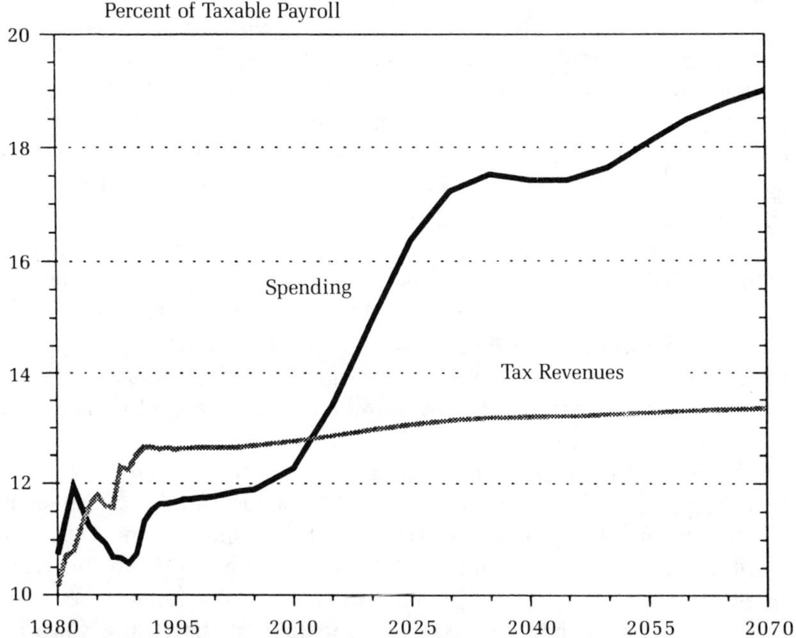

Source: U.S. Board of OASDI Trust Funds (1994), intermediate projections, adjusted to reflect 1994 reallocation of tax rates between OASI and DI.
Note: Tax revenues include payroll tax and income taxation of benefits.

2029, less than four decades from now (U.S. Board of Trustees of the OASDI Trust Funds 1994, pp. 23–24 and 106).

Under current law and best estimate assumptions as of 1994, OASDI faced a 75-year actuarial deficit equal to 2.13 percent of taxable payroll (U.S. Board of Trustees of the OASDI Trust Funds 1994, p. 109). This represents the amount by which the payroll tax rate would have to be increased immediately to establish actuarial balance in the OASDI portion of the system for the next 75 years. Balance could, of course, be restored through benefit reductions as well.

Restoring a 75-year actuarial balance to OASI, unfortunately, could still be inadequate for a number of reasons. First, some reforms that merely restore long-run actuarial balance would leave a problem for the longer run. Second, the much larger Medicare imbalance would remain. Finally, there exist other, more fundamental problems related to the broader fiscal situation of the federal government; Social Security cannot be separated from this broader fiscal dilemma.

The first problem is reflected in the trustees' reports (U.S. Board of Trustees of the Federal Hospital Insurance Trust Fund 1994; U.S. Board of Trustees of the Federal Old-Age and Survivors Insurance and Disability Insurance Trust Funds 1994; U.S. Board of Trustees of the Federal Supplemental Medical Insurance Trust Fund 1994). Benefit outlays are expected to continue to exceed tax revenues by a widening margin beyond the 75-year horizon (figure 2.2). Thus, as each year elapses, a past year of surplus drops out of the 75-year projection and a new year of deficit is added on. As a result, every year the size of the long-run actuarial deficit grows.

Suppose that the OASI system were brought back into exact 75-year actuarial balance with an increase in tax rates today. As soon as one more year passed, the trustees would issue a report stating that the system was out of balance once again. While projections so far in the future are always very tentative, the gap remains too substantial to ignore. Thus, something will eventually have to be done to bring long-run revenues and expenditures closer together.

Of more importance for the nearer term, Medicare is in poor financial shape. The Hospital Insurance (HI) portion of Medicare is financed primarily by a payroll tax, set at a combined employer and employee rate of 2.9 percent as of 1994. As with OASI, no increases in this tax rate are currently scheduled. HI tax revenues, however, were already less than expenditures by 1992.[13] The Health Care Finance Administration's best estimate projections in 1994 suggested that spending would continue to exceed tax receipts by a growing margin, and the HI trust fund would be fully exhausted just after the turn of the century.[14] The annual HI deficit was projected to balloon to 5.2 percent of taxable payroll by 2030 and 6.7 percent by 2050. The 75-year actuarial deficit for HI was estimated at 4.1 percent of taxable payroll (U.S. Board of Trustees of the Federal Hospital Insurance Trust Fund 1994, pp. 20 and 22). Legislators made only a small dent in this problem in a 1993 deficit reduction enactment, while health reform efforts in 1995 refused to deal fully with the long-run costs of Medicare.

Although these figures reflect an almost impossible scenario, they do not even include the effects of large increases in the Supplementary Medical Insurance (SMI) portion of Medicare. Calculations of SMI actuarial deficits are not performed, because general government funds, not Social Security taxes, already pay for nearly all costs above and beyond what enrollees contribute in premiums. In recent years, almost three-quarters of SMI funding comes from general federal tax revenues and deficit financing. SMI is expected to grow to be about as large as HI during the next century, implying that taxpayers will be required indirectly to come up with additional taxes equivalent to several more percentage points of their wages.

Finally, neither the HI nor the SMI calculations take into account the health costs being incurred under Medicaid. About one-third of Medicaid spending currently supports health care, particularly long-term nursing home care for the elderly. Barring any change, growth in these costs will also be substantial. Attempts to restrict total Medicaid expenditures in 1995 again do not deal with long-term demographic pressures.

Social Security and the Federal Budget

Measures of actuarial deficits within Social Security trust funds do not capture the full impact of Social Security on the broader federal budget. Social Security's surplus tax revenues are currently invested in government bonds, which provide a positive cash flow to the federal government. But the government is borrowing money both from Social Security and from the public to finance other activities.

When the time comes in the next century to draw down the trust funds to pay out benefits, the cash flow will be reversed, and the federal government will face a much more difficult fiscal situation. It will no longer have access to Social Security surpluses as a means of relieving fiscal pressures outside of Social Security.

One way to illustrate the full impact of Social Security's growth on the federal government's fiscal situation is to show how total Social

Security and Medicare spending is expected to change as a percentage of the national economy, or Gross Domestic Product (GDP). To give a rough impression of the magnitude of future fiscal problems, I provide two projections. One is based on the 1994 best estimates of the Social Security Administration and Health Care Finance Administration (HCFA), the other on some very conservative estimates that assume that growth in health costs is brought under control almost immediately (table 2.5). The real world is likely to be somewhere between the two estimates. These estimates of spending levels include outlays for OASDI and Medicare, but subtract out offsetting receipts paid by beneficiaries such as income taxes on Social Security benefits and SMI premiums, assumed to remain at 25 percent of costs.[15]

By themselves, OASDI outlays (less income taxes on benefits) are expected to rise from 4.7 percent of GDP in 1994 to about 6.4 percent of GDP in 2030. This amounts to an increase of about a quarter over today's spending levels, relative to GDP. Under these projections, OASDI would force the federal government to raise taxes, reduce other spending, and/or increase the deficit relative to 1994 levels by roughly 1.7 percent of GDP in 2030. This is equivalent to around $97 billion at 1994 levels of economic activity.

The potential fiscal impact of OASDI is significant but would probably be manageable by itself, especially if benefit and tax changes are

Table 2.5 OASDI AND MEDICARE SPENDING AS A PERCENTAGE OF GDP

		Assuming Medicare Grows According to HCFA 1994 Best Estimate		Assuming Medicare Cost per Enrollee Grows at the Same Rate as per Capita GDP After 1995	
Year	OASDI (SSA 1994 Best Estimate)	Medicare	OASDI & Medicare	Medicare	OASDI & Medicare
1950	0.3	0.0	0.3	0.0	0.3
1970	3.1	0.6	3.7	0.6	3.7
1994	4.7	2.1	6.8	2.1	6.8
2010	4.8	4.3	9.1	2.6	7.4
2030	6.4	7.0	13.4	3.8	10.2
2050	6.3	7.6	13.9	4.0	10.3

Source: Based on OMB and intermediate projections from the U.S. Board of Trustees of the OASDI, HI, and SMI Trust Funds (1994).
Note: Income taxes on benefits and SMI premiums are counted as expenditure reductions.
Figures assume that SMI premiums remain at 25 percent of program costs indefinitely. Years 1950 through 1994 are fiscal years; 2010 through 2050 are calendar years.

phased in over time. Potential problems arising from growth in Medicare costs, however, are much larger still. Although projections here are highly speculative, the 1994 best estimates of the HCFA actuaries suggest that total net Medicare spending will soar from about 2.1 percent of GDP in 1994 to about 7 percent in 2030, assuming SMI premiums remain at 25 percent of program costs (table 2.5). If we accept these numbers and add them to those for OASDI, we can see that in 2030, additional resources equal to roughly 6.6 percent of GDP would have to be diverted from other uses in order to provide the OASDI and Medicare benefits promised under current law.

Projections of Medicare spending are considerably less reliable than those for OASDI. Nonetheless, even if very strict cost-control measures were to limit growth in Medicare spending per enrollee to the rate of growth in per capita GDP (which would be well below the historical pace) after 1995, net Medicare spending would still rise to roughly 3.8 percent of GDP in 2030, simply because of demographic changes (table 2.5).

Figure 2.3 provides a hypothetical illustration of the bind that government will find itself in when projected growth in Social Security and Medicare is combined with already potent deficit pressures. Under the best estimate SSA and HCFA projections, OASDI and Medicare (less premiums and taxes on benefits) would increase from 6.8 percent of GDP today to 13.5 percent of GDP by 2030. On the one hand, if tax rates were to remain constant at 1998 levels (after full implementation of Clinton tax increases), spending on all other federal government functions—defense, federal aid to education, environment, assistance to children, interest on the debt, and so forth—would have to be squeezed from 15.4 percent of GDP in 1994 to 5.5 percent of GDP in 2030, in order to produce a balanced budget. On the other hand, if after 1998 all government spending other than OASDI and Medicare were to be held constant as a percentage of GDP, total federal taxes would have to be further increased above 1998 levels by 8.8 percent of GDP, in order to balance the budget in 2030. Even under the more optimistic assumption that Medicare spending per enrollee could be held to the rate of growth of per capita GDP, tax increases or expenditure cuts of close to 6 percent of GDP would be required to balance the budget in 2030.

These figures may even give an optimistic impression of the problem, since many other categories of government spending, such as Medicaid and interest on the federal debt, can also be expected to grow rapidly relative to the national economy unless major reforms

Figure 2.3 FUTURE GROWTH IN SOCIAL SECURITY AND MEDICARE MEANS HIGHER TAXES, LARGER DEFICITS, OR LOWER SPENDING ON EVERYTHING ELSE

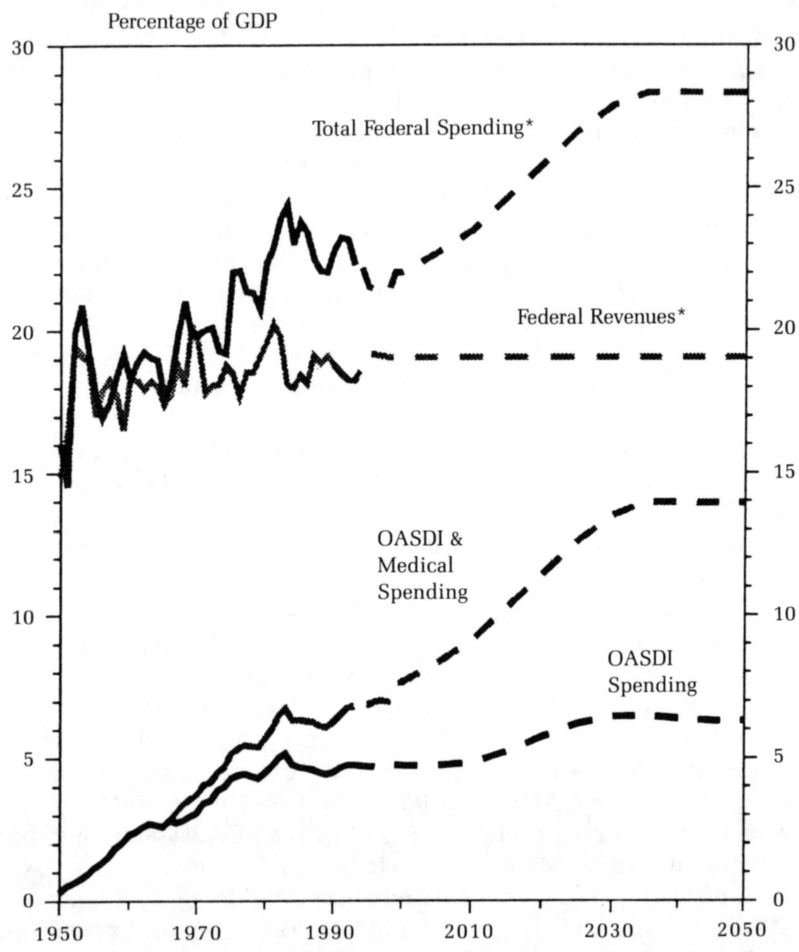

Source: Authors' calculations based on data from US Board of Trustees of the OASDI Trust Funds (1994) intermediate projections, and Office of Management and Budget (1994).

*Projections assume that spending—besides OASDI and Medicare—and taxes remain constant as a percentage of GDP after 1998.

Note: SMI premiums and income taxes on benefits are counted as expenditure reductions. Figures assume that SMI premiums remain at 25 percent of program costs indefinitely.

take place. The U.S. General Accounting Office estimated in a recent report that if current law were to remain unchanged, federal government spending would rise from about 23 percent of GNP today to 42 percent of GNP in 2020, while federal tax revenues would only rise from 20 to 22 percent of GNP over that same period (U.S. General Accounting Office 1992, p. 6). The report noted that spending on the elderly, health, and interest on the debt accounts for the vast majority of this expected rise in spending. This is an unsustainable situation.

Sharing the Government Pie. The share of the federal budget devoted to the elderly has grown enormously over the past four decades and is expected to grow still more. Spending on the elderly now accounts for nearly a third of the federal budget, and more than one-half of all federal domestic spending other than interest.[16] If expenditures on other important government functions are being "crowded out," it becomes all the more likely that some reform will have to occur.

Figure 2.4 shows how the composition of federal government spending has changed over the postwar period.[17] The bottom four categories in the chart are mainly pension and health programs that devote a large share of their budgets to the elderly and near-elderly. These include OASDI, Medicare, other retirement and disability (such as SSI and pensions for federal employees, veterans, and military personnel), and other health—mainly Medicaid and health benefits for civil servants and veterans. About three-quarters of aggregate outlays in these programs go to those who are elderly and/or retired.[18] Expenditures on these items grew from around 10 percent of the total federal budget in 1950 to about 48 percent in 1994. Under projections incorporating President Clinton's 1996 budget proposals, including significant Medicare cuts, these expenditures are expected to rise to approximately 53 percent by 2000. Similar results obtain under congressional Republican plans.

The fifth category in figure 2.4, which has also been consuming an increasing portion of the budget, is net interest on the public debt. Altogether, spending on the elderly and disabled, on health care, and on net interest is expected to account for slightly more than two-thirds of the federal budget by 1998.

As shown in the figure, much of the postwar growth in expenditures on these items has been offset by a decline in defense spending as a share of the budget. Defense spending decreased from more than two-thirds of the budget in the early 1950s to roughly a fifth today.

Figure 2.4 CHANGE IN THE COMPOSITION OF THE FEDERAL BUDGET, 1950–2000

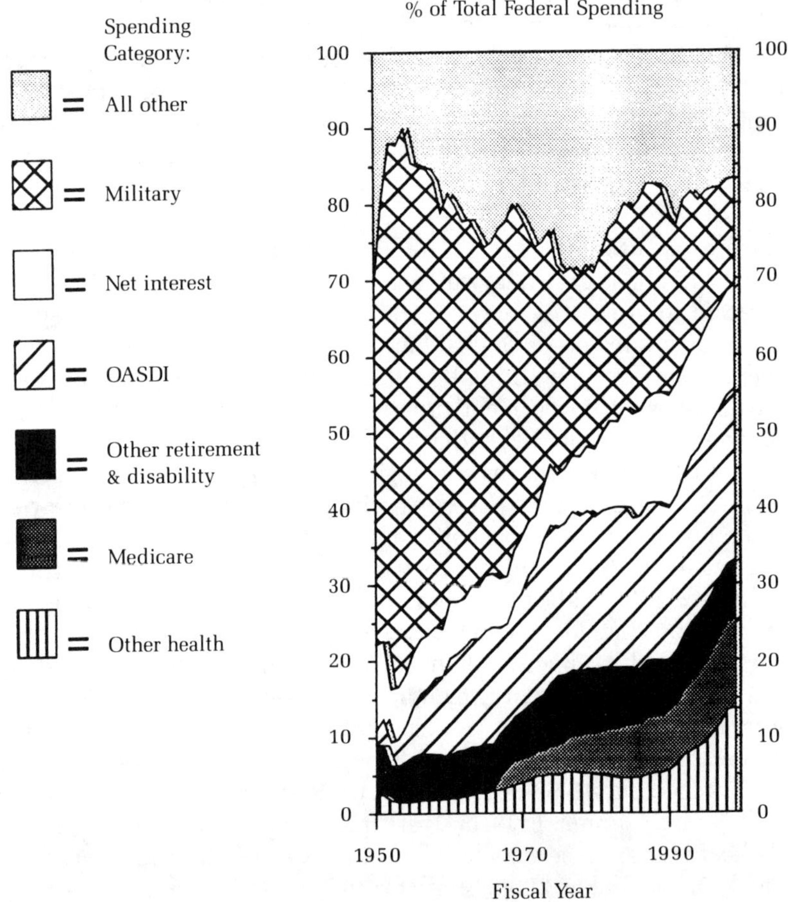

Source: Authors' calculations based on data from Office of Management and Budget (1995).

The final category, "all other" spending, is where pressure is being felt today. Included in this category is a vast array of functions such as welfare, unemployment insurance, investment in infrastructure, federal aid to education, foreign aid, administration of justice, the environment, agriculture, urban aid, disaster relief, and insurance of financial institutions.

Social Security and Economic Growth

Stronger economic growth always makes it easier to deal with budgetary pressures, whether they arise in Social Security, from the deficit itself, or from any other pressure on government. Likewise, slower economic growth tends to exacerbate fiscal problems. Many economists have noted that strong, sustained economic growth is crucial to our ability to meet future demands of an aging population, and have suggested a variety of measures, including deficit reduction and greater public investment, as means for achieving that goal.[19] It is indeed true that America's ability to provide for its elderly in the next century will depend heavily on the productivity of its economy at that time.

While economic growth is practically always advantageous, one should not be misled as to what it would achieve. Even very high rates of economic growth would not automatically solve the problems of imbalance in the Social Security system. Initially, higher than expected economic growth rates would increase Social Security tax receipts, but eventually benefit increases would work their way into the system and offset much of the gain in tax revenues. There would be some net improvement in the financial balance of the Social Security system, but not much. SSA actuarial analyses have demonstrated that even major improvements in rates of real wage growth, all else being equal, would have only a marginal effect on the long-run fiscal balance of the system.[20]

Better than expected economic growth might also improve somewhat the financial situation for Medicare. The demand for and cost of health care, however, have often risen more than proportionately to a rise in income. Hence, economic growth might simply allow greater dollar amounts of health care to be consumed, without necessarily improving Medicare's financial status or reducing its pressure on the budget.[21]

The estimates reported here already presume healthy rates of economic growth over the long-term future. Average wages are projected to grow at a rate of 1 percent per year in real (inflation-adjusted) terms.[22] This appears reasonable in relation to the average rate between 1951 and 1990, which was 1.04 percent. Some economists, however, believe that future growth rates will not be able to sustain this historic average.

Finally, healthy long-term economic growth doesn't just "happen." It is achieved partly through saving and investment. Achieving greater saving and investment means consuming less today—a temporary cost that all segments of American society, including Social Security recipients and taxpayers, may be called upon to share. If deficit reduction or investment in education are among the measures used to try to promote long-term growth, for instance, such efforts will create additional pressures to reduce other expenditures or to increase taxes.

Policy Adjustments

Given the imbalance in Social Security and Medicare trust funds, adjustments are inevitable. It is my view that programs for the elderly should be brought into line with a set of underlying principles. These principles, which sometimes conflict, include orienting payments more toward those who are needy, ensuring that those who are mandated to participate in a social insurance scheme still get some benefit from that system, treating similarly those in similar situations, and promoting efficiency—that is, comparing social benefits and costs.

Such principles demonstrate a strong case for benefit changes that include increasing and indexing the age of retirement for Social Security and Medicare, placing greater restrictions on early withdrawals, and counting *all* years of contributions in the formula by which benefits are calculated (currently only 35 years are counted). On the Medicare side, I would favor the adoption of more stringent rules limiting future payments for health care expenses, and encourage the adoption of vouchers and similar mechanisms that do not provide open-ended expenditures to cover health insurance. At the same time, I would increase minimum cash benefits in order to eventually remove all of the elderly from poverty. On the tax side, the government might both expand the tax base to include all forms of compensation—employee benefits continue to erode the Social Security tax base—and increase the income taxation of benefits, perhaps to include Medicare benefits. Some features of the U.S. system have tended to discriminate against working women and to favor high-income spouses who do not work, regardless of the amount of child rearing these spouses provide. These particular features also deserve reform.

These various reforms would go a long way toward bringing the Social Security and Medicare systems into balance. If such systematic reforms were enacted, it might still be necessary to decrease the real rate of growth of lifetime benefits from one cohort to the next, for example, by adjusting the index by which Social Security benefits are scheduled to grow in the future. Finally, the option of increasing the Social Security tax rate should not be cast aside, but other tax reforms suggested above should be considered first.

CONCLUSION

The demographic pressures on the United States budget cannot be avoided. Social Security and Medicare, the principal programs for the elderly, suffer from long-run actuarial deficits that will eventually require either tax increases or benefit reductions. When viewed in the broader context of the overall federal budget, the situation appears even more challenging.

Reform of the OASI retirement benefit system, by itself, is a manageable task, if dealt with in a timely and responsible fashion. Pressures in the United States are less pronounced than in many other industrial nations around the world, partly because birth rates have not dropped as far and immigration rates are higher. The tremendous growth expected in Medicare and other health programs, however, creates much more difficult fiscal pressures. This growth will force painful choices not only within our health care programs, but in all government programs, including OASI.

Reform must be a multiyear effort that should begin soon. The issues stretch far beyond the budget to individual decisions about age of retirement, private saving patterns, and consumption levels before and after retirement. Changes in retirement ages and rates of growth of benefits should be implemented gradually rather than suddenly. In addition, reforms in public pension systems could require alteration in the design of private pension plans. That itself could take years to be put in place.

In 1993, a U.S. Entitlement Commission was created to assess the need for entitlement and tax reform and to make specific recommendations to President Clinton. The Commission gave serious consideration to my research and some of the reforms that I, among others, suggested (see Steuerle 1994)—in particular, increasing the retirement age. Its concern was similar: that the issue is a pressing one that cannot be delayed to the future without a cost to society.

The next few years provide a crucial period of opportunity during which the United States should be preparing itself for the demands of the future. The nation should not be lulled into inaction by the relative stability of retiree-to-worker ratios in the near term, while a potent demographic challenge looms right around the corner.

Notes

1. Much of the material in this paper is derived from Steuerle and Bakija (1994). I would also like to thank Gordon Mermin for his assistance in the preparation of this report.

2. Author's calculations based on SSA cohort life tables in U.S. Social Security Administration (1992b), and unpublished tables. These same probabilities were used for the intermediate assumptions in the 1992 OASDI Trustees report.

3. For further discussion, see chapter 3 of Steuerle and Bakija (1994).

4. The average remaining life expectancy for people turning 62 in 1992 is estimated at 17 years for males, 21.6 years for females, and 25.2 years for the longest living member of a couple (Steuerle and Bakija 1994).

5. Even when benefits are reduced actuarially, earlier retirement reduces tax collections to the government, increases the likelihood that individuals will fall back on the government for assistance, and leads to demands for higher benefit payments to support those who have less income as a result of the earlier retirement.

6. See Steuerle and Bakija (1994) and note 5 above.

7. The SSA's 1994 intermediate projections assume that total net immigration (legal and non-legal immigration less emigration) will ultimately rise to 850,000 per year. During the 1980s, it is estimated that the total net immigration rate hovered around 650,000 per year. A sensitivity analysis conducted by the SSA suggests that OASDI's 75-year actuarial balance would improve by 0.07 percent of taxable payroll for each 100,000 increase in the net immigration assumption. A larger than expected increase in immigration would thus improve Social Security's financial situation, but the increase would have to be extremely large to have a very significant impact (U.S. Board of Trustees of the OASDI Trust Funds 1994, pp. 57 and 133–134).

8. Studies suggest that female labor force participation rates are likely to level off (Johnston and Packer 1987, chapter 3; and Fullerton 1991, pp. 33–34).

9. Authors' calculations based on data from the U.S. Board of Trustees of the OASDI Trust Funds (1994), pp. 119 and 144.

10. "OASI beneficiaries" includes some "nonelderly" people such as young dependents and survivors.

11. This simple statement ignores some complicating factors such as early retirement penalties, income taxation of benefits, and growth in nontaxable employee benefits. These factors help explain why, between now and 2030, the ratio of OASDI beneficiaries to covered workers is projected to increase by about 60 percent, while the ratio of OASDI benefits (less income taxes on benefits) to GDP is projected to increase by only 25 percent.

12. Total health expenditures in the U.S. grew from 5.3 percent of GDP in 1960 to 13.9 percent of GDP in 1993 (Levit et al. 1994).

13. HI benefit expenditures were 3.03 percent of taxable payroll in calendar year 1992, while the payroll tax rate was 2.9 percent (U.S. Board of Trustees of the Federal Hospital Insurance Trust Fund 1994, p. 19).

14. In the 1994 HI Trustees report (p. 3), the intermediate projections estimate trust fund exhaustion in 2001.

15. SMI premiums and income taxes on OASDI benefits are treated here as reductions in net spending. Data for years 1950 to 1999 are on a fiscal year basis and are derived from OMB historical tables and Clinton's FY 1995 budget estimates (OMB 1994). Data for years after 1999 are on a calendar year basis and come from the annual reports of the U.S. Board of Trustees of the OASDI, HI, and SMI Trust Funds (all 1994), intermediate projections.

16. For a fuller discussion of growth in spending on the elderly, see Penner (1994) and U.S. Congress (1992, p. 1579).

17. The historical data and projections in figure 2.4 are derived from Office of Management and Budget 1995. These projections include the estimated effects of presidential proposals contained in Clinton's fiscal year 1995 budget.

18. In fiscal year 1990, we estimate that 69.4 percent of spending in these bottom four categories (except veteran's health benefits, for which estimates are not available) went to individuals age 65 or over (based on U.S. Congress 1992, p. 1579). An additional several percent went to near-elderly retirees and pensioners.

19. See, for example, Aaron, Bosworth, and Burtless (1989) and Weaver (1990) for further discussion.

20. The long-run average real wage growth assumption underlying the SSA's intermediate projections is 1 percent per year. If average real wages were to grow instead at 1.53 percent per year, the 75-year actuarial deficit of the OASDI system would be reduced by 0.55 percent of taxable payroll. If real wages were to grow at a lower average annual rate of 0.5 percent, OASDI's 75-year actuarial deficit would be increased by 0.55 percent of taxable payroll (U.S. Board of Trustees of the OASDI Trust Funds 1994, p. 135).

21. For a discussion of the demand for medical care, see Newhouse (1992).

22. The average wage measure used here is the same one used to index the Social Security benefit formulas. It is currently derived by dividing the total amount of wages and salaries reported on W-2 forms by the total number of full- and part-time employees. For the historical series and an explanation of the methodology behind this wage measure, see U.S. Social Security Administration (1993a, p. 22).

References

Aaron, Henry J., Barry P. Bosworth, and Gary Burtless. 1989. *Can America Afford to Grow Old? Paying for Social Security.* Washington, D.C.: Brookings Institution.

Economic Report of the President. 1993. Washington, D.C.: U.S. Government Printing Office.

Fullerton, Howard N. 1991. "Labor Force Projections: The Baby Boom Moves On." *Monthly Labor Review* 114, 1 (November): 31–44.

Johnston, William B., and Arnold H. Packer. 1987. *Workforce 2000: Work and Workers for the 21st Century.* Indianapolis, In.: Hudson Institute.

Levit, Katherine R., Arthur L. Sensenig, Cathy A. Cowan et al. 1994. "National Health Expenditures, 1993." *Health Care Financing Review* 16:1 (Fall): 247–294.

Newhouse, Joseph P. 1992. "Medical Care Costs: How Much Welfare Loss?" *Journal of Economic Perspectives* 6, 3 (Summer): 3–21.

Office of Management and Budget (OMB). 1995. *Budget of the United States Government, Fiscal Year 1996.* Washington, D.C.: U.S. Government Printing Office, February.

———. 1994. *Budget of the United States Government, Fiscal Year 1995.* Washington, D.C.: U.S. Government Printing Office, April.

———. 1993. *Budget Baselines, Historical Data, and Alternatives for the Future.* Washington, D.C.: U.S. Government Printing Office, January.

Penner, Rudolph. 1994. *Dealing with the Retirement of the Baby Boomers.* Washington, D.C.: Urban Institute.

Steuerle, C. Eugene. 1994. "*Implications of Entitlement Growth.*" Statement before the Bipartisan Committee on Entitlement and Tax Reform.

Steuerle, C. Eugene, and Jon M. Bakija. 1994. *Retooling Social Security for the 21st Century.* Washington, D.C.: Urban Institute Press.

U.S. Board of Trustees of the Federal Hospital Insurance Trust Fund. 1994. *Annual Report.* Washington, D.C.: U.S. Government Printing Office.

U.S. Board of Trustees of the Federal Old-Age and Survivors Insurance and Disability Insurance Trust Funds. 1994. *Annual Report.* Washington, D.C.: U.S. Government Printing Office.

U.S. Board of Trustees of the Federal Supplemental Medical Insurance Trust Fund. 1994. *Annual Report.* Washington, D.C.: U.S. Government Printing Office.

U.S. Bureau of Labor Statistics. 1993. *Employment and Earnings.* Washington, D.C.: U.S. Government Printing Office, January.

———. 1992. *Employment and Earnings.* Washington, D.C.: U.S. Government Printing Office, January.

———. 1989. *Handbook of Labor Statistics.* Washington, D.C.: U.S. Government Printing Office.

U.S. Congress, Committee on House Ways and Means. 1992. *Green Book: Overview of Entitlement Programs.* Washington, D.C.: U.S. Government Printing Office.

U.S. General Accounting Office. 1992. Budget Policy: *Prompt Action Necessary to Avert Long-Term Damage to the Economy.* Washington, D.C.: Superintendent of Documents.

U.S. Social Security Administration. 1993. *Social Security Bulletin Annual Statistical Supplement, 1992.* Washington, D.C.: U.S. Government Printing Office.

———. 1992a. *Life Tables for the United States Social Security Area, 1900–2080*. Actuarial Study, No. 107. Baltimore Md.: U.S. Social Security Administration.

———. 1992b. *Social Security Area Population Projections: 1991*. Baltimore, Md.: U.S. Social Security Administration.

Weaver, Carolyn L., ed. 1990. *Social Security's Looming Surpluses: Prospects and Implications*. American Enterprise Institute Study, No. 511. Washington, D.C.: American Enterprise Institute Press.

Chapter Three

THE FISCAL IMPERATIVES OF CHANGING DEMOGRAPHICS IN JAPAN

Naohiro Yashiro

In this chapter I analyze the macroeconomic and fiscal impacts of Japan's aging population and examine the possible policy alternatives to help alleviate these impacts. While growing government expenditures are a major problem in many OECD countries, a unique characteristic of Japan is that the size of its government, measured by its total expenditures as a proportion of GDP, remains relatively small (table 3.1). There has even been substantial improvement in the *general government* balance over the last decade, which has gone from a deficit of 4 percent of GDP to a surplus of 3 percent of GDP. However, this does not imply that Japan's fiscal situation is a healthy one, because Japan already has a large *overall* fiscal deficit that threatens to grow larger unless certain actions are taken to contain it. Thus, the rapid aging of the Japanese population and the burdens this poses on society have important macroeconomic as well as fiscal implications.

Below I summarize the major factors underlying the rapid aging of Japan's population, investigate the macroeconomic effects of population aging, discuss the fiscal impacts of an aging population (focusing on public pensions and health insurance), and end by examining possibilities for reducing the excessive burden on the working generation in its support of the elderly. I also offer some of my own recommendations concerning fiscal policy options.

THE REASONS BEHIND JAPAN'S RAPIDLY AGING POPULATION

Although the share of the elderly in the total population is growing in many developed countries, the most striking feature of this phenomenon in Japan is the high speed at which it is occurring. The reasons are closely related to Japan's swift economic development, which has triggered rapid social changes. Japan's fertility ratio fell sharply from

Table 3.1 COMPARISON OF GOVERNMENT SIZE OF SELECTED INDUSTRIALIZED COUNTRIES BY SPENDING COMPONENT MEASURED BY EXPENDITURES AS A PROPORTION OF GDP, 1993

	Japan	U.S.A.	U.K.	Germany	France
Total Expenditures	32.3%	36.0%	42.5%	45.9%	51.1%
Consumption	9.1	17.8	20.0	18.3	18.1
Investment	5.2	1.6	2.3	2.3	3.3
Social Security	11.0	10.7	12.3	15.2	21.5

Source: OECD, *Main Economic Indicators.*

4.5 in 1947 (the postwar baby boom) to 2.1 in the 1960s, and to 1.5 in 1993.[1] The initial postwar decline in the fertility ratio was mainly due to a fall in the average number of children per family, reflecting a further shift from an agricultural to a service sector economy, and the migration of the population from rural to urban areas.

In contrast, the decline in fertility that has taken place from the early 1970s to the present has been mainly due to a later average age for women's first marriages. This age is now 26 years, the second highest in the world after Sweden. The major factors behind women delaying marriages are their rising enrollment in colleges and their expanded job opportunities. There is no indication that Japan's fertility rates will stop falling, in contrast to the recovery of fertility rates in other OECD countries such as the United States and Sweden.

Another reason for Japan's increasingly large elderly population is that Japan has the highest life expectancy of all major industrial countries. Average life expectancy for males has increased from 50.1 years in 1947 to 76.3 years in 1993, and for females from 54 years to 82.5 years during the same period.[2] Initially, increased life expectancy was due to a sharp fall in the mortality rate among children under one year old—thanks to improvements in nutrition and sanitary conditions. Better health care for the elderly has also significantly increased life expectancy at retirement age and beyond. In Japan, average expected years remaining at age 65 for males and females were 16.4 and 20.6 in 1993, respectively. Increased life expectancy reflects a rapid rise in Japanese average per capita income and in medical standards in the postwar period. The more equal distribution of both income and medical services since World War II has contributed to Japan's population having the longest life expectancy of all OECD countries.

Declining Labor Force Growth

In the early phase of this type of population aging process, the ratio of the young to total population falls more rapidly than the ratio of elderly to total population rises. The initial result is a decline in the total dependency ratio—defined as the ratio of the sum of the population below 15 years and above 64 years to the working-age population (those between ages 15 and 64). Thus, Japan currently has the lowest total dependency ratio among major OECD countries (figure 3.1, panel A), but this ratio is projected to rise steadily into the 21st century. As shown in panel B of the same figure, by 2000 the young dependency ratio is expected to bottom out while the aged dependency ratio will more than double.

Falling fertility rates have actually resulted in a declining population from one generation to the next. The population of those under age 30 has declined since the 1960s, and the working-age population is projected to decline beyond 1995. Although this trend will be partly offset by Japan's rising female labor force participation—the total labor force will continue to grow in the latter half of the 1990s—the workforce will grow at a much lower rate than in the past few decades. For instance, as shown in table 3.2, total labor force growth rates per

Figure 3.1 COMPARISON OF DEPENDENCY RATIOS OF SELECTED INDUSTRIALIZED COUNTRIES, 1965–2025

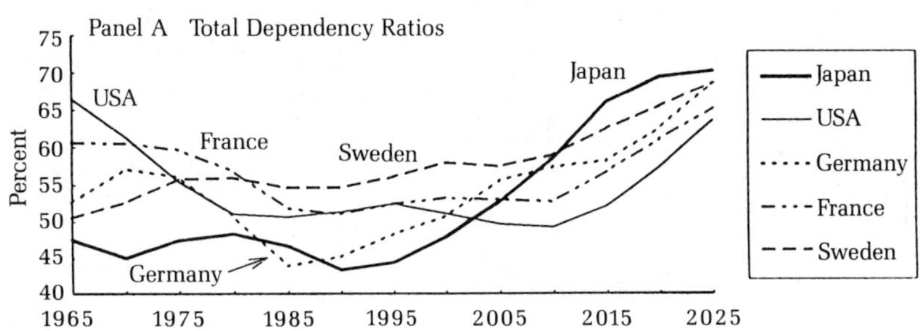

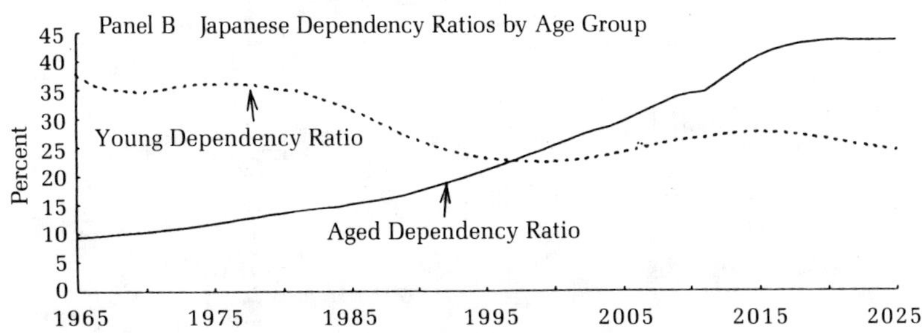

Sources: Bos et al. 1992; Ministry of Health and Welfare, *Population Projections for Japan* 1992.

Table 3.2 PROJECTIONS FOR JAPAN'S LABOR FORCE, 1980–2020 (IN MILLIONS)

						Growth Rate Per Year (%)			
	1980	1990	2000	2010	2020	1980–1990	1990–2000	2000–2010	2010–2020
Total	5,650	6,384	6,875	6,691	6,363	1.23%	0.74%	−0.27%	−0.50%
Male	3,465	3,791	4,099	3,977	3,715	0.90	0.78	−0.30	−0.68
Age 15–24	352	421	408	313	295	1.81	−0.31	−2.62	−0.59
Age 55–64	379	582	696	829	696	4.38	1.80	1.76	−1.73
Female	2,185	2,593	2,776	2,714	2,648	1.73	0.68	−0.23	−0.25
Age 15–24	347	413	359	284	275	1.76	−1.39	−2.32	−0.32
Age 55–64	253	350	398	458	391	3.30	1.29	1.41	−1.57

Source: Japan Center for Economic Research 1995.

year are projected to be 0.7 between 1990 and 2000, declining to minus 0.5 between 2010 and 2020.

One major uncertainty is the labor force trends of older workers. In Japan, like other OECD countries, the labor force participation of older workers fell until the mid-1980s, when the trend reversed itself. Between 1987 and 1993, the share of working males age 60 to 64 years relative to total population rose from 71.1 percent to 75.6 percent, while the share of working males age 65 and above rose from 35.6 percent to 37.9 percent.[3] This trend, if sustained, will affect total labor force and macroeconomic developments.

THE MACROECONOMIC CONSEQUENCES OF AN AGING POPULATION

The extent of fiscal burden associated with an aging population largely depends on macroeconomic factors. The higher a country's per capita income growth, the lower the burden of the working-age population. A decreased labor force beyond the year 2000 and an increased ratio of elderly to total population are likely to have negative impacts on macroeconomic developments in two ways.

First, the impact of an aging population on labor productivity growth and investment is the result of two counteracting forces. Declining labor force growth, other things being equal, discourages business investment due to a drop in capital profitability. However, this negative impact on investment can be partly offset by labor-enhancing technological development. Though it is not easy to measure the quantitative impact of a declining labor supply on stimulating labor-enhancing technology, past experiences in major OECD countries imply that labor shortage is an important impetus for more efficient utilization of the existing labor force.[4]

Second, household savings are likely to fall as the proportion of elderly rises, resulting in a gradual increase in dissavers as a share of total population. Because Japan's elderly do save significantly, on first glance it may seem that this life cycle hypothesis on household savings may not apply to Japan. However, there are two types of Japanese elderly: those who are economically independent and are likely to save, and those who are dependent on their children and who account for 65 percent of the total elderly. The latter type of elderly are taken care of by their children and are thus excluded from statistics on a household basis. If we take this sample selection bias into account,

Japan's elderly as a whole does indeed dissave, as predicted by life cycle theory (Yashiro and Maeda 1994).

Thus, the aging of Japan's population will lower the nation's propensities for investing and for saving. How this will affect Japan's current external account will depend on the extent of decline in savings and investment. Although empirical evidence is scant, it is possible that the decline in investment could be slower than that in savings, mainly due to the development of labor-enhancing technology, which is induced by an increasing labor shortage. If so, an aging population will reduce Japan's current external surplus (Yoshitomi and Yashiro 1992; Yashiro and Oishi 1993).[5] Real GDP growth may well decline from the 4 percent average growth between 1970 and 1990, to an average growth rate of 1.2 percent between 2000 and 2020. At the same time, per capita income may grow higher even as the population decreases by 0.4 percent between 2010 and 2020 (table 3.3).

THE FISCAL IMPACT OF JAPAN'S AGING POPULATION

Below I focus on the fiscal effects of Japan's growing elderly population on social security, including public pensions, health care expenditures, and unemployment compensation (see table 3.4 for a brief outline of Japan's pension system).

Social Security

In industrialized countries, one major fiscal impact of population aging is substantial increases in public pension benefits for the re-

Table 3.3 PROJECTIONS FOR JAPAN'S GDP GROWTH (PERCENT)

	1980–1990	1990–2000	2000–2010	2010–2020
Real GDP growth	4.1%	2.6%	1.9%	0.5%
Of which:				
Labor force growth	0.8	0.5	−0.3	−0.4
Capital stock growth	2.1	1.7	1.1	0.5
Total factor productivity growth	1.2	0.4	1.1	0.4
Per capita GDP growth	3.6	2.4	1.9	0.9
Population growth	0.5	0.2	0.0	−0.4

Source: Japan Center for Economic Research 1995.

Table 3.4 JAPAN'S PENSION SYSTEM

Japan has a two-tiered pension system: a *national program* pays a flat rate to all residents, and an *employees' pension insurance* pays out earnings-related benefits.

	National Program	Employees' Pension Insurance[a,b]
Source of Funds		
Insured person	Employed persons and their dependent spouses, included in employee contributions to employee pension insurance.	7.250% of earnings (men) or 7.225% of earnings (women) according to 30 wage classes. If contracted out, 5.65% (men) and 5.625% (women), respectively.
Employer	Included in employer contribution to employee pension insurance.	Same as for insured persons.
Government	One-third of benefit cost, plus administrative costs.	Administrative costs.
Qualifying Conditions	Age 65, and 25 years' contribution (including for dependent spouse of employee, years of own coverage plus years married to an employee who is covered by an employment-related program). Pension payable at age 60–64 with actuarial reduction. Pension increased if first paid at age 66 or later.	Age 60 (men),[c] 58 (women), or 55 (seamen and miners); 25 years of coverage, including years covered by National Pension program. Age 60–64 pension reduced 20%–100% if monthly basic wage (i.e., excluding bonuses, etc.) equals 95,000–250,000 yen ($769–$2,024).
Benefits	If fully insured (480 months of contributions), 737,300 yen ($5,968) a year (as of April 1, 1993), plus 200 yen ($1.62) for each contribution month if self-employed.	0.75% of indexed monthly wages multiplied by the number of months of coverage. Age 60–64: insured receives an added 1,463 yen ($11.80) a month for each month of coverage.

Source: U.S. Department of Health and Human Services 1994.

a. Contracting out from employee pension insurance allowed if corporate plan provides equivalent benefits.

b. Maximum earnings for contribution purposes: 530,000 yen ($4,290 at 1993 exchange rates) a month.

c. These age arequirements were recently increased.

tired. Both savings and investment are also affected by an aging population through associated increases in the tax and social security burdens of the working-age population. There is a tendency in the OECD countries for those with a relatively high proportion of elderly to have larger government sectors—measured by the ratio of social transfers or by the tax and social burden relative to GDP.

Though government size varies with an aging population, mainly through changes in transfer payments, there are many differences among countries and regions. First, consider European countries, along with Japan. After attempting to take into account differences that are unique to each country, the rate of total transfers (to all age groups) to income seems to rise with the elderly ratio, and the rate of increase of total transfers seems to accelerate as the elderly ratio rises. In contrast, the Pacific Rim countries—the United States, Canada, Australia, and Japan—still show some increase in transfers as their elderly proportion of the population increases, but the rate of increase seems to become more moderate over time as higher elderly rates are achieved. Taxes, as might be expected, show roughly the same pattern as transfers (these results can be seen by plugging relevant elderly ratios into the equations in table 3.5).

One explanation might simply be that the Pacific Rim countries lag behind the European countries in the aging of their populations. When the aging of the population is more modest, transfers rise in a different pattern than when the aging is more severe. The adjustment process is different in the two stages.

When all OECD countries are considered together, the ratio of transfer payments usually appears lower than in Japan *after* taking into account differences in elderly ratios. These results might be interpreted to mean that Japan *potentially* has a larger government, but that its relatively younger age structure, at least by international standards, tends to obscure this fact. Interestingly, Japan will increase its elderly ratio in the near future far ahead of other OECD countries.

However, as C. Eugene Steuerle argues earlier in this volume vis-à-vis the United States, there is still time to put into place policies that can effectively work to restrain the expansion of social transfers. There are various explanations for the dichotomy between trends in social security transfers and burdens between European countries, on the one hand, and the United States, Japan, Canada, and Australia, on the other. Some of these differences are obviously due to historical and cultural variance—for instance, the creation of the "welfare state" in the West. An alternative hypothesis is that there is a "threshold elderly ratio" below which government social security benefits

Table 3.5 TAXES AND TRANSFERS AS A FUNCTION OF THE ELDERLY RATIO[a]

	Transfers			Taxes		
	Pacific Countries	European Countries	Total OECD	Pacific Countries	European Countries	Total OECD
Constant	−30.02**	12.22**	3.92**	−20.07**	37.08**	18.58**
Elderly Ratio	7.03**	−1.46*		7.90**	−1.77*	
(Elderly Ratio)^2	−0.29**	0.11**	0.06**	−0.31**	0.14**	0.08**
Dummy						
USA	−2.19**		−2.07**	−0.80*		−0.45
CANADA	0.66**		1.18**	6.04**		6.66**
AUSTRALIA	−1.38**		−0.72*	3.42**		4.20**
AUSTRIA			−2.32**			5.19**
BELGIUM			4.63**			8.73**
FRANCE		5.75**	3.49**		1.55**	6.88**
GERMANY		−0.56*	−2.86**		−0.22	4.99**
SWITZERLAND		−0.07	−2.26**		−8.10**	−2.67**
UK		−4.09**	−6.38**		−5.06**	0.17
IRELAND		3.83**	2.18**		1.76*	7.95**
FINLAND		−2.57**	−4.39**		0.10	6.05**
DENMARK		1.49**	−0.79*		5.27**	10.54**
NORWAY		0.53*	−1.73**		6.51**	11.77**
SWEDEN		−1.57**	−3.68**		4.28**	9.63**
R^2	0.85	0.85	0.88	0.90	0.88	0.92

Source: OECD, *Main Economic Indicators*.
a. Elderly ratio = number of persons age 65 or older divided by total population.
Note: ** and * indicate significance at 99 percent and 95 percent level, respectively.

can be constrained and the private sector will kick in to provide similar services. Once the elderly ratio goes above this threshold, however, the public sector crowds out private sector activities. In the West, growing political resistance among an increasingly large elderly population to the curtailment of welfare services may be another explanation for the different degrees of social security transfers in the West and in the Pacific Rim countries.

Public Pensions. Projections indicate that the aging of Japan's population and the resulting higher ratio of pension beneficiaries to contributors will lead to a higher ratio of pension expenditures to GDP. Recently, the Japan Center for Economic Research (1995) projected that social security benefits as a percentage of national income will rise from 15 percent in 1992 to 24 percent in 2020, while public pension expenditures as a percentage of national income will rise from 7.7 percent to 13.2 percent. This rapid rise in public pension expenditures has been due to the increasing "maturity" of the public pension fund, which will account for roughly half of the projected pension expenditure increase between 1990 and 2020.

Japan's public pension scheme was initially designed to be a "fully funded" scheme, meaning that contributors accumulate their own savings that they then withdraw after retirement. Under this system, both accumulated contributions and benefits per person are relatively low in the beginning. The average benefit per beneficiary increases with time as the average period of contribution becomes longer or the public pension fund becomes more "mature."[6] Under such a scheme, variations in the age structure of the population lead to corresponding variations in the fund's net assets, thus lessening the burdens associated with an aging population.

However, this "fully funded principle" regarding pensions in Japan has gradually been eroded, and the system has shifted to a *de facto* "pay-as-you-go" scheme. This means that present beneficiaries are directly supported by present contributors through taxes. This shift is mainly the result of a generous increase in pension benefits brought about by political pressures—a generosity not bolstered by sufficiently higher premiums in the 1970s. Moreover, benefits had to be paid for longer periods of time, due to unforeseen increases in life expectancy of the elderly (discussed earlier). This situation has been exacerbated by Japan's low, by international standards, eligibility age for public pensions, which is 60 for males and 55 for females.[7]

These factors naturally produce a "potential deficit" in the public pension balance—that is, future promised benefits unmatched by future fund accumulation—even though an actual surplus has been accumulated. According to estimates, the accumulated "potential debt" amounts to 110 percent of GDP in 1990, compared with actual assets of the Social Security Fund, which comprise 20 percent of GDP (Hatta and Oguchi 1993).

This situation has led to a substantial increase in intergenerational transfers. Indeed, current public pension beneficiaries on average have contributed only 30 percent of the benefits actually received (Takayama 1992). As the elderly ratio increases, public pension fund reserves will eventually be exhausted even before population aging reaches its peak, putting a greater burden on current contributors.

Without a substantial revision of the current system, the size of social security transfers will automatically increase, reaching the same proportions as those in current European countries by 2020—just as Japan's ratio of the elderly to the total population reaches its peak of 25 percent. According to official projections, in order to have adequate reserves to keep currently promised benefits flowing, public pension premiums would need to rise from 14.5 percent of regular wages in 1994 to 29.5 percent in 2020. There would also need to be a gradual rise in the statutory age of pension eligibility from the current 60 to 65 (Management and Coordination Agency 1994).[8] Thus, demographic changes require adjustments of benefits and contributions in order to mitigate an increased burden on the working generation as the share of the elderly population rises.

Health Care and Medical Services. In Japan, health care comes second after public pensions as an important social expenditure, accounting for over one-third of total social security and welfare expenditures. Although Japan's total social transfer payments are relatively low, medical expenditures, which represented 5.8 percent of national income in 1992, are comparable in size to those of other industrialized countries. The concentration of public health care services on the elderly is particularly prominent in Japan. Costs of medical care for the elderly (age 70 and above) now account for nearly one-fourth of total health care expenditures. Patients age 65 and above utilize 3.2 times more medical services than the average, making Japan's gap between average versus elderly use of medical services one of the largest of the seven major OECD countries. This is due in part to Japan's generous health insurance system, which provides nearly unlimited free health care services to those 70 years and above.[9]

The lack of a mechanism for discouraging demand for medical services is aggravated by insufficient information on prices of medical services, since services are directly supplied, absent reimbursements by public health insurance schemes. Another problem is Japan's relatively large share of drug costs as a proportion of total medical expenditures.[10] This occurs because drug dispensing is encouraged through discounted prices granted to doctors by pharmaceutical companies.

While the ratio of total medical expenses (both public and private) relative to national income stabilized in the 1980s at 6 percent, the share of elderly medical expenses rose continuously, reaching nearly 30 percent in 1991. It is likely that medical expenditures on the elderly will expand more rapidly in the future with the increase in the elderly population. Such spending will account for nearly half of total medical expenditures in Japan by 2020 (Japan Center for Economic Research 1995).

Unemployment Compensation. Although the average rate of unemployment in Japan has been quite low by international standards, rates for older workers are higher than the average. The unemployment rate of males age 60 to 64 years was 6.1 percent in 1993, much higher than the average rate of 2.4 percent. In addition, the duration of older males' unemployment is also much longer than the average, thus government expenditures for their unemployment compensation are larger. A major factor behind older workers being more prone to unemployment lies in Japan's seniority-based wage structure. Older workers cost more, but come at a cost not necessarily commensurate with their productivity. So, although they come in large supply—because of major firms' mandatory retirement age of 60 years—demand for them is relatively weak.

Increasing the eligibility age for old-age pensions beyond the normal mandatory retirement age of 60 years will result in more older job seekers, because retirement from a particular firm does not necessarily imply retirement from the labor market in Japan. Unless the mismatch between demand for and supply of elderly workers is addressed, an increase in the share of the older labor force will entail a parallel increase in structural unemployment, resulting in increased expenditures for unemployment compensation.

THE VALIDITY OF ALTERNATIVE STRATEGIES FOR EASING THE BURDEN

Although the causal relationships between the size of government and economic efficiency in the OECD countries are not necessarily clear, the continued expansion of the public sector is of concern for various reasons (OECD 1985). An increasing share of government transfer payments and an associated larger tax and social security burden will reduce economic efficiency in several ways. First, those who bear the burden, both employers and employees, will find it more profitable to make efforts to avoid increased tax burdens, for example, by hiring tax consultants or starting tax-saving businesses, rather than investing in more productive activities. Second, once retired, those who receive benefits will find it difficult to go back to work or accept a lower level of benefits—a "trap" from which they cannot easily emerge. Finally, the administrative procedures associated with imposing and distributing taxes are also costly, particularly when labor supply is declining.

Relying on the Family

If excessive expansion of the government sector has unfavorable effects on the economy, what are the alternatives? The extent to which government must increase social transfers to the elderly depends on their family support and their ability to help themselves. In traditional societies such as pre-war Japan, the family was the major entity supporting the needs of the elderly. This family function remains important in today's Japan, as reflected in the high proportion of Japanese elderly being cared for by their children. For example, 57 percent of elderly Japanese males live with their relatives, compared with only 7 percent in the United States (Yashiro 1993). This is one of the major factors preventing the incidence of poverty among the elderly.

However, we cannot expect too much from family altruism in the future. Japanese family structure has been changing rapidly, and elderly people are increasingly less likely to be living together with their children than in the past. The changing industrial structure and the associated concentration of the population in urban areas have geographically separated parents from their grown children. In addition, the share of self-employed families—wherein implicit contracts that children will inherit their parents' household assets in return for providing care for them are most prominent—has declined.[11]

Increasing the Employment of Older Workers

Following the tendency toward early retirement of many European countries and the United States would impose large costs on the Japanese economy. As discussed earlier, the labor force participation rate for Japanese males age 65 to 69 was 55.3 percent in 1993—twice as high as the same rate for U.S. males (25.9 percent). This partly reflects Japan's large proportion of self-employed males (more than 50 percent between age 60 and 69), but even for Japanese male wage and salary workers, there is only a minor drop in the labor force participation rate at age 60 (the normal mandatory retirement age), after which the rate declines only gradually (figure 3.2). Moreover, there are recent signs that the elderly are increasing their labor force participation, regardless of age.

There are several factors behind the high labor market attachment of the Japanese elderly, an attachment likely to continue in the future. First, life expectancy after age 65, which increased from 11.6 years to 16.4 years for males and from 14.1 years to 20.6 years for females between 1960 and 1993, is likely to extend further. Longer life expec-

Figure 3.2 LABOR FORCE PARTICIPATION OF JAPANESE ELDERLY MALES

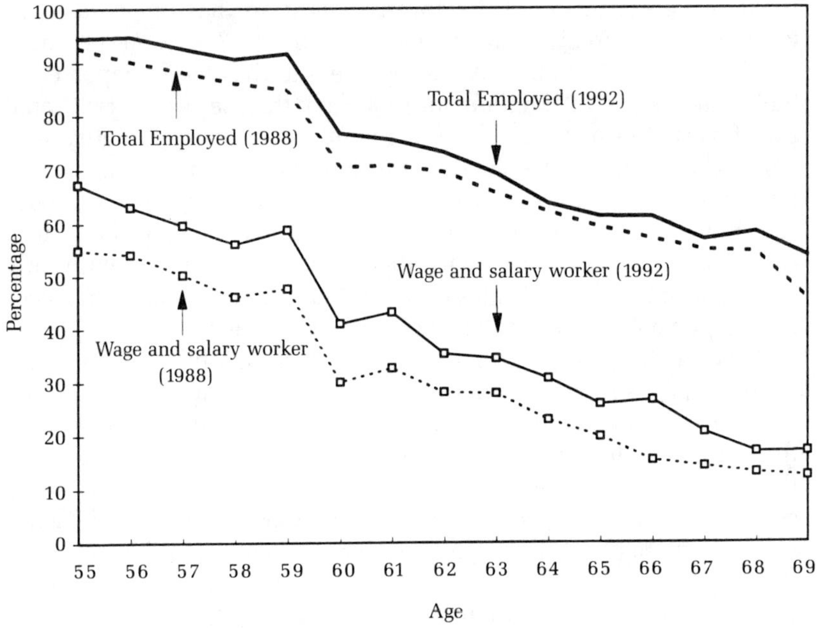

tancies may imply better health at age 65, and may stimulate employees to continue to work to accumulate additional savings for retirement. Second, financial pressures on the public pension system will require an extension of the eligibility age for collecting pensions, as well as other cost-saving policy reforms. Third, the share of the college-educated (including junior colleges) in the total labor force will rise from 20 percent in 1990 to 40 percent in 2010. The better educated generally have better job opportunities, even at older ages. Finally, Japan's upcoming labor shortage, due mainly to a declining labor force, will create a favorable working environment for the elderly.

Having more older workers remain in the labor market will substantially reduce the social security burden of the working-age population. The definition of the "elderly" need not be fixed at age 65 in a society where a further extension of life expectancy is expected. In my view, we should adopt a newer definition of "elderly" than the one based on the economic capability of a 65-year-old person in 1955. In 1990, that same capability could be applied to someone 67 years old, and in 2025 to someone 70 years old. Using this new definition, the ratio of the "elderly" to total population in the year 2025 would be

20.6 percent, rather than the 25.8 percent conventionally used (Yashiro and Oishi 1993).

Creating New Methods of Intragenerational Income Transfers

There is, of course, a limit on how long the elderly will continue working. The growing number of the very elderly (age 75 years and above) would expand the demand for medical, welfare, and other public services, while, as discussed above, the traditional role of the family in Japan in taking care of the elderly has declined over time. However, the role of the family can be partly replaced by the increased role of the market in supplying welfare services. Most elderly people in Japan are not poor; their average per capita income is equivalent to that of the national average. Also, the average value of elderly household assets—including that of the single elderly—is twice as large as that of the non-elderly. This reflects the elderly's high rate of homeownership, which exceeds 80 percent, and the high value of land on which those homes are located.

One method that would allow the elderly to purchase welfare services in the market would be a system of annuitization of household assets, for example, through a "reverse-mortgage" (Noguchi 1993).[12] This would substantially increase the annual incomes of the elderly. One could also purchase insurance against the risk of living after the loan reaches the value of the home. Combining a reverse mortgage with insurance against the risk of "living longer than originally expected," however, would result in intragenerational income transfers, contrary to the current method within the Japanese family. The present transfer involves an implicit contract that children will receive bequests in exchange for taking care of their parents. The new method, however, would entail fewer bequests from old to young, but would also reduce intergenerational transfers required from young to old.

FISCAL POLICY RECOMMENDATIONS

Population aging does not create new problems, but simply aggravates the current dilemma concerning economic efficiency and equity. Japan must reform its overly generous social security system and reduce excessive intergenerational income transfers. There are several options that can be used to alleviate the negative impacts on macroeconomic activities arising from higher tax and social security premiums: modifying the public pension system by basing it on an "actuarially fair" principle, broadening the tax base, and reforming the health care system.

Along with the rising life expectancies of the elderly, the "equivalent retirement age" that is necessary to maintain the financial balance of the pension system without disturbing fixed benefits and premiums must also be raised. Increasing the statutory age of pension eligibility would reduce the number of beneficiaries while increasing contributors, thereby substantially helping to improve the fiscal balance of the pension fund.

Reforming the social security system alone is not sufficient; the tax base must also be broadened in order to maintain the pension system. This can be done by increasing the consumption tax, which is currently 3 percent, and by increasing the capital gains tax. Both these actions would distribute the tax burden more toward the elderly, whose income is mainly based on net wealth and other non-wage income. Also, net increases in social security premiums are required in order for today's older workers to pay sufficiently for the costs of their pension benefits. Without such increases in social security premiums, later generations will be left with a large deficit in the pension fund.

Reforming the current health care system is also required. Although government health expenditures as a proportion of GDP recently have stabilized, as previously discussed, health care expenditures for the elderly have continued to expand. Japan's health care system can be made more efficient by increasing the share of the patient's financial burden and/or introducing a pre-paid system for medical fees. Also, because the very elderly are major consumers of medical resources, improved coordination between welfare and medical services for the elderly would contribute to reducing total medical costs by shifting demand from hospitals to nursing homes for the elderly.

Rapid population aging is a major challenge to Japan's economy, which has long enjoyed an abundant labor force supply and a low old-age dependency ratio. Now, however, the increased burdens soon to be brought on by an aging society must be overcome by improving resource allocation through structural reforms in the tax and social security systems. In particular, providing better employment opportunities for the elderly will increase the number of social security contributors, while reducing the number of beneficiaries, thus helping to prevent negative impacts on the economy and on society.

Notes

1. The fertility ratio here is defined as the average number of children born to a woman during her lifetime. Recent corresponding fertility ratios in other OECD countries are 2.0 for the United States, 1.8 for France and Canada, and 1.5 for Germany (OECD 1990). The ratio is particularly low in Japan's urban areas; for example, in Tokyo Prefecture it was 1.1 in 1993.

2. This refers to the average life expectancy at birth. Corresponding ratios for males (females) in other OECD countries are 72.2 (79.1) in the United States in 1991, 72.8 (80.9) in France in 1990, and 72.6 (79.0) in Germany from 1988 to 1990 (OECD 1990).

3. These figures include self-employed older workers, many of whom are in the agricultural sector. Although the average rate of labor force participation of the self-employed is higher, their share in total labor is now shrinking in size, resulting in a downward bias in the average participation ratio. Because of this, the ratio of employees (rather than total workers) to the population is a better indicator for the labor force behavior of older workers. Between 1987 and 1993, the comparable ratios of male employees (i.e., excluding the self-employed) age 60 to 64 to the population went from 38 percent to 46.5 percent; the same ratios for male workers age 65 and above went from 13.3 percent to 17 percent (Management and Coordination Agency 1994).

4. Throughout the 1980s, countries with relatively high labor force growth such as the United States and Australia had low rates of total factor productivity (TFP) growth, while major European countries with relatively low rates of labor force growth had high TFP growth (Yashiro and Oishi 1993).

5. The logic behind the projected decline in the external surplus is that household savings are more dependent on the life cycle patterns of household members, while business investment is primarily affected by changes in labor force growth and quality, which can be enhanced by technology.

6. For example, in 1992 an average public pension benefit for a couple in Japan was 151,000 yen per month (about US$ 1,192), which is roughly 20 percent lower than a similar pension in Sweden. In contrast, the full pension granted to Japanese who have contributed into the fund for 35 years would be 43 percent larger, a figure well exceeding the current pension level in Sweden.

7. The majority of OECD countries, except France, Italy, and New Zealand, set the eligibility age for males and females at 65 years and 60 years or above, respectively (OECD 1990). In Japan the eligibility age for public pensions for the self-employed is set at 65 years.

8. The public pension premium is shared equally between employers and employees in Japan.

9. Recently, nominal user charges of 1,000 yen (roughly US$ 10.00) per month and 700 yen (roughly US$ 7.00) per day for hospitalization were introduced.

10. The proportion of drug costs relative to total medical expenditures was 18 percent in 1986, compared to 7 percent in the United States (Schieber and Poullier 1989).

11. "Three generation families" in which parents, children, and grandchildren live together and share the family budget accounted for nearly 50 percent of agricultural households in 1990. The equivalent ratios for non-agricultural households and employee households were 16 percent and 11 percent, respectively (Management and Coordination Agency 1990).

12. This works in an opposite way from a housing loan. The owner of a house borrows from a financial institution annually until the accumulated amount reaches the value of the house.

References

Bos, Eduard et al. 1992. *World Population Projections: 1992–93 Edition*. Baltimore, MD.: The Johns Hopkins University Press.

Hatta, Tatsuo, and Noriyuki Oguchi. 1993. *The Public Pension Debt of the Japanese Government*. Mimeo. Paper presented at the Joint Conference of the National Bureau of Economic Research and the Japan Center for Economic Research, September, Tokyo.

Japan Center for Economic Research. 1995. *Japan in the Year 2020: Complementarity between the Aging of the Population and the Internationalization of Economic Activities*. Tokyo: JCER.

Management and Coordination Agency. 1990. *Basic Survey of People's Welfare*. Tokyo: Government Printing Office.

———. 1994. *Annual Survey of Labor Force*. Tokyo: Government Printing Office.

Ministry of Health and Welfare. 1992. *Population Projections for Japan*. Tokyo: Government Printing Office [in Japanese].

Noguchi, Yukio. 1993. *After-Retirement Income Maintenance by Home Equity Conversion: Possibility in Japan*. Mimeo. Paper presented at the Joint Conference of the National Bureau of Economic Research and the Japan Center for Economic Research, September, Tokyo.

OECD. 1985. *The Role of the Public Sector*. Paris, France: OECD.

———. 1990. *The Economic Survey of Japan* (1989–90). Paris, France: OECD.

Schieber, G.S., and J.P. Poullier. 1989. "Overview of International Comparisons of Health Care Expenditures." *Health Care Financing Review, (Annual Supplement)*.

Takayama, Noriyuki. 1992. *The Graying of Japan: An Economic Perspective on Public Pensions*. Tokyo: Kinokuniya and Oxford University Press.

U.S. Department of Health and Human Services. 1994. *Social Security Programs Throughout the World—1993*. Social Security Administration, Office of Research and Statistics. SSA Publication No. 13-11805. Research Report no. 63. May.

Yashiro, Naohiro. 1993. *The Economic Position of the Elderly in Japan with Specific Reference to Sample Selection Bias*. Mimeo. Paper presented at the Joint Conference of the National Bureau of Economic Research and the Japan Center for Economic Research, September, Tokyo.

Yashiro, Naohiro, and Akiko Oishi. 1993. *Population Aging and the Saving and Investment Balance in Japan*. Mimeo. Paper presented at the Joint Conference of the National Bureau of Economic Research and the Japan Center for Economic Research, September, Tokyo.

Yashiro, Naohiro, and Yoshiaki Maeda. 1994. "The Applicability of Life Cycle Hypothesis to Japan" [in Japanese]. *Nihonkeizaikenkyuu*, no. 27.

Yoshitomi, Masaru, and Naohiro Yashiro. 1992. "Long-term Economic Issues in Japan and the Asia-Pacific Region." In *Long-term Prospects for the World Economy*, ed. OECD. Paris, France: OECD.

Chapter Four

THE MYTH OF THE DEMOGRAPHIC IMPERATIVE

Peter Scherer

Below I examine with a critical eye the concept of the demographic imperative as it pertains to OECD countries. I argue that, although there is a relationship between aging and the extent of public transfer, governments react to make the link less stark and less mechanical than is often maintained. I also maintain that economic activity within demographic groups, particularly the growth in non-employment among adult males, is the main cause of strain on OECD nations' social protection systems. After discussing the growing demand for long-term care for the frail elderly—a very real burden resulting from demographic change—I conclude by drawing parallels between the debate about demographic pressures and the "Club of Rome" debate of the 1970s about scarcity of natural resources.

WHAT MIGHT THE DEMOGRAPHIC IMPERATIVE MEAN?

One of the policy myths that has arisen in the course of domestic policy debates is the idea that demographic changes will necessarily constrain fiscal policy over the next half century. Particular concern lies with the expected increase in the proportion of the population no longer working and eligible to draw a public pension.

The reason for this concern is summarized in table 4.1. In the sample of OECD countries covered, the ratio of people of "working age" (15 to 64) to those above that age, was 7.5 on average in 1960. By 1990 it had fallen to 5.4, and by 2020 it is projected to drop to 3.8. Unless there are massive unanticipated migration flows or changes in mortality, these projections are likely to be fulfilled. Although this aging ratio is affected by future birth rates, about which it is prudent to be cautious, assuring current projections, the ratio can be expected to decline to 2.5 in less than 50 years from now.

Table 4.1 WORKING-AGE POPULATION PER ELDERLY PERSON IN SELECTED OECD COUNTRIES (RATIO OF THOSE AGE 15–64 TO THOSE AGE 65+)

	1960	1980	1990	2000	2020	2040
Australia	7.2 (1961)	6.6 (1981)	6.0	5.5 (2001)	3.7 (2021)	2.9 (2031)
Austria	5.4	4.2	4.5	4.3	3.3	2.1
Belgium	5.2 (1961)	4.6 (1981)	4.5	3.9	3.1	2.2
Canada	7.7 (1961)	7.0 (1981)	5.9[a]	4.9 (2001)	3.1 (2021)	2.3 (2036)
Denmark	6.0	4.5	4.3	4.4	3.3	N/A
Finland	8.5	5.6	5.0	4.6	2.9	2.7
France	N/A	4.6	4.7	N/A	N/A	N/A
Greece	N/A	5.0	4.9 (1988)	N/A	N/A	N/A
Japan	11.2	7.4	5.8	4.0	2.4	2.1
New Zealand	9.0 (1961)	6.4 (1981)	5.8 (1991)	5.6 (2001)	4.1 (2021)	2.7 (2031)
Norway	5.7	4.3	4.0	4.3	3.6	2.8
Portugal	7.9	5.5 (1981)	5.0[a]	4.6	3.1 (2025)	2.6 (2035)
Spain	7.6	5.6	5.0	4.2	3.7	2.1
Sweden	5.5	3.9	3.6	3.7	3.0	N/A
Switzerland	6.2	4.7	4.5	4.2	3.2	2.6
Turkey	15.1	11.3	13.8	11.3	11.0 (2005)	N/A
United Kingdom[b]	5.5	4.3	4.2	4.1	3.5	2.8
United States	6.5	5.9	5.3	5.4	3.6	2.7
GROUP AVERAGE[c]	7.5	5.6	5.4	5.0	3.8	2.5

Source: OECD, 1994a, p. 100.
a. Estimated ratio.
b. In the United Kingdom, elderly refers to women 60+ and men 65+.
c. Non-weighted averages.

At any point in time, public pension regulations prescribe a certain rate of pension to be paid for given work experience and earnings histories.[1] Other expenditures are associated with age. In particular, health care needs and costs are greater for the elderly than for younger people in any given country. It is therefore true in a mechanical sense that if *per capita* transfers to and expenditures on the elderly retain their value relative to average incomes of the working-age population, the aging process will lead to higher expenditures, both on public pensions and on other forms of service provision. Several researchers have used such scenarios to explore the possible implications for public finances of aging populations in industrialized countries (see, for example, Hageman and Nicoletti 1989; and Van den Noord and Herd 1993). Such exercises always show that if policies and behavior remain unchanged, the aging of the population will result in an increase in transfers over the course of the decade and a resultant worsening in public finances.

However, it is important not to confuse this mechanical process with the actual public policy choices that countries face. The crucial question is: How much discretion do countries have to vary their rates of transfers and of direct expenditures in light of aging populations? One way to test this is to see whether countries that already have relatively elderly populations also have relatively high levels of expenditure on transfers. Figure 4.1 shows publicly financed direct expenditures and transfers as a percentage of GDP in OECD countries.[2]

On the surface, this figure indicates that there is indeed a strong relationship. Across the 21 OECD countries included, each one percentage increase in the proportion of the elderly population is associated with an increase of 2.27 percent in public social protection transfers and expenditures as a proportion of GDP. The relationship is statistically significant, although there are clearly other explanatory factors at work, as illustrated by the many countries that lie a long way from the central slope.

Figure 4.1 PUBLIC SOCIAL PROTECTION TRANSFERS AND EXPENDITURES, AND EXTENT OF AGING, OECD, 1990

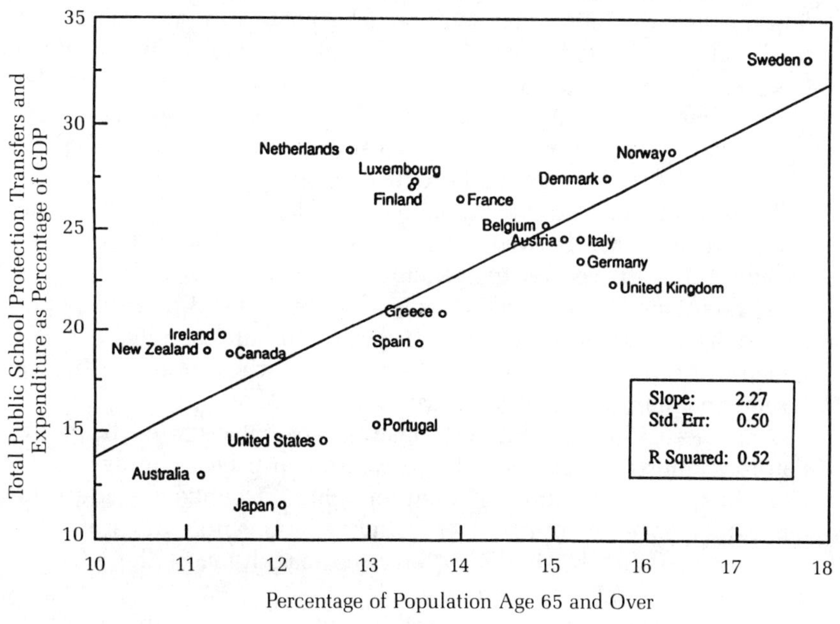

Source: OECD 1994a, d.

Does this relationship impose a similar burden in most countries? Figure 4.1 includes *all* public transfers and expenditures. However, it is easy to think that the relationship it shows is due to transfers to the elderly—in particular, public pensions. On this issue, the work of Van den Noord and Herd (1993) is suggestive. They show that, under particular assumptions made for the purposes of the exercise,[3] the net present value of future pension liabilities ranges from 43 percent of GDP (in the United States) to 250 percent (in Canada).

The range of these estimates shows that there is considerable variation across countries in pension systems, so that the fiscal liabilities they represent are as much a function of design as of the inherent nature of the aging process. Another way to demonstrate this is to look at how expenditures on pensions vary with the extent of aging. If the aging process were the major factor determining expenditures on pensions, one might expect that the proportion of elderly people in the population would largely determine the proportion of GDP that is transferred to them.

In fact, looking across OECD countries today it is clear that there is a link between the proportion of GDP spent on public support for the elderly and the proportion of the population that is elderly (figure 4.2). On average, each extra one percentage increase in the elderly population is associated with an additional 1.2 percent in public transfers to the elderly. Furthermore, some countries (notably, Austria, Italy, Greece, Luxembourg, and France)[4] show a rate of transfers to the elderly that is much higher than that of other countries. If these "outlying" countries are excluded, the result (see dotted line on figure 4.2) is a better fit and a slightly reduced slope.

Transfers to the elderly, therefore, account for less than half the overall relationship between total transfers and aging that is shown in figure 4.1. To what is the remainder attributable? Health care is often mentioned as a possible cause of higher expenditures as populations age. It is certainly the case that within any national system, expenditure increases with age, and that most health expenditures are attributable to the last few years of life. However, as figure 4.3 shows, these intranational relationships are not reflected in cross-country comparisons: there is no relationship between aggregate health expenditures and the extent of aging.[5] If public expenditures alone are considered (figure 4.4), a slight relationship is apparent, but it is not statistically significant and the magnitude of the effect is slight.

Clearly, within each of the countries shown in the figure, the costs of medical care are higher for the elderly than for the nonelderly.

Figure 4.2 PUBLIC TRANSFERS TO THE ELDERLY AND EXTENT OF AGING, OECD, 1990

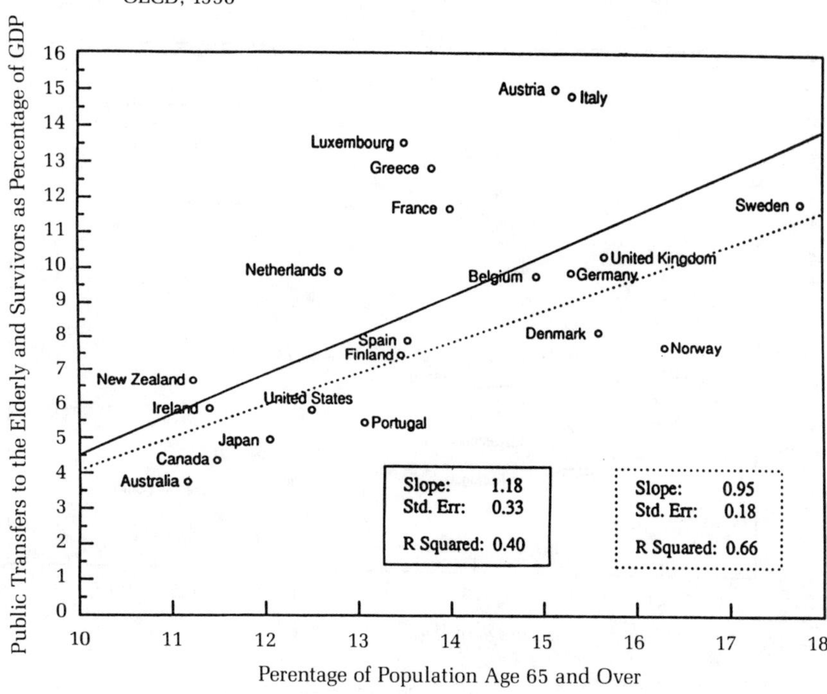

Source: OECD 1994a, d.

However, the range of rates of expenditure suggests that countries can address potentially higher costs of health care for the elderly by rationalizing their health care systems. There is no need for the burden to become unmanageable.

This leaves transfers to the nonelderly. Figure 4.5 shows that these are also correlated with the extent of population aging: the slope of the relationship (one additional percentage point in the ratio of transfers to GDP for each additional percentage in the population who are elderly) is similar to that for transfers to the elderly (figure 4.2). However, in this case the relationship is due to the fact that five countries with extensive welfare transfers to the nonelderly (the four Nordic countries plus the Netherlands) also have relatively elderly populations. When these five countries are excluded (see dotted line on figure 4.5), the relationship disappears.

Figure 4.3 HEALTH EXPENDITURES (PUBLIC AND PRIVATE) AND EXTENT OF AGING, OECD, 1990

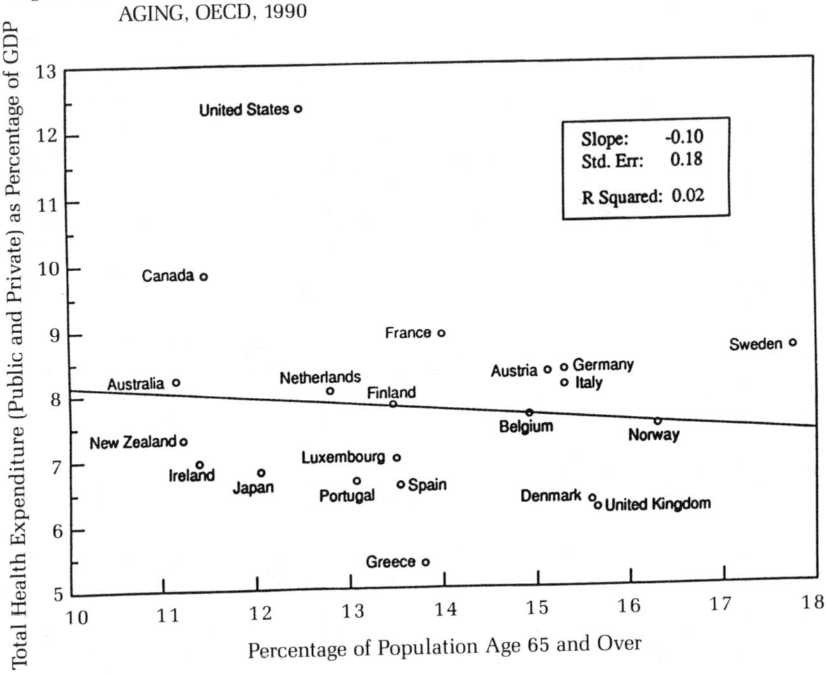

Source: OECD 1994a, d.

Figure 4.6 shows preliminary data on the purposes of these transfers to and expenditures on the nonelderly. Some categories, notably services for the disabled, do include expenditures that relate to the elderly. But taken as a whole, the four "high-expenditure" nations shown (Sweden, Denmark, the Netherlands, and Finland—data are not available for Norway) have made a policy choice that is not the result of demographic constraints and that to some extent runs counter to them. The extent of social expenditures is governed by decisions based on considerations much wider than purely demographic factors. The Nordic countries, while having the highest proportion of elderly people, generally are transferring less through public pension systems than might be expected when their age structure is taken into account. Rather, these countries have high rates of transfer to the nonelderly. Clearly, it is social choice, not demographics, that drives these expenditures. By the same token, there are a number of European countries where *high* rates of income transfers to the elderly are clearly the result of policy choices, and are not demographically determined.

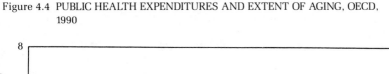

Figure 4.4 PUBLIC HEALTH EXPENDITURES AND EXTENT OF AGING, OECD, 1990

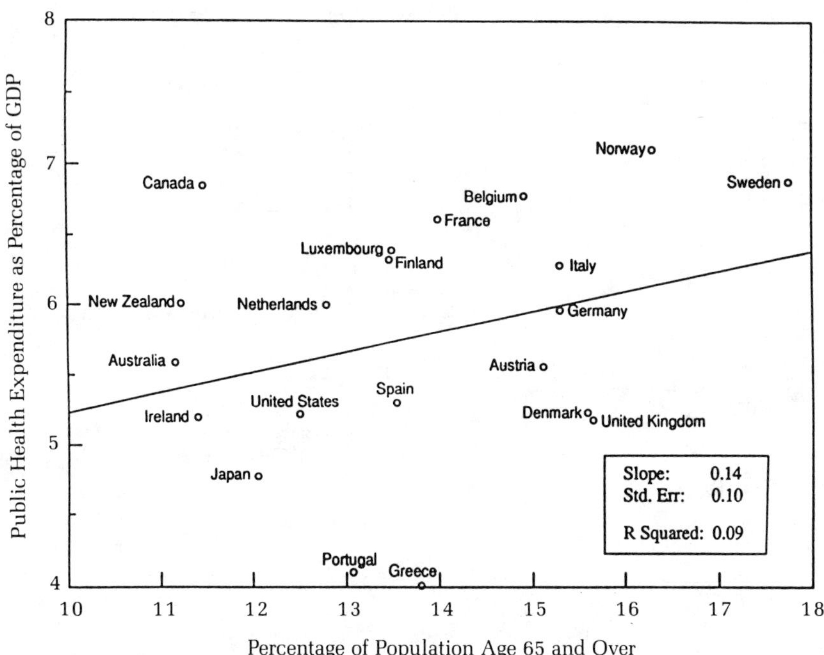

Source: OECD 1994a, d.

The proportion of the population that is elderly will increase in all OECD countries over the next thirty years. By the year 2020, this proportion is expected to be (on average) similar to Sweden's proportion of elderly today, about 3.8 (table 4.1). If the cross-country pattern shown in figure 4.2 were to persist over time, this would lead to an increase in transfers to the elderly by about 5 percent of GDP, which is by no means inconsiderable. However, this is much less than would be predicted from the overall relationship shown in figure 4.1, or from projecting forward current rates of pension expenditure.[6]

Furthermore, any discussion of demographic strains should take account of the whole dependent population. Aging will be accompanied by (in fact, its continuation to the year 2040 will in part be caused by) a low and falling proportion of children in the population. As table 4.2 shows, the working-age population per dependent person will not fall nearly as rapidly. Thus, while pension systems will clearly have to be adjusted to cater to the greater proportion of the

Figure 4.5 PUBLIC TRANSFERS (OTHER THAN FOR HEALTH) TO THE NONELDERLY, AND EXTENT OF AGING, OECD, 1990

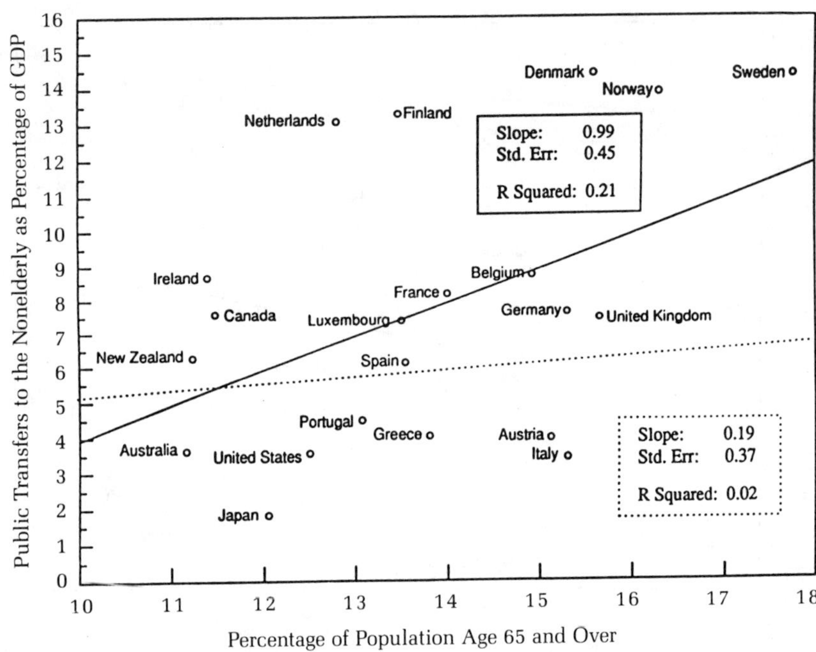

Regression excluding Denmark, Finland, Norway, Sweden, and the Netherlands.

Source: OECD 1994a, d.

population that is aged, some wiggle room will be provided by the decline in the demographic pressure from the young. Of course, some of the investment currently being made in educating children will have to be diverted to adult continuing education if the overall rate of skill formation is to be maintained. Otherwise, long-term growth rates may not be sustained (see also the caution noted in the Steuerle essay, this volume).

ECONOMIC ACTIVITY AMONG DEMOGRAPHIC GROUPS

At least historically, a main threat to fiscal balance in OECD countries has not come from demographic change, but from changes in the economic performance among demographic groups, which in turn is

Figure 4.6 MAIN PURPOSES OF PUBLIC TRANSFERS OTHER THAN FOR HEALTH TO THE NONELDERLY, AS A PERCENTAGE OF GDP, 1989

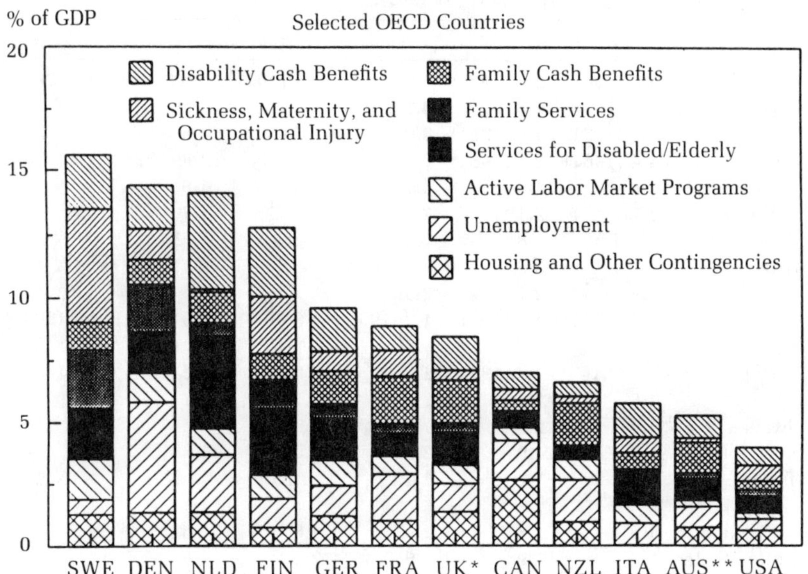

Source: OEDC Social Data Base.
*United Kingdom = 1988.
**AUS = Australia.
European Union countries exclude expenditure on sickness benefits.

related partly to retirement policy independently from aging patterns. Male employment has fallen as a percentage of the working-age population, while female employment has risen in most OECD countries (figures 4.7 and 4.8). The rise in non-employment among males that this implies has been largely due to delayed entry into the labor force by the young and a tendency for a larger proportion of the age group 55–64 to retire. Among women, the same tendencies are evident but are countered by increasing labor force participation by women in their adult years (figures 4.9 and 4.10). It is these changes in activity among the nonelderly, combined with the inherited structure of pension systems, that determine this source of fiscal pressure.

The growth in early retirement has been facilitated by the growing availability of pension wealth for two reasons. First, individuals who have a preference for leisure have been able to divert savings that would otherwise have been used to support them in their old age to finance earlier retirement. Second, a consensus grew that if there was

Table 4.2 WORKING-AGE POPULATION PER DEPENDENT PERSON IN SELECTED OECD COUNTRIES (RATIO OF THOSE AGE 15–64 TO THOSE WHO ARE YOUNG—AGE 0–14—AND OLD—AGE 65+)

	1960	1980	1990	2000	2020	2040
Australia	1.6 (1961)	1.9 (1981)	2.0	2.1 (2001)	1.9 (2021)	1.7 (2031)
Austria	1.9	1.8	2.1	N/A	N/A	N/A
Belgium	1.8 (1961)	1.9 (1981)	2.0	2.0	1.8	1.4
Canada	1.4 (1961)	2.1 (1981)	2.1[a]	2.1 (2001)	1.8 (2021)	1.5 (2036)
Denmark	1.8	1.8	2.1	2.0	1.8	N/A
Finland	1.7	2.1	2.1	2.1	1.7	1.6
France	N/A	1.8	1.9	N/A	N/A	N/A
Greece	N/A	2.8	N/A	N/A	N/A	N/A
Japan	1.8	2.1	2.3	2.1	1.5	1.3
New Zealand	1.4 (1961)	1.7 (1981)	1.9 (1991)	1.9 (2001)	1.9 (2021)	1.1 (2031)
Norway	1.7	1.7	1.8	N/A	N/A	N/A
Portugal	N/A	1.7 (1981)	1.9[a]	2.0	1.8 (2025)	1.6 (2035)
Spain	1.8	1.7	2.0	2.1	2.2	1.5
Sweden	1.9	1.8	1.8	1.6	1.6	N/A
Switzerland	1.8	1.9	2.0	2.0	1.8	1.6
Turkey	1.1	1.2	1.4	N/A	N/A	N/A
United Kingdom[b]	1.9	1.8	1.9	1.8	1.8	1.5
United States	1.5	1.9	1.9	2.3	1.8	1.6
GROUP AVERAGE[c]	1.7	1.9	2.0	2.0	1.8	1.5

Source: OECD 1994a, p. 100.
a. Estimated ratio.
b. In the United Kingdom, elderly refers to women 60+ and men 65+.
c. Non-weighted averages.

to be a retrenchment of labor it should be concentrated on those eligible for income support through early retirement. In particular, public pensions often offer benefits to those who have lost their jobs, while employer-sponsored pension funds (which often receive considerable tax benefits) are another important source of such income support. Pension systems that distort working life patterns in this way would need to be reformed even if populations were not aging, although it is of course true that as populations age, the cost of subsidized early retirement may become unsupportable.[7]

In general, the high rates of non-employment among working-age men and particularly the persistence of long-term unemployment is a major policy concern (see OECD 1994b, 1994c). It represents a failure to use to the fullest extent the potential of the workforce. But from the demographic perspective, it is a positive sign. OECD economies are at the moment nowhere near any *demographic* constraint. There are

Figure 4.7 EMPLOYMENT POPULATION RATIOS[a], 1980–1991 (AVERAGES AND PERCENTAGE POINT CHANGES[b])

Source: OECD 1994a.

a. An employment ratio is defined as the sum of persons in employment (part-time and full-time) as a percentage of the working-age population (age 15–64). It is calculated over the period 1980–1991 unless otherwise specified.

b. Changes is defined as 1991 less 1980 unless otherwise specified.

c. 1981 to 1990.

d. 1981 to 1990 excluding 1982.

e. 1981 to 1989 excluding 1982.

f. 1981 to 1988 excluding 1982.

g. 1983 to 1990.

h. 1983 to 1988.

i. 1981 to 1991 excluding 1982, 1984, and 1986.

j. 1980 to 1991 excluding 1981 to 1985.

k. 1987 to 1991.

Figure 4.8 EMPLOYMENT POPULATION RATIOS[a], 1980–1991 (AVERAGES AND PERCENTAGE POINT CHANGES[b])

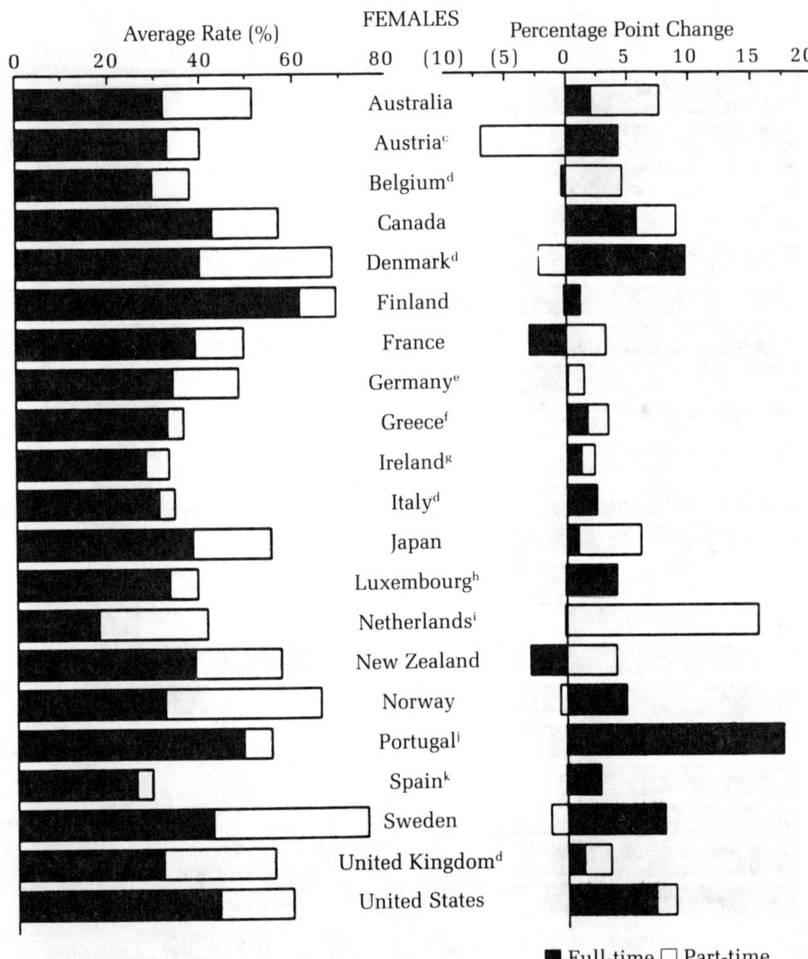

Source: OECD 1994a.

a. An employment ratio is defined as the sum of persons in employment (part-time and full-time) as a percentage of the working-age population (age 15–64). It is calculated over the period 1980–1991 unless otherwise specified.

b. Change is defined as 1991 less 1980 unless otherwise specified.

c. 1981 to 1990.

d. 1981 to 1990 excluding 1982.

e. 1981 to 1989 excluding 1982.

f. 1981 to 1988 excluding 1982.

g. 1983 to 1990.

h. 1983 to 1988.

i. 1981 to 1991 excluding 1982, 1984, and 1986.

j. 1980 to 1991 excluding 1981 to 1985.

k. 1987 to 1991.

many working-age resources that are not being used. Clearly, this underutilization of human resources may be reducing the total resources available to support dependents.[8] While the fall in the labor force participation of men has been accompanied by an increase in participation of women, this has at best maintained the overall ratio of workers to the working-age population. A revival in total employment rate among the non-elderly would do much to relieve the fiscal pressures that even soundly designed public pension systems are experiencing.

A REAL DEMOGRAPHIC DILEMMA: LONG-TERM CARE FOR THE ELDERLY

Nonetheless, it is true that OECD populations can be expected to age considerably over the next decade and that, in particular, the number of people age 80 and above is almost certain to rise dramatically from present levels, as it has done over the past three decades (table 4.3). The cost of providing care for the elderly rises dramatically when they enter institutions, and thus it is alarming that the proportion of the institutionalized elderly has been rising in a number of countries (figure 4.11). If this trend continues, the cost of care for the very elderly will rise sharply. Moreover, the costs of institutional care, unlike those of pension payments, are not cash transfers that may or may not increase consumption. Institutional care costs represent real resource usage that often leaves the community with lower *per capita* incomes to be spent on other items.

One reason for the growth in nursing home care provision is that it has replaced the even higher costs of placing elderly people in hospitals designed for acute care. Despite the growth in nursing home care provision, the elderly often resist nursing home stays because, while hospital care is usually covered by health insurance, long-term care for chronic conditions often is not. Hence, elderly patients in OECD countries tend to resist being moved into long-term care institutions.

Long-term care provision is less expensive than the provision of hospital care, but still more expensive than the average pension. Thus, in countries in which the recipients of long-term care are expected to pay for it themselves, those who need it can quickly become impoverished. Their homes can be sold (or mortgaged to the authorities and sold after the death of their surviving spouse), and in countries such

Figure 4.9 NON-EMPLOYMENT RATES[a], 1980–1991 (AVERAGES AND PERCENTAGE POINT CHANGES[b])

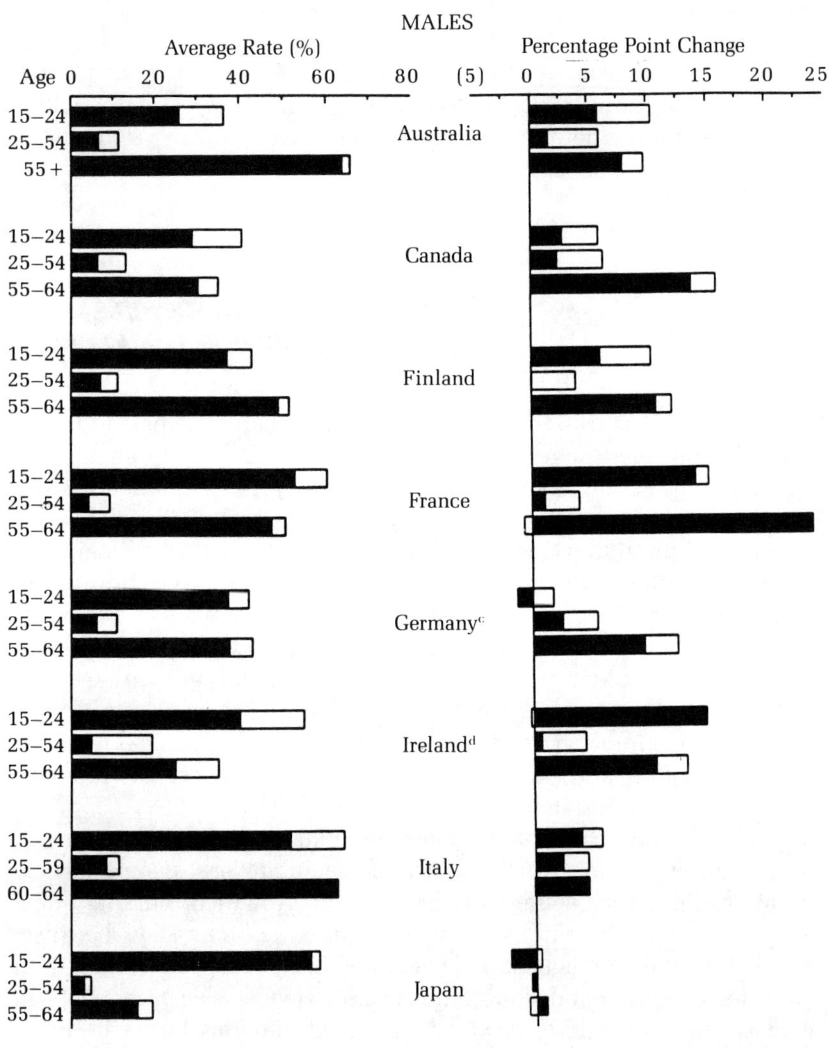

Figure 4.9 (continued) NON-EMPLOYMENT RATES[a], 1980–1991 (AVERAGES AND PERCENTAGE POINT CHANGES[b])

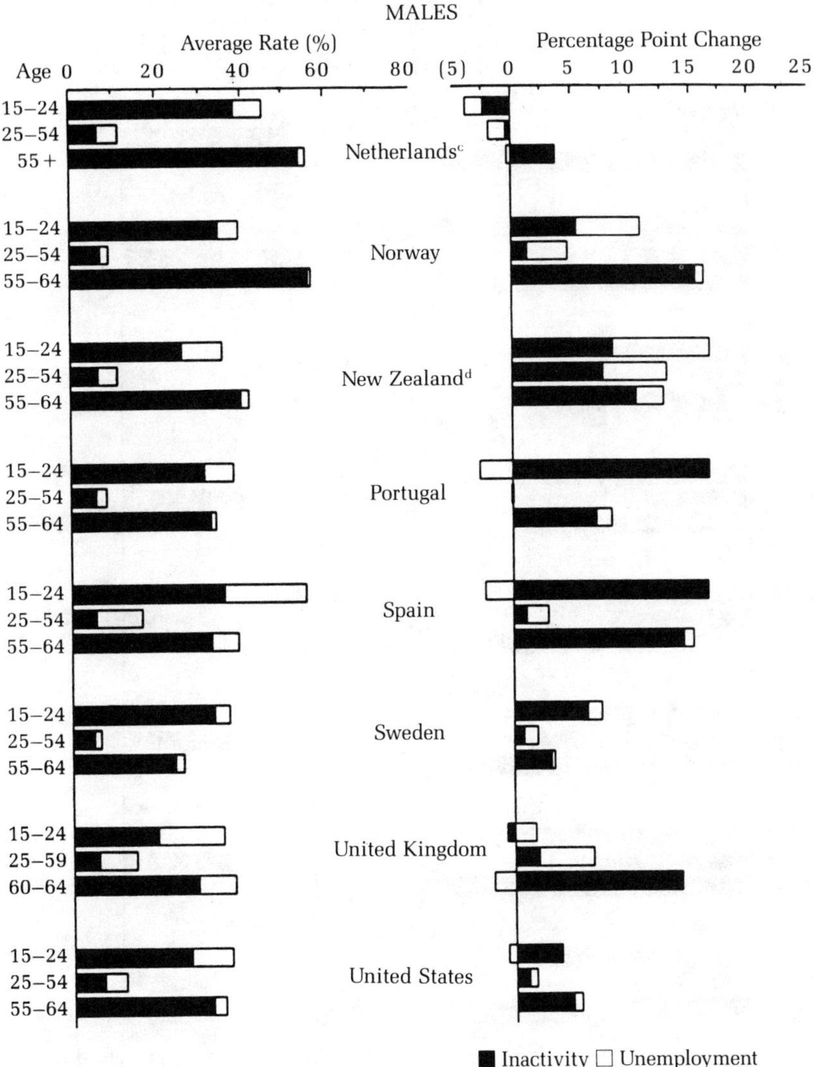

Source: OECD 1994a.

a. A non-employment rate is defined as the sum of persons not in employment (unemployed and inactive) as a percentage of the population specified. It is calculated over the period 1980–1991 unless otherwise specified.

b. Change is defined as 1991 less 1980 unless otherwise specified.

c. Netherlands: 1987 to 1989.

d. New Zealand: 1986 to 1991.

Figure 4.10 NON-EMPLOYMENT RATES[a], 1980–1991 (AVERAGES AND PERCENTAGE POINT CHANGES[b])

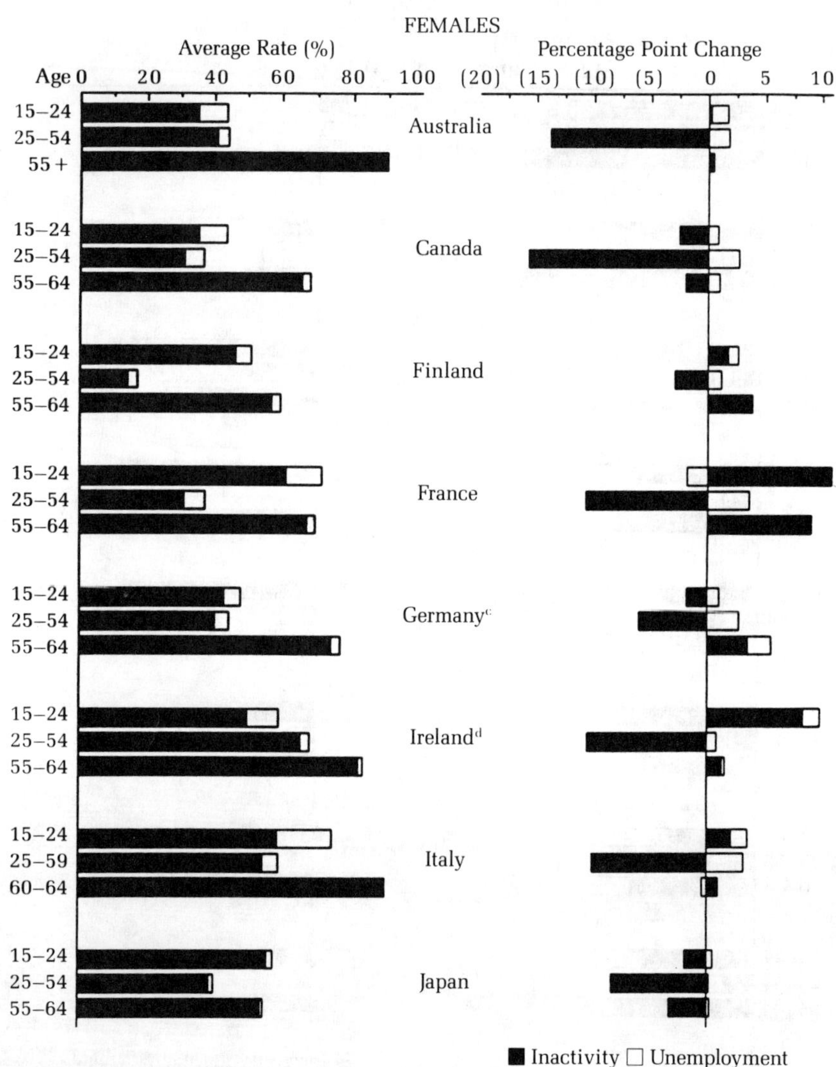

Figure 4.10 (continued) NON-EMPLOYMENT RATES[a], 1980–1991 (AVERAGES AND PERCENTAGE POINT CHANGES[b])

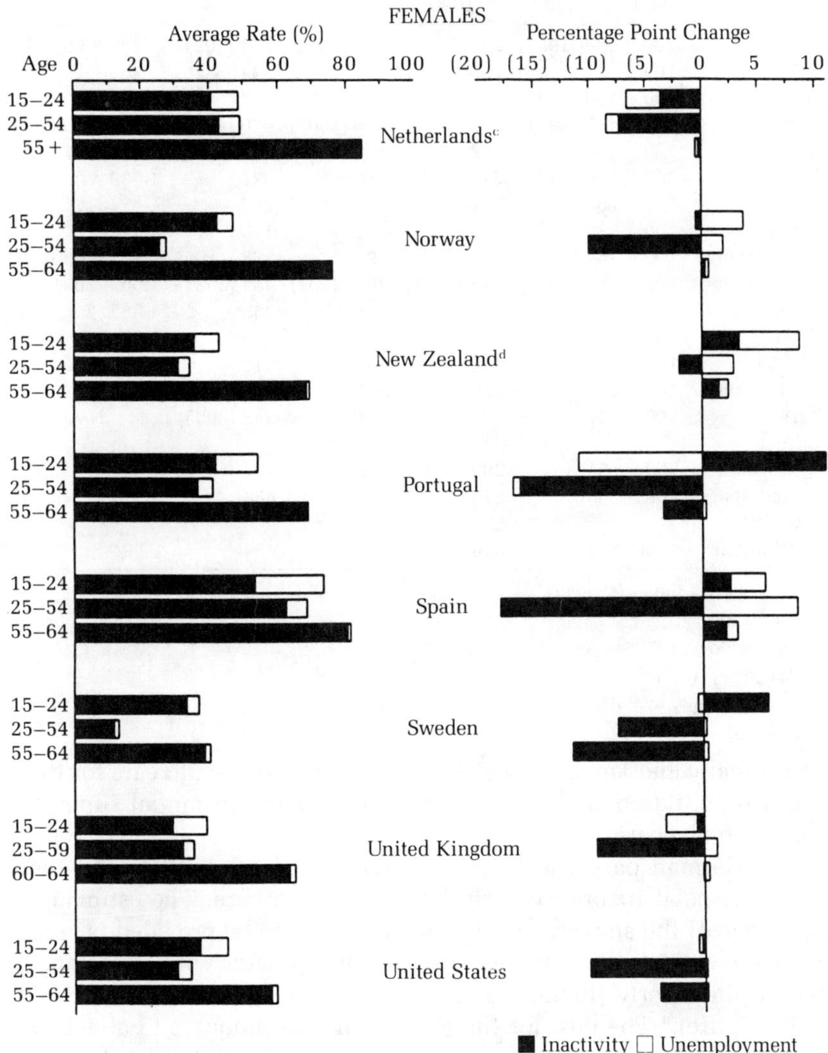

Source: OECD 1994a.

a. A non-employment rate is defined as the sum of persons not in employment (unemployed and inactive) as a percentage of the population specified. It is calculated over the period 1980–1991 unless otherwise specified.

b. Change is defined as 1991 less 1980 unless otherwise specified.

c. Netherlands: 1987 to 1989.

d. New Zealand: 1986 to 1991.

Table 4.3 GROWTH IN NUMBER OF PEOPLE AGE 80 AND ABOVE IN SELECTED OECD COUNTRIES, 1980–2040

	1960	1980	1990	2000	2020	2040
Australia	100[a]	194 (1981)	286	445 (2001)	705 (2021)	1,062 (2031)
Austria	100	162	228	226	334	494
Belgium	100[a]	150 (1981)	193	202	293	396
Canada	100[a]	198 (1981)	277[b]	446 (2001)	690 (2021)	1,075 (2036)
Denmark	100	190	252	286	285	N/A
Finland	100	210	349	410	521	723
France[c]	100	156	192	197	242	N/A
Japan	100	239	435	673	1,327	1,480
Luxembourg[c]	100	164 (1981)	190 (1987)	199	268	313 (2030)
New Zealand	100[a]	148 (1981)	212 (1991)	292 (2001)	434 (2021)	605 (2031)
Norway	100	170	225	268	255	385
Spain	100	170	260	314	384	474
Sweden	100	181	255	309	312	N/A
Switzerland	100	203	296	324	403	522
Turkey[c]	100	227	285	331	442 (2005)	N/A
United Kingdom	100	151	209	239	274	357
United States	100	206	276	373	483	918
GROUP AVERAGE[d]	100	184	260	326	454	694

Source: OECD 1994a, p. 103.
a. 1961 = 100.
b. Estimated.
c. Age group is 75+.
d. Non-weighted average.

as Germany and Japan, in which relatives are required to care for the indigent, children can be required to contribute substantial sums to their parents' care.

The German parliament has recently passed a law to extend the German social insurance system to cover such care. The estimated total cost of the subsidy for the long-term care to be provided is estimated to be 27 billion DM per year, which compares with total transfers to the elderly (including survivors' benefits) of 240 billion DM (1988 figure).[9] The cost for the expansion thus amounts to about 10 percent of the pension income of the elderly. It should be noted, however, that this subsidy will not cover all expenditures; a part will still be payable by the recipient or the local authority (Alber 1994).

Germany's expansion of its social insurance system to cover long-term care is to be financed not by a charge on the elderly, but by a compulsory charge paid by all contributors to the insurance funds, of whom the majority are employees and their employers. The result is yet another net transfer of income flows from the active population to the inactive. This will only exacerbate the tendency to move out of the labor force, a tendency illustrated in figures 4.7 through 4.10.

This is not to deny that long-term care poses a considerable potential burden on the elderly, and that it may not be feasible to expect them to bear the cost themselves, even if the burden is distributed evenly. This problem is illustrated by the case of the United States, where the issue of cost has been better researched than in many other countries. Rivlin and Wiener (1988) have estimated that expenditure for long-term care already exceeded $1,300 per capita in 1987, at a time when average income per elderly person was $6,009. Hence, aggregate long-term care costs already amounted to over 21 percent of aggregate income of the elderly, and can be expected to increase at a faster rate than incomes in the future.[10]

This example illustrates that even a measure such as provision for long-term care, which is closely associated with a sharp demographic change, is a matter of choice. Long-term care represents a real economic burden, and meeting it will require resources. However, the incomes of the elderly themselves are sufficient to meet a large part of this burden—provided adequate insurance programs are in place to share the cost. If the cost of long-term care is to be met by the general population, another layer of transfers from the working-age population will be necessary, whether financed from specific taxes or, as is proposed in Japan, from a general consumption tax. But at least part of this burden will be the result of a decision not to tax the incomes of the elderly. It is the politics of demographic change, not demographic change itself, which is at issue.

CONCLUSION

I have argued in this paper that much of the debate on demographic pressures on our societies is reminiscent of the "Club of Rome" debate on natural resources 25 years ago.[11] As argued by the authors of the "Club of Rome" study, it is true that if we assume that the coefficients of consumption of resources per unit of output are fixed, growth of natural resources will quickly become impossible. Likewise, if demands on economic resources by various age groups are immutable, the burden of aging populations will start to erode economic incentives for the working-age population. But economic systems, governments, and the societies of which they are a part are more flexible

Figure 4.11 ELDERLY PEOPLE RESIDING IN INSTITUTIONS, 1960s–1990s (CHANGE IN PERCENTAGE OF EACH AGE GROUP)

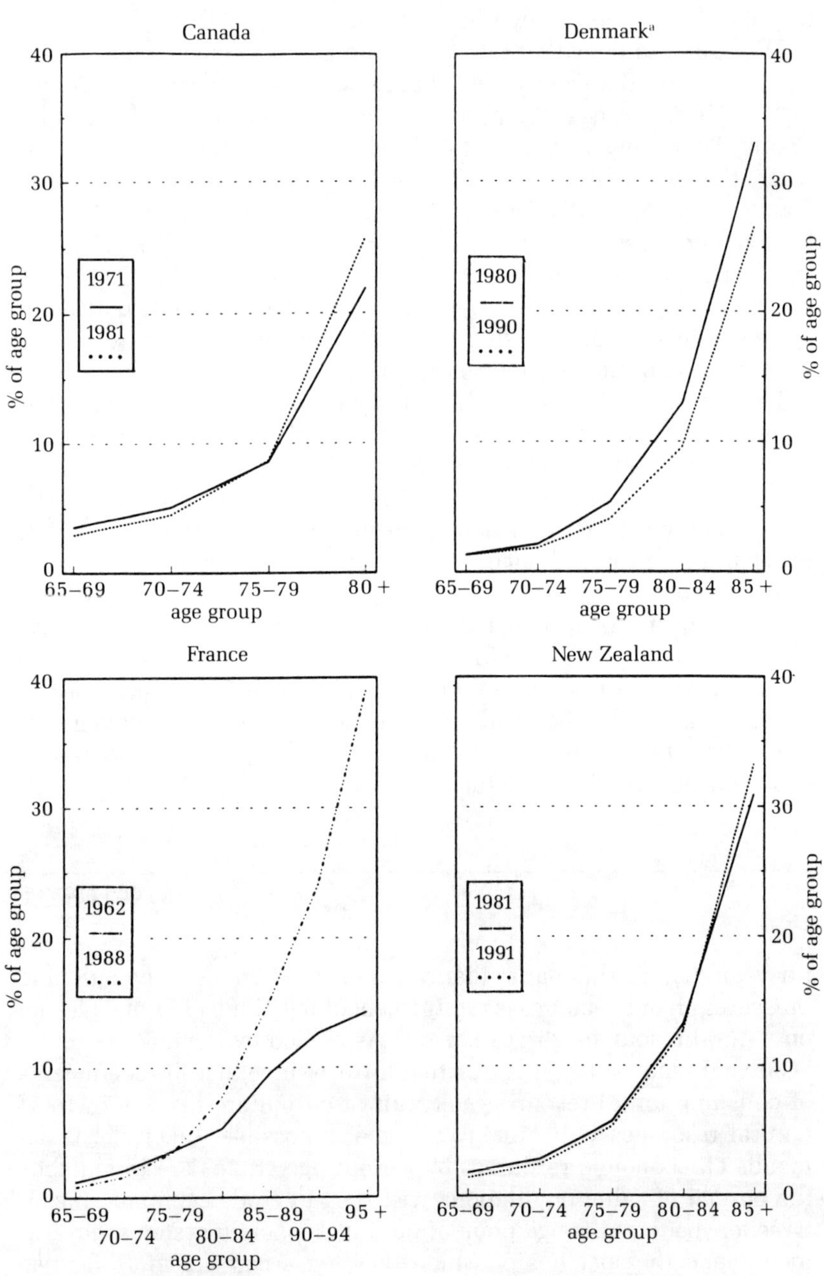

Source OECD (1994a).

a. Nursing homes only.

Figure 4.11 (continued) ELDERLY PEOPLE RESIDING IN INSTITUTIONS, 1960s–1990s (CHANGE IN PERCENTAGE OF EACH AGE GROUP)

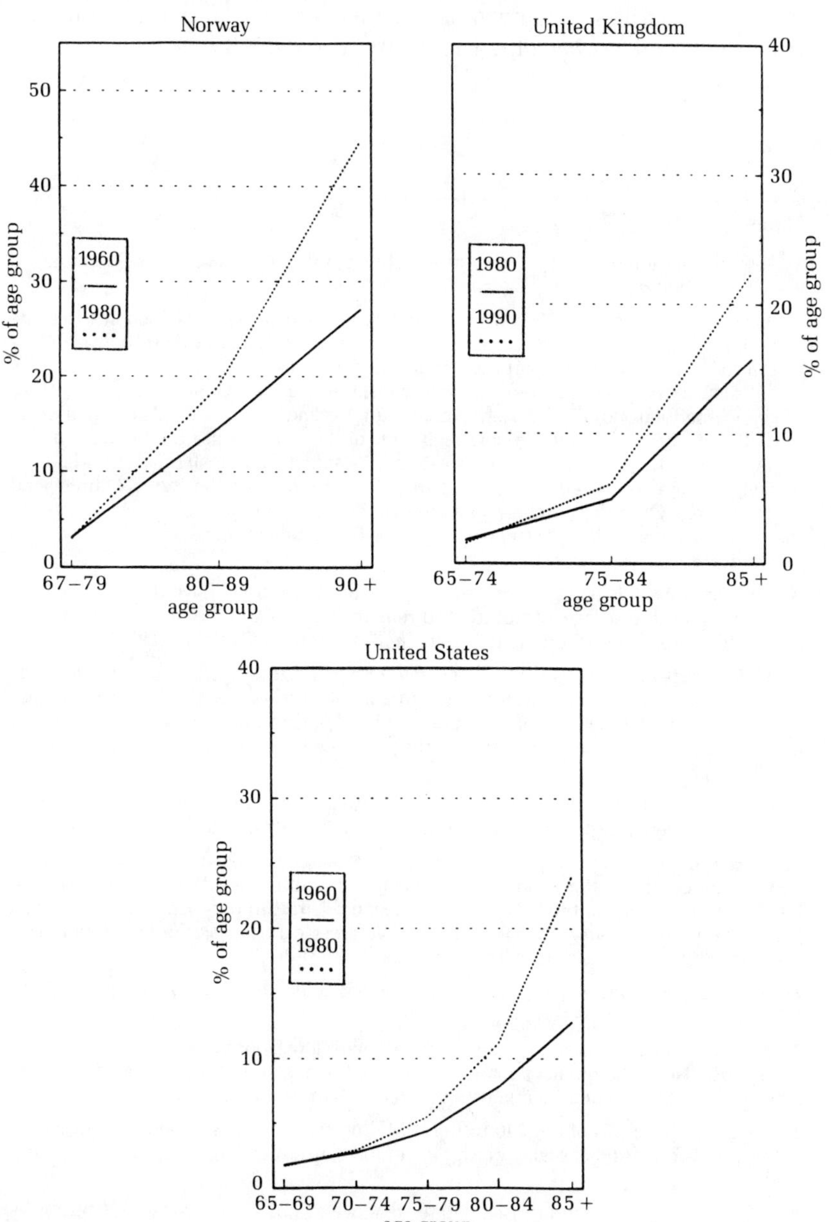

than such fixed coefficient models would suggest. There is only a need to see the future in terms of demographic imperatives if current transfer ratios are allowed to become dogma—a situation that most industrialized countries have the capability to avoid.

Notes

1. For a discussion of the rules governing public pension provision in OECD countries, see OECD (1988).

2. These figures are often described as the proportion of national incomes that are "expended" on social protection. However, this is a very misleading definition: transfers in the form of cash income support financed out of taxation, including compulsory social security charges, may represent expenditures as far as the budgetary authorities are concerned, but do not themselves constitute expenditure of GDP. The expenditure of GDP that results depends on how recipients of the transfers use the funds, and will always be less than the transfers. For example, some of the transfers will not be consumed, but will be saved or returned to the government in the form of direct and indirect taxes. Only the purchase of actual goods and services (such as health care in the United Kingdom) by governments and quasi-government organizations constitutes expenditure of GDP.

3. They assume that pension schemes in all countries studied have the same accrual structure, that this accrual structure will remain in place into the future, and that the aggregate value of contributions will remain at their current ratio to GDP.

4. There are three reasons for the high rate of expenditure in these countries. These include generous pension formula (see Eurostat 1993); low standard retirement ages (60 in France, 60 for men and 55 for women in Italy); and even lower effective retirement ages due to the ready availability of early pensions for those who have accrued full pension rights.

5. Cross-national variation in health expenditure per capita is very closely correlated with total domestic expenditure per capita (see OECD 1993, p. 15).

6. The German pension reform of 1989, and that passed in Japan in 1994, both show how policy can limit the escalation of transfers. In both cases, the intention more or less was to hold constant the ratio of net pension receipts to net earnings—implying a *fall* in the ratio of average pensions to average gross earnings as the population ages and contributions increase (see Takayama 1994).

7. The tendency to retire at earlier ages is explored at length in OECD (1992) and OECD (1994a).

8. But even this is not certain. Some countries with low labor force participation rates, such as the Netherlands, have maintained a continuous growth in average *per capita* incomes, and have maintained substantial redistributive flows.

9. About 6 billion DM of the 240 billion DM represent social assistance, out of which public provision of social assistance for the indigent needing long-term care is currently paid.

10. My colleague Mr. Hennessy calculates that average income per elderly family was $9,314. By using estimates from a 1984 survey of the proportion of elderly people who were married, he derives an average income per elderly person of $6,009.

11. This debate originated with the publication of Meadows et al. (1972), who presented a variety of catastrophic scenarios for the exhaustion of the world's resources and a consequent collapse of food supplies and living standards over the course of the next 100 years.

References

Alber, Jens. 1994. "The Debate Over Long-Term Care Insurance in Germany." Mimeo. Presented to OECD seminar on the care of the frail elderly, July.

Eurostat. 1993. *Old Age Replacement Ratios*, Volume 1. Luxembourg: Statistical Office of the European Communities.

Hageman, Robert P., and Giuseppe Nicoletti. 1989. "Population Aging: Economic Effects and Some Policy Implications for Financing Public Pensions." *OECD Economic Studies*, no. 12 (Spring).

Meadows, Donella H. et al. 1972. *The Limits to Growth: A Report for the Club of Rome's Project of the Predicament of Mankind*. New York: Universe Books.

OECD (Organization for Economic Cooperation and Development). 1994a. *New Orientations for Social Policy*. Paris: OECD.

________. 1994b. *The OECD Jobs Study: Facts, Analysis, Strategies*. Paris: OECD.

________. 1994c. *The OECD Jobs Study: Evidence and Explanations*. Paris: OECD.

________. 1994d. *Labor Force Statistics 1972–1992*. Paris: OECD.

________. 1993. *OECD Health Systems: Facts and Trends*. Vol. 1. Paris: OECD.

________. 1992. *Employment Outlook, July 1992* (Chapter 5, Labour Market Participation and Retirement of Older Workers). Paris: OECD

________. 1988. *Reforming Public Pensions*. Paris: OECD.

Rivlin, Alice M., and Joshua M. Wiener. 1988. *Caring for the Disabled Elderly: Who Will Pay?* Washington, D.C.: Brookings Institution.

Takayama, Moriyuki. 1994. "Preparing Public Pensions for an Old-Aged Society." *Japan Echo*, vol. XXI (Special Issue).

Van den Noord, Paul, and Richard Herd. 1993. *Pension Liabilities in Seven Major Economies*. Paris: OECD Economic Department Working Papers, no. 142.

COMMENTS ON "THE FISCAL IMPLICATIONS OF CHANGING DEMOGRAPHICS"

COMMENT BY STANFORD G. ROSS

The papers in this volume carefully delineate the long-term fiscal imbalance faced by all of the OECD countries. Although configurations of the imbalance vary depending on the individual country's demographics and design of social welfare and tax systems, the strategic problem is more or less universal.

There are a variety of ways to address the problem of fiscal imbalance. As a lawyer and former government official, I would like to focus my comments on the issue of the process of addressing the problem. How will change occur? When will it occur and why? Will change be orderly and based on reasoned policy development, or will it be abrupt and reflect extreme political pressures? If done in an orderly way with adequate lead time for transitions, the kinds of adjustments needed may not cause major societal dislocations. However, if change is delayed and done under great pressure, it could result in great hardships for individuals. Is there any reason to believe that orderly change will take place in any particular country?

The experience of the United States may be instructive. At almost every key juncture, the major changes in both the creation of our social welfare systems and their adjustment have taken place at the last minute and under extreme political pressure. The Social Security system was created in 1935 in response to the Great Depression and political developments that suggested the possibility of more radical approaches if action was not taken promptly. The expansions of the system were incremental from 1939 on, including the final major expansion in 1972, when benefits were raised 20 percent and indexed to inflation. However, changes since then—in response to stagflation in the 1970s, changing demographics, and other adverse conditions—have been anything but orderly.

It was clear almost immediately following the 1972 expansion, for instance, that the indexing of benefits was done improperly. Social Security beneficiaries wound up with a form of excessive indexing that was not addressed until 1977 remedial legislation. By then the Social Security system was facing extreme financial imbalances that required large tax increases and benefit cuts including a substantial reduction in the indexing formulas. However, the legislative change was done hurriedly and left the system with a financial structure that, despite politicians' claims that it had been fixed for at least the next half century, was in serious financial trouble within two years.

The 1983 adjustment of the system again was not carried out until the last minute—when benefit checks could not have been sent out without some legislation. At this point, the normal political process largely failed and an ad hoc commission of executive branch and congressional appointees came up with a package of revenue increases and benefit cuts that reset the system. The financing was designed to produce large surpluses that have, in fact, begun to materialize. However, these surpluses have masked the government's general deficit and may be seen as having had detrimental effects on the overall fiscal situation of the United States.

What, then, are the sources of the fiscal imbalance in the United States? First, we have revenue systems sometimes poorly matched to the expenditures they support. The United States, particularly, at the federal level, has established a *de facto* segregation of sources of revenue. The payroll tax largely supports social insurance entitlements, primarily Old-Age, Survivors, and Disability Insurance; health insurance for the elderly and disabled; and unemployment compensation. The federal individual and corporate income taxes support the general expenditure budget, which is running chronic deficits. The federal government imposes relatively few transactions taxes, which are largely the prerogative of the states, but increasingly has mandated social welfare expenditures for the states. Thus, the states, many of which are required to run a balanced budget, have revenue systems that also are matched poorly to expenditure obligations.

Second, as described by Professor Cordes in this volume, there are "over-promised benefit systems." Legally, Social Security Old-Age, Survivors, and Disability benefits can be changed, but it is difficult to make adjustments because of the strong political support these programs command and the clear moral promise that underlies the system. The same is true with health care for the elderly and disabled.

Third, there are weak political mechanisms for securing change of the revenue and benefit systems. A president has a four-year horizon, and sometimes as long as eight years, but members of the House of Representative have two-year terms. It is very difficult for congressmen to come to grips with problems that may involve a great deal of political difficulty during their short terms and even destroy possibilities for reelection, while the political beneficiaries will be persons who have yet to run for office. Generally speaking, most politicians deal only at the last minute with "crisis"-level problems, as exemplified in the Clinton administration's budget legislation, the North American Free Trade Act, and GATT implementation.

The public generally is aware of the difficulties that the Social Security system is facing. Polling shows that over half of the people in the younger age groups do not expect to receive Social Security benefits at retirement. And yet, these very same people do not take the time to learn about what needs to be done. Whether politicians as a group can contribute to filling the "public's attention deficit" and educating the voters is uncertain.

To give some concrete examples of the long-term fiscal problem in the United States, the Public Trustees of Social Security and Medicare have issued reports for the past several years showing that the disability insurance program needs substantive changes. In fact, the disability fund would have been exhausted in 1995 were it not for temporary corrective action. The Medicare program is extremely underfinanced and will run out of funds in the next five to ten years unless change takes place. The Old-Age and Survivors Insurance program has adequate funds for about 30 years, but will be exhausted within the 75-year period for which trust fund reports are issued.

The most promising step recently taken to address the disconnect between financial imbalances and action to address them is legislation that makes the Social Security Administration an independent agency. It is entirely possible that, once separated from the U.S. Department of Health and Human Services, more public and therefore political attention will be give to the Social Security program. Apart from this institutional change, there seems little on the horizon to greatly improve the situation.

The state of affairs does not seem very different in other OECD countries. Despite the professional analysts in Japan knowing that retirement ages must be raised and other necessary reforms made, it has been difficult to achieve legislative change from the Diet, although that was recently accomplished. The European countries tend not to issue long-term projections or to worry as much in public about the imbalances as do the professional analysts in the United States and Japan, but there is no evidence that nations in Europe are better situated to make changes.

The countries that make the necessary changes earlier may well be pathfinders for those that make them later. One way or another, there is no question that today's social welfare systems will be dramatically different in the future. One hopes that change will come within the framework of orderly democratic decisionmaking and will reflect fairness and consideration for the well-being of those affected. It would be naive, however, not to recognize that this may not happen and that there may even be occasions when the politics of extremism are fueled by the failure to have changed in a fair way these systems that lie so much at the core of OECD societies.

COMMENT BY KATSUHIRO HORI

There is no doubt that the aging of the population increases social security expenditures and total public expenditures. I agree with Mr. Steuerle's opinion that a decrease in the 0–14 year old population will not necessarily mitigate the burden on the working-age population. I also acknowledge Mr. Scherer's view that political decisions influence the ratio of social security expenditures to GDP, because decisions regarding social security are based more on politics than on market economics.

It is not clear whether an increase in social security expenditures or an increase in total public expenditures reduces economic growth. Economic growth is determined by many factors. For example, the economic growth rate of Sweden has been higher than that of the United Kingdom, which has spent less than Sweden on social security. It is more accurate to say that economic growth makes possible increases in social security expenditures and that a slowing down of economic growth hinders such increases.

The social security system has been reformed many times in the past in order to adapt to changing social and economic structures. The reform of social security should be done according to public consensus, in light of stability of lifetime consumption, equity of benefits and burden, efficiency and coordination of the system, and similar standards.

I agree with most of the social security reform proposals made in these papers. For example, the age at which people can get social security benefits should be flexible. The older generation should share the burden of social security costs and the tax base should be enlarged. Japan should also consolidate its complex social security schemes, lower the benefit level of public pensions (which I believe is still too high), and improve long-term care policy for the elderly.

Mr. Yashiro reported that last year's Japanese pension reform was made to balance the total amount of contributions paid during working age and the total amount of benefits received after retirement, and that pension reform must try to attain intergenerational equity. But I cannot agree, because intergenerational equity should be interpreted in a much broader sense. For example, the older generation paid the cost of rearing and educating the younger generation. The elderly often leave houses, bequests, and social capital such as school buildings, roads, and so on, for which the latter pay no cost. Members of the older generation also maintained parents in their homes, though they paid fewer social insurance taxes or contributions than the younger generation, which doesn't always take care of its parents.

It is possible, of course, to mitigate the burden of social security cost by achieving high economic growth. But it is not easy to attain that objective because of lower savings (investment), a diminishing workforce resulting from an aging population, natural resource restraints, global environmental problems, international economic frictions, and so on.

It is not necessarily desirable that countries such as Japan maintain high economic growth, if we think of the problems of environment, energy, and food. But it is necessary to attain moderate economic growth to cope with the problems generated by population aging. Consequently, we have to stimulate technology innovation, improve productivity, and heighten savings and investment.

More people in their sixties and more women in Japan should be encouraged to enter the labor force in order to solve the future labor shortage problem. This year's public pension reform in Japan should be highly valued, as it has made it easier for people in their sixties to work. Although many measures to help women both work and raise children have been taken, the special treatment of housewives in the tax and pension systems still hampers women's entry into the labor force.

COMMENT BY JOHN B. SHOVEN

I am among those who feel that the demographic developments of the next 20 to 50 years will have a major impact on the economies of industrial nations. Most of my research has been on the United States, where the impact of improving mortality, declining birthrates, and the aging of the baby boom generation will be felt by both government finances and by the economy as a whole.

Michael Topper, David Wise, and I have looked at all the federal, state, and local programs whose beneficiaries could be identified.* The programs included Social Security, federal Civil Service, Medicare and Medicaid, Railroad Retirement, Worker's Compensation, Aid for Families with Dependent Children, Food Stamps, education, Veterans' Benefits, and so on. We then asked what the cost would be of offering the same benefits at each age in the future, assuming no change in relative prices. The answer was that the cost of these programs can be expected to go up by over 65 percent by 2040. The adult population is expected to grow approximately 32 percent by then. The difference is due solely to the changing composition of the population and the benefits that we offer the elderly. Peter Scherer has stated that such exercises are simply arithmetic—and he is right—but the arithmetic is dramatic nonetheless.

The demographic changes will, in fact, probably be accommodated by a scaling back of government transfer programs and by tax increases. Recognizing the necessity of these adjustments earlier rather than later will tend to make them less painful.

The point that concerns me most about the economy and demographic changes is the saving and investment balance. In the United States, we have a chronic imbalance between saving and investment leading to our importation of capital. Much of the saving that is done is carried out through the vehicle of pension funds. It is hard to exaggerate how large and important pension funds have become. Their assets exceed $4 trillion, and are roughly comparable to the value of the nation's housing stock (also roughly equal to the total capitalization of the New York Stock Exchange). Pension assets have climbed from 2 percent of the nation's net worth in 1950 to almost 25 percent by 1994, according to the national balance sheets of the Flow of Funds Division of the Federal Reserve Board. By some accounts, all of the nation's saving in the 1980s could be attributed to pensions.

The problem is that changing demographics, and the aging of the baby boom generation in particular, will have a profound impact on the saving provided through the pension system. Recall that the huge baby boom generation caused great strain on the education system in

*See "The Impact of Demographic Changes on Government Spending," in *Studies in the Economics of Aging*, ed. David Wise, NBER-University of Chicago Press, 1994.

the 1950s and 1960s; the same generation drove up housing prices and retarded the growth of real wages in the 1970s. It is not difficult to predict that the retirement of the baby boom generation will cause dramatic changes in the U.S. pension and health care delivery systems.

We know that the baby boom generation will also put pressure on the Social Security system. According to the latest forecasts from the Social Security Administration, the Retirement Trust Fund will grow until 2020, when it will peak at around $4 trillion. After that, the trust fund will be rapidly depleted by the numerous baby boom retirees and completely exhausted by 2030, when the baby boom generation is still in the middle of its retirement years. We know that this will force adjustments in the Social Security program itself, almost surely including tax increases and benefit curtailments. The point that I want to emphasize is that the cash flow surpluses of the system, which contribute to national saving, will disappear by 2020.

The same demographic forces that will deplete the Social Security Trust Fund will also impact the funded pension system. In recent years, the pension system has contributed a staggering amount to national saving—approximately 3.5 percent of national payroll, or 2.5 percent of GNP. Sylvester Schieber and I forecast that the saving provided by the pension system will begin to noticeably decline by 2010 and will cease by 2024.** After that the pension system will become a net dissaver. In fact, by 2040 it will become a fairly massive liquidator of assets (of the order of 2 percent of GNP per year). The potential impact of this on asset prices is troubling.

The demographic future presents a lot of serious economic questions. What will replace pensions as our primary generator of national saving? Will net national saving be much lower than now, perhaps even negative? What will the impact be on real interest rates and on asset prices? Are these effects magnified because Japan and Europe will have similar demographic developments to our own? Can immigration alleviate some of these problems for the United States and can East Asia and China in particular be a source of saving for the world? We need answers to these questions, the sooner the better.

**See "The Consequences of Population Aging on Private Pension Fund Saving and Asset Markets." NBER Working Paper no. 4665, April 1994.

Part Two

THE YOKE OF PRIOR COMMITMENTS

Chapter Five

HOW YESTERDAY'S DECISIONS AFFECT TODAY'S BUDGET AND FISCAL OPTIONS

Joseph J. Cordes

INTRODUCTION

In the 1980s and 1990s, American politicians and policymakers became ever more aware of the limits that confront fiscal decision-making in the modern welfare state. In the past, questions of how to pay for new or expanded government initiatives often seemed to take second place to questions about the desirability and scope of the initiatives themselves. This is clearly not so in current budget debates, where answering the question "How do we pay for it?" can be as decisive in determining the legislative fate of an initiative as its substantive merits. Thus, in submitting his annual budget, President Clinton, like President Bush, felt it necessary to explain how new or expanded initiatives would be funded by reduced spending on other programs; and despite broad agreement about the need to provide disaster relief to earthquake victims, there was a serious, if short-lived, debate about whether such relief spending should be offset by cuts in other government spending programs, or simply added to the current budget deficit.

The greater attention paid to financing reflects the expansion and maturation of the modern public sector. Although there is always a constraint on resources available for public spending, the constraint can be relatively "soft" or "hard" depending on the amount of fiscal slack. The degree of fiscal slack depends on the size of the revenue increment that results both from growth in the share of national income shifted from private to public use and from growth in national income, as well as on the size of existing claims on that revenue increment.

In the earlier stages of its development, the modern welfare state benefitted from the presence of considerable fiscal slack resulting from two sources.[1] Voters were willing to support shifting a larger share of national income to public uses when the share was perceived to be low. There were also fewer claims on added revenues—even from a stable public share—when programs were new, relatively small in scope, and relatively few in number.

Growth in public spending programs, however, began to reduce, if not eliminate, the very fiscal slack that helped facilitate their creation and expansion. As the share of national income claimed by the government has risen, voters have become less willing to support further increases in that share, thereby limiting, perhaps eliminating, this source of revenue growth. Higher tax collections resulting from economic growth have thus become the main source of added revenue.

Revenue increments from this source can be significant. For example, Congressional Budget Office (CBO) projections imply that between 1994 and 1999, growth in gross domestic product alone would increase federal tax collections by roughly $300 billion in 1993 dollars, thereby permitting real government spending to grow by about 25 percent.[2] At the same time, claims to these additional revenues have also expanded as programs have increased in number and scope, leaving less room to accommodate new programs, or changes in existing ones.

The decline of fiscal slack has affected budget policy in several ways. For a time, the political process accommodated demands for program expansion and change by allowing annual spending to exceed receipts on a "permanent" or "structural" basis. However, "softening" the spending constraint in this fashion has encountered resistance from voters and politicians alike, as the consequences of structural deficit finance became evident.

As resistance to deficit finance has mounted, pressures have increased for "budget-neutral" finance of policy changes. In such an environment, policymakers face strong incentives to link proposals for new programs with proposals to provide offsetting sources of financing, either by raising taxes, or by shifting resources from elsewhere in the budget. To the extent that voters are reluctant to support significant increases in taxes, the resources needed to respond to changing needs must increasingly come from reallocating resources among existing and proposed spending programs.

The erosion of fiscal slack has the salutary effect of forcing those involved in the budget process to think more explicitly about budget trade-offs among existing and new policies. At the same time, the effects of the new fiscal discipline depend on the ability to make trade-offs in ways that are not only politically feasible, but also distributionally fair and that use scarce resources wisely.

The process of reallocating budgetary resources among competing uses would be difficult enough if policymakers had the flexibility to do so. In practice, however, this flexibility is limited to the extent that past decisions pre-commit budgetary resources to particular ends. Such prior commitments impose a yoke on the ability of policymakers to shift resources—a yoke that makes responding to the new fiscal discipline especially challenging.

What are the principal ways in which budgetary resources are pre-committed by past decisions? How important and confining are such pre-commitments? What implications do they hold for the future? Finally, how might policies be modified to give policymakers the flexibility needed to reallocate scarce fiscal resources? These are the questions considered in the remainder of this paper.

FORMS OF PRIOR COMMITMENT

Because government programs evolve over time incrementally, the range of politically feasible options is always shaped by past decisions. This being said, some past actions create special claims on the public purse that impose more binding constraints on current actions than do others. Of particular interest and importance are: (1) pre-commitments to spend for specific purposes, (2) pre-commitments to set aside designated tax revenue for specific purposes, and (3) the pre-commitment to maintain the real tax burden and the real value of benefits received from certain spending programs by means of indexation.

Pre-Committed Expenditures

Some government actions create prior obligations to spend that must be honored in the present. Important examples of such actions include enacting and expanding income redistribution programs, increasing the amount of government borrowing, and providing government loan and other guarantees in and credit markets.

Income Transfers and Entitlements. Programs that provide income support to groups such as farmers, or cash and in-kind benefits to the aged, the sick and disabled, the poor, and the unemployed, are perhaps the single most important source of prior spending commitments. Once set up, such programs create future obligations to spend for several reasons.

First, the amount that is to be spent once a transfer program is enacted does not lend itself well to annual budget control. When legislators set up a transfer program, they can limit both who qualifies for the transfer and the size of the transfer payment made to individuals or households. But, once such limits are established, the total number of persons or families who become eligible in any given year, and hence the total amount to be spent, depends on factors such as age, health, and labor market status that are beyond legislative control.

Moreover, support for many (though not all) transfer programs is frequently mobilized by describing such programs as providing social insurance that protects all citizens from income loss.[3] Portraying transfer programs in this light carries with it the promise that taxpayers who finance transfers to others can expect to receive benefits themselves if or, in the case of old age pensions, when they become eligible. To make good on this promise, in turn, requires a fairly open-ended commitment to spend the sums needed to provide benefits to all those who qualify for such social insurance benefits.

Growth in Government Debt. Payments to service past government borrowing also have a special claim on current public financial resources. As noted above, as fiscal slack shrinks, a natural political response is to turn to government borrowing to accommodate pressures for growth and change in government spending programs. Although increased government borrowing helps keep the government budget constraint "soft" for a time, such borrowing also creates future claims on tax revenues in the form of principal and interest that must be paid if the government is to remain a credible borrower. The relative magnitude of such claims depends both on the rate of growth in government debt, and on the real interest that must be paid to government bondholders.

Contingent Liabilities Guarantees that governments make to individual lenders and to financial institutions also create future obligations to spend that can be as binding as those just described. Although loan and other credit guarantees do not obligate future spending with certainty, they create contingent claims on government resources. As in the case of spending on transfer programs, the amount needed to honor such claims if they come due depends on factors that are largely (though not entirely) beyond legislative control. And, like obligations incurred in connection with public borrowing, the contingent claim must be honored if the government is to maintain its credibility.

Pre-Committed Tax Revenues

Earmarking of tax revenues for specific purposes is another way in which some forms of spending can exert special claims on government financial resources. Under such arrangements, the revenue collected from a particular tax or set of taxes is set aside for specific purposes. Typically in the United States, these revenues are placed in a government trust fund which receives income from earmarked revenue sources and then spends such income on programs financed by the trust fund.

Earmarking creates a prior commitment to spend in two ways. Programs financed from earmarked revenue have access to a guaranteed source of financing, which gives them a favored position in the queue of annual spending priorities. This budgetary claim is reinforced by a political promise to spend earmarked revenues for designated purposes which is generally part of the bargain that secures political support for levying earmarked taxes.

Though earmarking imposes constraints on spending flexibility that are very similar to those imposed by pre-committed expenditures, there are also some differences. While earmarking reduces budgetary flexibility, it does not eliminate budgetary control, since there is nothing about earmarking *per se* that requires legislators to spend a fixed amount of earmarked revenues on the designated program. Although a decision not to spend the "full amount" of earmarked revenue for its designated purpose does not directly release such revenue for other uses, it can do so indirectly. For example, earmarked revenue that is not spent may permit spending on other non-designated programs to increase by the amount of the "trust fund surplus" without changing the size of the total deficit. Nonetheless, despite the fact that earmarked revenues are "fungible" to a degree, earmarking tends to assure an automatic flow of revenue to a program, regardless of how spending on that program would be ranked against alternative uses of funds.

Indexation

Indexation of taxes and/or spending for inflation can be a further important source of pre-commitment in public budgets. Indexing tax brackets and exemptions prevents inflation from increasing average tax rates. Thus, indexing of taxes obligates the government to hold the share of national income claimed by taxes roughly constant, barring explicit legislative action to increase the tax burden.

Although indexing of taxes does not constrain how revenues are to be spent, it can make the yoke imposed by prior commitments harder to bear because it reduces the amount of fiscal slack available for financing both prior claims and new needs. In other words, just as some past actions such as the creation of entitlement programs tie the hands of legislators on the spending side, indexing of taxes ties legislators' hands on the revenue side by ensuring that real tax collections do not grow faster than the rate of economic growth, without the explicit consent of taxpayers.

On the spending side, indexation reinforces the future obligations to spend that are created by certain forms of pre-committed expenditures, notably income redistribution programs. While setting up an income transfer program creates a future obligation to make benefit payments to those who qualify, the real value of these payments depends on whether they are automatically adjusted for inflation. If they are not, the real value of any prior commitment to spend depends on inflation rates and the willingness of legislators to make discretionary increases in benefits to offset the effects of inflation.

Without automatic inflation adjustments, inflation may loosen the yoke of prior commitments to spend. Legislators can, for example, decide not to increase benefits of transfer and other income-support programs by the full amount of inflation, thereby effectively shifting real budgetary resources away from such spending to other uses.

Such leeway, however, is either eliminated altogether, or greatly reduced, if the initial commitment to spend is backed by automatic inflation adjustments.[4] As Allen Schick (1990, p. 43) notes, once such adjustments are provided, the "right to have benefits protected against price increases . . . [comes to be] . . . regarded almost as much an entitlement as the core benefits themselves."

This perceived "right" to fully indexed benefits is further reinforced by the fact that indexing benefits can cause otherwise equivalent spending decisions to be framed in fundamentally different terms. As Schick notes, while a decision to increase unindexed benefits by 2 percent in the face of 4 percent inflation has the same real effect on benefits as a decision to reduce otherwise fully indexed benefits from 4 percent to 2 percent, the two actions are likely to viewed in different lights. The former action is likely to be perceived as raising benefits, and hence garner political support, while the latter would be seen as a cut and thus meet opposition.[5]

PRIOR COMMITMENTS AND THE UNITED STATES FEDERAL BUDGET

To what extent do prior commitments of the sort described above limit the ability of politicians and policymakers in the U.S. to make trade-offs among competing uses of scarce public funds? To provide an institutional context for discussing this question, it is helpful to start by briefly describing the main features of the current budget landscape.

In 1993, federal outlays claimed slightly more than $1.4 trillion, or 22.4 percent of GDP. For over a decade, it has been common practice to break down this total among several broad spending categories, which have recently attained formal status in the 1990 Budget Enforcement Act.[6]

Discretionary Spending

Discretionary spending comprises programs whose funding levels are determined every year through the appropriation process. The broad category of discretionary spending can be further broken down into three functional categories.

Defense discretionary spending, which presently accounts for over 55 percent of discretionary spending, includes the military activities of the Department of Defense, as well as defense-related functions of other agencies, such as the Department of Energy's nuclear weapons programs. *Domestic discretionary spending* which accounts for two-fifths of all discretionary spending includes federal spending on most federal activities in areas such as science, space, transportation, medical research, environmental protection, and law enforcement. The remaining component is *international discretionary spending*, which includes all spending for foreign economic and military aid, as well as the activities of the Department of State and the U.S. Information Agency, and international financial programs, such as the Export-Import Bank of the United States.

Though the above-mentioned programs encompass a wide range of different government activities, they have one important feature in common. Namely, each year the President and the Congress must decide how much money is to be appropriated for each of these activities. Thus, decisionmakers must make explicit choices about whether to reduce, increase, or to maintain funding of these programs at current levels. Moreover, making such choices does not require legislators to change existing law. It is, therefore, possible to shift funds among competing discretionary programs by the relatively "simple" legislative act of appropriating more funds for some programs and less for others.[7]

Entitlement and Other Mandatory Spending

Entitlement and other mandatory spending spending comprises programs that make payments to any person, business, or unit of government that seeks the payments and meets the criteria set by law. Almost three-fifths of entitlement spending is attributable to the *Social Security* and *Medicare* programs which provide income security and health benefits to the aged without regard to the economic need or means of the recipient. Programs that provide benefits based on economic need or means such as *Aid to Families with Dependent Children (AFDC)*, *Food Stamps*, *Medicaid*, *Supplemental Security Income*, and the *Earned Income Tax Credit* account for another fifth of entitlement spending. The remainder includes programs that provide income support to designated population groups such as veterans and farmers.

As noted by Schick (1990), entitlement programs share several important attributes. First, any person or family who meets the eligibility criteria of a particular entitlement program has a legal right to receive benefits, which the federal government must honor. Second, the size of the benefit which eligible recipients are entitled to receive is determined by administrative rules and criteria that are enacted into law.

Reflecting these attributes, entitlement spending is treated differently than discretionary spending in the budget process. The largest entitlement programs, Social Security and Medicare, have permanent appropriations that are completely open-ended, so that payments to recipients are made automatically each year without any direct action by Congress. The amount that must be spent on these payments depends entirely on the number of eligible recipients and on the amount spent per recipient. These variables, in turn, are determined by a combination of (a) past legislative actions that define both who is eligible and the size of the benefit, (b) demographic factors, such as the age structure of the population, and (c) in the case of Medicare, costs of providing services, and the behavior of health care providers.

None of the aforementioned factors is susceptible to current budgetary control. This is perhaps most obvious in the case of demographics, but is also true in practice, if not in principle, in the case of the other factors that determine current spending on Social Security and Medicare. Although Congress and the President have the authority to change both the size of Social Security and Medicare benefits and who is eligible to receive them, doing so requires changing the underlying laws that authorize and govern these programs. Securing political agreement for changes that would limit spending by tightening eligibility criteria and/or reducing benefits is hard enough when the proposed changes would affect *future* but not current recipients, and is all but impossible in the case of proposed changes that would reduce or limit *current* benefits.

Some entitlement programs have legislated caps on amounts that can be spent in each year, while others, such as veterans benefits and Medicaid are formally subject to the appropriations process in each year. Although spending on these programs is not "automatic" because they do not have open-ended appropriations as do Social Security and Medicare, lawmakers are required by law to appropriate sufficient funds to cover benefits paid under these programs. Thus, although such programs may be formally subject to budgetary control each year, in practice the amount spent is ultimately determined by hard-to-control factors similar to those discussed in connection with Social Security and Medicare.[8]

Net Interest

Net interest consists of interest payments made by the federal government to the public less interest income received by the government on loans and cash balances. As noted above, the amount of net interest that must be paid in any given year depends on the amount of government debt outstanding and the interest that must be paid on that debt. These factors (e.g., the amount of debt that is outstanding and interest payments on old debt) depend either entirely on past decisions, or at best are only indirectly affected by current legislative actions (e.g., the amount of interest paid on new government debt).[9]

Deposit Insurance and Offsetting Receipts

The remaining budget categories consist of deposit insurance and offsetting receipts, though neither item receives extensive treatment in the remainder of this paper. *Deposit insurance* consists of payments made by financial institutions to finance the guarantee by a federal agency that individual depositors will receive the full amount of their deposits (up to $100,000) if the institution becomes insolvent. *Offset-*

ting receipts are funds collected by the federal government that are treated as "negative spending" and are credited to separate accounts. Within this category, *proprietary receipts* are payments made by the public for specific services received from the government.

Trends in the Composition of Federal Spending

Table 5.1 presents the share of GDP claimed by federal spending as well as the distribution of federal spending among the outlay categories described above, over the past 30 years and as projected in the year 2004. The story told by table 5.1 is by now a familiar one.

In 1965, federal spending claimed almost 19 percent of GDP.[10] Of this total, about 65 percent represented discretionary spending subject to the annual appropriation process, while mandatory spending on entitlements and net interest accounted for 28 percent and 7 percent, respectively. Put slightly differently, in 1965, prior obligations to spend claimed about $.35 of each $1.00 of federal financial resources.

Between 1965 and 1975, however, both the level and the mix of federal spending shifted markedly. By 1975, federal spending as a share of GDP had risen by 4.4 percentage points to just over 23 percent, of which just over half was devoted to spending on entitlements and net interest, and slightly less than half represented discretionary spending.

In the ensuing two decades since 1975, federal spending has continued to claim between 23 and 25 percent of GDP, while the share of federal spending devoted to spending on entitlements and net interest has continued to rise. The upshot is that by 1993, the relative budgetary importance of pre-committed spending and discretionary spending was almost the exact reverse of what it was 30 years ago. That is, in 1993, spending to honor prior obligations in the form of entitlements and net interest payments claimed roughly $.65 of each $1.00 of federal spending, while discretionary spending accounted for only $.35.[11]

Sources of Growth in Pre-Committed Spending

There are several reasons for the shift toward forms of government spending that are less susceptible to budgetary control. First, in the United States, as in other modern industrial democracies, much of the recent growth in government spending reflects a significant expansion in the redistributional role of government.[12] Between 1955 and 1965, for example, federal spending on income transfers rose by

Table 5.1 COMPOSITION OF FEDERAL SPENDING[a]

	Total	Discretionary	Entitlements and Other Mandatory	Net Interest
1965				
Billions of $	126.5	81.8	36.1	8.6
Share of GDP	18.9%	12.2%	5.4%	1.3%
Share of spending	100.0%	64.7%	28.5%	6.8%
1970				
Billions of $	207.7	124.6	68.7	14.4
Share of GDP	21.1%	12.6%	7.0%	1.5%
Share of spending	100.0%	59.9%	33.0%	6.9%
1975				
Billions of $	350.1	162.5	164.4	23.2
Share of GDP	23.2%	10.8%	10.9%	1.5%
Share of spending	100.0%	46.4%	46.9%	6.6%
1980				
Billions of $	620.5	276.5	291.5	52.5
Share of GDP	23.5%	10.5%	11.0%	2.0%
Share of spending	100.0%	44.5%	46.9%	8.4%
1985				
Billions of $	995.7	416.2	450.0	129.5
Share of GDP	25.1%	10.5%	11.3%	3.3%
Share of spending	100.0%	41.7%	45.0%	13.0%
1990				
Billions of $	1,253.3	501.7	567.4	184.2
Share of GDP	22.9%	9.2%	10.3%	3.4%
Share of spending	100.0%	40.0%	45.2%	14.6%
1993				
Billions of $	1,503.2	543.4	760.9	198.9
Share of GDP	23.9%	8.6%	12.1%	3.2%
Share of spending	100.0%	36.0%	50.6%	13.2%
2004				
Billions of $	2,528.0	658.0	1,536.0	334.0
Share of GDP	23.2%	6.0%	14.1%	3.1%
Share of spending	100.0%	26.0%	60.7%	13.2%

Source: Congressional Budget Office 1994a, Appendix E and Box 2-1 with accompanying table.

a. Spending equals the sum of discretionary and entitlement spending plus net interest. Totals exclude offsetting receipts and deposit insurance.

230 percent, compared with federal spending on goods and services, which grew by 160 percent. Between 1965 and 1975, spending on transfers grew almost five-fold, while spending on goods and services only doubled. The upshot was that over a 20-year period, the ratio of spending on transfer payments to spending on purchases of goods and services rose from .27 to 1.12. In other words, whereas in 1955 the federal government spent $.27 on transfers for each $1.00 spent on purchases of goods and services, by 1975, it was spending $1.16 in transfers for each $1.00 spent on goods and services.

As seen in table 5.2, the shift in the composition of federal spending away from goods and services toward transfers continued in the 1970s, 1980s, and 1990s, and mirrors the shift away from discretionary spending toward entitlements shown in table 5.1. This is hardly surprising since for reasons given above, income redistribution programs create obligations to spend that must be honored when they come due.

A second reason for the growth in pre-committed spending is that much of the increase in spending on transfers was for programs such as Social Security, Medicare, and Medicaid, which had built-in tendencies to grow over time once enacted. In other words, expansion of redistributive activities was done in a way that not only created obligations to spend in the future, but created obligations that would grow over time as the population grew older and as medical technology became more expansive and expensive.

The increased propensity toward deficit finance is a third factor behind the growth in prior claims on current budgetary resources. As

Table 5.2 RATIO OF SPENDING ON TRANSFERS TO PERSONS TO SPENDING ON GOODS AND SERVICES

	Spending on Goods and Services (Billions of $)	Spending on Transfers to Persons (Billions of $)	Ratio (2)/(1)
1955	51.2	14.3	0.28
1965	75.4	32.8	0.43
1970	99.8	55.3	0.55
1975	123.9	131.9	1.06
1980	201.0	235.4	1.16
1985	335.2	360.7	1.07
1990	418.1	491.3	1.18
1993	445.0	630.2	1.42

Source: Data for 1955 and 1965 are taken from U.S. Office of Management and Budget (1986). Data from 1970 onward are taken from *Economic Report of the President* (1990, 1994).

is shown in table 5.3, the fraction of federal outlays financed by taxes declined significantly between 1970 and 1975, and continued falling thereafter until 1985.

As noted above, borrowing to finance current spending is politically appealing because it appears to soften the government's budget constraint. The effect, however, is temporary, since the obligation to service the higher level of government debt creates future claims that must be honored.

Borrowing does not eliminate trade-offs that must be made between raising taxes or reducing spending on some programs in order to add new programs or expand existing ones; it merely shifts these trade-offs forward into the future. Taxes that are not raised or spending that is not cut in the present show up as future interest payments that exert prior claims on tax revenues, making it harder to fund future spending needs. Thus, increased reliance on deficit finance in the late 1970s and 1980s temporarily allowed lawmakers to simultaneously honor growing prior commitments to spend on entitlement programs, maintain existing programs, and add new ones, but at the price of having to confront these trade-offs in starker form in the late 1980s, 1990s, and into the next century.

Did Spending on Entitlements Crowd Out Other Spending?

A question raised by the shift in federal outlays toward entitlements and away from discretionary spending is whether prior obligations to spend on the former have crowded out spending on the latter. The answer to the question is far from obvious.

Table 5.3 RATIO OF TAX REVENUE TO FEDERAL OUTLAYS

	Tax Revenue (Billions of $) (1)	Federal Outlays (Billions of $) (2)	Ratio/ (1)/(2) (3)
1965	116.8	118.2	.99
1970	192.8	195.6	.99
1975	279.1	332.3	.84
1980	517.1	590.9	.88
1985	734.1	946.4	.78
1990	1,031.3	1,252.7	.82
1993	1,153.2	1,408.1	.82

Source: Congressional Budget Office 1994a, Table E-2.

On the one hand, expansion of entitlements could simply reflect a desire on the part of the public to expand the scope of what Richard Musgrave has termed the redistribution branch of the government (e.g. income transfers to persons), while leaving the overall scope of the allocation branch (e.g. spending on goods and services) unchanged. If this were the case, one would observe a rising share of government spending that was pre-committed in the sense described in this paper, but this pre-commitment to spend would not limit resources that would otherwise have been available to lawmakers to respond to changing needs elsewhere in the budget. On the other hand, expansion of entitlements could have the (presumably unintended) effect of crowding out other forms of spending if, for example, such spending grew more rapidly than was intended at the time such programs were put in place.

Tables 5.4 and 5.5 try to shed some further light on this issue. Table 5.4 presents data in real levels of discretionary and entitlement spending and on the share of GDP claimed by each of these budget categories. Table 5.5 presents comparable data on the various components of discretionary spending.

Trends in Real Discretionary Spending. Table 5.4 shows that between 1965 and 1993, the overall effect of federal spending decisions has been to commit a growing share of an expanding economic pie to spending on entitlements, and a declining share to discretionary spending. As a result, though discretionary spending grew steadily in real terms, with one interruption, between 1965 and 1985, growth in such spending lagged behind that of the economy at large. From 1985 to 1993, discretionary spending has actually stayed flat in real terms.

Based on the data in table 5.4, one cannot reject the hypothesis that prior obligations to spend on entitlements have crowded out at least some spending in other areas. The data do not, however, "prove" that this was the case. The key issue is whether past decisions to expand entitlement programs have forced lawmakers to devote less of the revenue increment from real economic growth to non-entitlement spending than they would have otherwise desired.

Shifts Within Discretionary Spending. Table 5.5 shows how changing spending priorities have been accommodated within the portion of the federal budget that is not constrained by prior commitments. Although discretionary spending has grown more slowly than has national income, at various times the ability to shift spending within the discretionary category has enabled spending on defense or on domestic programs to grow as fast or faster than the economy as a

Table 5.4 TRENDS IN DISCRETIONARY VERSUS ENTITLEMENTS AND OTHER MANDATORY SPENDING

	Discretionary	Entitlements and other mandatory
1965		
Billions of 1993 $	358.4	157.7
Share of GDP	12.2%	5.4%
1970		
Billions of 1993 $	439.3	242.2
Share of GDP	12.6%	7.0%
1975		
Billions of 1993 $	409.9	414.6
Share of GDP	10.8%	10.9%
1980		
Billions of 1993 $	478.5	504.6
Share of GDP	10.5%	11.0%
1985		
Billions of 1993 $	547.2	591.6
Share of GDP	10.5%	11.3%
1990		
Billions of 1993 $	549.5	621.5
Share of GDP	9.2%	10.3%
1993		
Billions of 1993 $	543.4	760.2
Share of GDP	8.6%	12.1%
2004		
Billions of 1993 $	476.8	1,113.0
Share of GDP	6.0%	14.1%

Source: Congressional Budget Office 1994a, Tables E-5 (for the years 1965–1993), and Box 2-1 (for 2004). Data are converted to 1993 dollars using the price deflator for GDP published in the 1994 *Economic Report of the President*. Data for 2004 are converted to 1993 dollars by assuming an annual inflation rate of 3 percent from 1993 onward. CBO projections for 2004 assume that discretionary spending would be held essentially flat in nominal terms between 1994 and 1998 by spending caps specified in the Balanced Budget Act of 1990.

whole. Most recently, for example, though total real discretionary spending declined by about $6 billion between 1990 and 1993, real spending on domestic and international programs rose by a little over $29 billion, "financed" by real reductions in defense spending of $37 billion.

The Political Economy of Pre-Commitment. The data summarized in this section show that there has been a shift in the mix of federal

Table 5.5 TRENDS IN COMPONENTS OF DISCRETIONARY SPENDING

	Defense	International	Domestic
1965			
Billions of 1993 $	223.0	20.6	114.1
Share of GDP	7.6%	0.7%	3.9%
Share of total	62.3%	5.7%	31.9%
1970			
Billions of 1993 $	288.9	14.1	136.5
Share of GDP	8.3%	0.4%	3.9%
Share of total	65.7%	3.2%	31.1%
1975			
Billions of 1993 $	221.1	20.7	168.4
Share of GDP	5.8%	0.5%	4.4%
Share of total	53.9%	5.0%	41.0%
1980			
Billions of 1993 $	233.2	22.2	223.6
Share of GDP	5.1%	0.5%	4.4%
Share of total	48.6%	4.6%	46.6%
1985			
Billions of 1993 $	333.0	22.9	191.7
Share of GDP	6.4%	0.4%	3.7%
Share of total	60.8%	4.2%	35.0%
1990			
Billions of 1993 $	329.8	21.0	200.6
Share of GDP	5.5%	0.3%	3.3%
Share of total	59.8%	3.8%	36.4%
1993			
Billions of 1993 $	292.5	21.6	229.4
Share of GDP	4.6%	0.3%	3.6%
Share of total	53.8%	4.0%	42.2%

Source: Congressional Budget Office 1994a, Tables E-8 (for 1965–1993), and 2-4 (for 1999). Data are converted to 1993 dollars using the method described in the previous table.

spending toward redistributive transfers, which tend to exact future claims on budgetary resources. An interesting question is why such a shift took place. Although a full treatment of this issue is beyond the scope of the paper, the pressure group model of redistribution posited by Becker (1983) is a potentially useful framework for exploring the subject.

In the basic pressure group model, groups of voters invest resources of time, money, and effort in order to influence aggregate expenditures on redistributive transfers. A prediction of this model is that the level of transfers supported by the political system will reflect a balancing of the benefits received from transfers by some groups, with what Kristov, Lindert, and McClelland (1990, 1992) have termed the "side-costs" of redistribution, beyond the visible budgetary amount of transfers.

Enacting transfer programs that exact future claims to budgetary resources effectively raises the deadweight loss of financing other forms of spending, which can be seen as a type of side-cost. Given these side-costs, the enactment of transfer programs could command political support in several circumstances.

Pressure groups and politicians may fully anticipate future side-costs at the time that future budgetary resources are pre-committed, but nonetheless support the creation of new entitlement programs because the benefits of redistribution are seen to compare favorably with the costs. Pressure groups and politicians could also fully anticipate the side-costs of redistribution, but discount these costs because the yoke of prior commitments will be borne by future generations of taxpayers. Finally, the well-being of future generations could be taken into account by the political process, but the ultimate consequences of enacting programs with prior claims to future budgetary resources may be underestimated.

THE OUTLOOK FOR THE FUTURE

Forecasts of future trends indicate that the yoke of prior commitments will become still more burdensome over the next decade. CBO projections indicate that, by the year 2004, *if current policies remain unchanged*, federal spending will continue to claim about 23 percent of GDP. But, almost three-fourths of all federal spending will be devoted to meeting prior obligations to fund entitlement programs and to pay net interest on the federal debt, with the remaining one-fourth of the budget available to be allocated among various competing spending priorities through the appropriations process.

CBO's projections include the anticipated effects of the Balanced Budget Act, which effectively would hold discretionary spending constant in nominal terms between 1994 and 1998. Even if such caps were not in place, however, and discretionary spending grew at the inflation rate, the fraction of federal spending devoted to funding entitlement programs and paying net interest would still be projected to exceed 70 percent of all spending by 2004.

The outlook beyond the year 2000 indicates that the yoke of prior commitments in the U.S. budget will become still heavier if current policies are allowed to run their course. This possibility has been documented in different ways by several studies that look at future directions in U.S. budget and fiscal policy.

Steuerle and Bakija (1994) project that, if the current structure of Social Security and Medicaid is left unchanged, lawmakers will be obligated to spend 13 percent of GDP in the year 2030 on these programs, compared with about 7 percent of GDP today. The effect would be to raise the share of total entitlement spending in GDP by 6.0 percentage points.

If tax burdens are not allowed to rise to offset this increase, the remaining alternatives would be to increase the government budget deficit, or further reduce the share of discretionary spending in GDP below its present level. If the former alternative were ruled out, then discretionary spending would need to fall to roughly 2.7 percent of GDP from its current level of 8.6 percent. Under plausible assumptions, this would mean a reduction in the *absolute* level of real discretionary spending of roughly 10 percent, or $50 billion in current dollars.

This broad conclusion is echoed in other studies. Using an intergenerational accounting framework developed by Auerbach, Kotlikoff, and Gohkale (1994), the U.S. Office of Management and Budget (OMB) (1994) estimates that current federal spending will impose a lifetime net tax burden on future taxpayers equal to an eye-catching 93 percent of their lifetime income. As is pointed out in the OMB report, this number assumes that all of the burden of paying for the current set of programs would be shifted to as-yet-unborn generations of taxpayers. It is therefore best seen as a measure of the degree of fiscal imbalance built into current programs rather than as an estimate of the net tax burden that will actually be passed on. The OMB estimate, however, does imply that, at some point in the not-too-distant future, steps will need to be taken to either reduce benefits promised under current law or to increase taxes.

The General Accounting Office (1992) has also projected that if current policies are maintained, federal spending and the federal deficit would increase, respectively, to 40 percent and 20 percent of GDP by the year 2020, again in large measure because of projected growth in entitlement spending, especially Medicare. Since neither of these alternatives seems plausible, the more realistic alternatives are to raise taxes or reduce spending.

CONCLUSIONS AND FUTURE DIRECTIONS

The analysis presented above suggests that prior spending commitments have exerted a grip on the federal budget that is likely become tighter as time passes. Projected increases in spending that would be required to meet promises that are embedded in existing entitlement programs could potentially squeeze other forms of spending.

In the near term, lawmakers may be able to address changing spending priorities by shifting spending within the discretionary category among defense, domestic, and international spending. But there is likely to be a limit to the size of any "peace dividend." To the extent that there is little or no political support for significant tax increases, the remaining alternative is to seek ways of controlling entitlement spending.

A detailed discussion of how to control spending on entitlements is beyond the scope of this paper. Nonetheless, it is appropriate to conclude by outlining some directions for future policy.[13] First, where possible, efforts should be made to reduce the cost of meeting promises that are currently enacted into law. Health care is probably the best example. Most of the projected growth in future entitlement spending is based on escalating costs of providing medical care. Controlling such costs is one way of simultaneously lightening the yoke of future commitments and meeting current promises.

Second, if the only way to control entitlement spending is to tighten eligibility and/or reduce currently promised benefits, such changes need to be made prospectively. This is necessary to give those affected time to adjust their behavior in order to minimize the adverse effects, and to make such changes politically viable. The future increase in the Social Security retirement age is a good example of a change enacted in this fashion. In this respect, the United States may be better positioned than many other countries to make adjustments of this type because it already has a well-developed set of private sector arrangements, such as private pensions, that can substitute for public spending.

Serious consideration should also be given to backing off from the commitment to fully index income security programs, especially those that are not means-tested. Though such a change in policy would be controversial, it would give lawmakers at least some discretion in setting real levels of spending for income transfers.

Finally, lawmakers should more carefully scrutinize the extent to which current actions impose significant prior obligations to spend. Although the time may not have come for generational accounts (of the sort proposed by Auerbach, Gokhale, and Kotlikoff 1994) to replace conventional budget measures, there is certainly merit in adopting the more farsighted mode of thinking about fiscal actions that is implied by a generational accounting framework. If nothing else, information of this sort would serve to better highlight the side cost of enacting redistributive programs that exact future claims to scarce budgetary resources.

Notes

1. For a related discussion of the role of fiscal slack in facilitating the expansion of public spending programs, see Schick (1990), Cordes and Steuerle (1989), and Steuerle (1992), and Steuerle and Bakija (1994).

2. These numbers are based on projections presented in Congressional Budget Office (1994a).

3. For an extended discussion of the implications of portraying income transfer programs as social insurance, see Steuerle and Bakija (1994), chapter 1. See also Kingson and Berkowitz (1993).

4. The leeway would be reduced but not eliminated if the automatic adjustment factor fell short of the relevant rate of inflation. For example, since health care costs have risen at rates faster than inflation, increasing government spending on health benefits by a factor equal to the general inflation rate would amount to a real cut in the value of such benefits.

5. There is an interesting and growing literature in economics which suggests that people will frame or perceive otherwise economically identical situations differently, leading to differences in behavior. For example, see Kahneman and Tversky (1984), and Sheffrin (1993).

6. The definitions of different spending categories provided in this section draw heavily, and in some cases directly from the glossary in Congressional Budget Office (1993).

7. The word simple appears in quotes because politically, it is usually anything but simple to shift resources away from existing programs.

8. This section focuses on the federal budget of the United States, which accounts for roughly two thirds of all government spending. Spending by state and local governments in the United States tends to be largely for goods and services, and therefore is less likely to involve a pre-commitment to spend in the future. However, some federal entitlement programs such as Medicaid have the effect of imposing future obligations to spend on state and local governments and may, therefore, crowd out other forms of spending at the state and local level.

9. In the opinion of many economists, credible actions taken by the government to reduce the government's budget deficit can reduce interest rates. Other economists

argue that there is little or no relationship between the deficit and interest rates. The empirical evidence is mixed. See, for example, Kotlikoff (1993).

10. Offsetting receipts, which typically flow through to finance spending, and deposit insurance are excluded from the calculation of total spending. Their inclusion would not affect the main patterns and trends presented in table 5.1.

11. This shift and its budgetary implications are also discussed in U.S. General Accounting Office (1992).

12. For an excellent discussion of historical trends in government spending in a number of different countries, see Tanzi (1986).

13. For an excellent discussion of this issue, see Congressional Budget Office (1994b).

References

Auerbach, Alan, Jagadeesh Gokhale, and Lawrence Kotlikoff. 1994. "Generational Accounts: A Meaningful Alternative to Deficit Accounting," *Journal of Economic Perspectives* 8 (Winter).

Becker, Gary. 1983. "A Theory of Competition Among Pressure Groups for Political Influence." *Quarterly Journal of Economics* 98 (August).

Congressional Budget Office. 1994a. *The Economic and Budget Outlook: Fiscal Years 1995–1999*. U.S. Government Printing Office, January.

________. 1994b. *Reduced Entitlement Spending*. U.S. Government Printing Office, September.

________. 1993. *The Economic and Budget Outlook: Fiscal Years 1994–1998*. U.S. Government Printing Office, January.

Cordes, Joseph J., and C. Eugene Steuerle, "The Effects of Tax Reform on Budget, Tax, and Social Policymaking," *Papers and Proceedings of the National Tax Association-Tax Institute of America*.

The Economic Report of the President: 1994. Washington, D.C.: U.S. Government Printing Office.

The Economic Report of the President: 1990. Washington, D.C.: U.S. Government Printing Office.

Kahneman, Daniel, and Amos Tversky. 1984. "Choices, Values, and Frames," *American Psychologist* 39 (April) 341–50.

Kingson, Eric R., and Edward D. Berkowitz. 1993. *Social Security and Medicare: A Policy Primer*. Westport, Ct.: Auburn House.

Kotlikoff, Laurence. 1993. *Generational Accounting: Knowing Who Pays, and When, for What We Spend*. New York: Free Press.

Kristov, L., P. Lindert, and R. McClelland. 1992. "Pressure Groups and Redistribution," *Journal of Public Economics*, 48, No. 2. Washington, D.C.

________. 1990. "Pressure Groups and Redistribution," Working Paper Series No. 65, Department of Economics, University of California at Davis, January.

Musgrave, Richard. 1959. *The Theory of Public Finance*. New York: McGraw-Hill.

Schick, Allen. 1990. *The Capacity to Budget*. Washington, D.C.: The Urban Institute Press.

Sheffrin, Steven M. 1993. "What Does the Public Believe About Tax Fairness?" *National Tax Journal* 46 (September): 301–308.

Steuerle, C. Eugene. 1992. *The Tax Decade*. Washington, D.C.: The Urban Institute Press.

Steuerle, C. Eugene, and Jon Bakija. 1994. *Retooling Social Security for the 21st Century: Right and Wrong Approaches to Reform*. Washington, D.C.: The Urban Institute Press.

Tanzi, Vito. 1986. "The Growth of Public Expenditures in Industrial Countries: An International and Historical Perspective." Mimeo.

U.S. General Accounting Office. 1992. *Budget Policy: Prompt Action Necessary to Avoid Long-Term Damage to the Economy*. GAO/OCG-92-2 June 5.

U.S. Office of Management and Budget. 1994. *Analytical Perspectives, Budget of the United States Government, Fiscal Year 1995*. Washington, D.C.: U.S. Government Printing Office.

Chapter Six

PRIOR COMMITMENTS, SUSTAINABILITY, AND INTERGENERATIONAL REDISTRIBUTION IN JAPAN

Toshihiro Ihori

As detailed by Professor Cordes in the previous chapter, most public spending and tax revenues are fixed by commitments made by previous generations of policymakers. Thus, when governments have become strapped for funds in recent years, they have tended to finance additional public spending in part by borrowing from the capital market rather than raising taxes or reducing spending. Must governments eventually repay public debt or can they keep refinancing it in perpetuity, issuing new liabilities to repay maturing debt? What sort of fiscal reforms should be implemented to avoid fiscal bankruptcy? Given the current state of prior commitments, how feasible are fiscal reforms such as increasing taxes or decreasing public expenditures? These questions occur to anyone who has witnessed the rapid worldwide growth of deficit finance.

In this chapter I discuss how Japan has handled its "prior commitments" and budget deficits since the mid-1970s, define the concept of "sustainability" of public debt and consider how the highest sustainable level of public debt may be affected by various fiscal actions, and suggest what austerity measures might be taken to alleviate the pressure on sustainability arising from major prior commitments.

JAPAN'S GOVERNMENT DEFICITS

The discussion below focuses on Japan's general account, which is the nation's basic account.[1] The budget process for any fiscal year T (which runs from April 1 of calendar year T to March 31 of the following calendar year) begins about nine months before the start of the fiscal year. In July of the year before year T the Ministry of Finance (MOF) issues guidelines that set ceilings for the total budget of each ministry and government agency. Subject to these guidelines, each ministry submits its budget proposals to the MOF by the end of August. The MOF and the ministries and government agencies then negotiate over the budget plan during the fall of the year before year T. At the end of December or the beginning of January, the Cabinet approves the tentative government budget plan. Although the details of the plan may not yet be worked out, total budget size seldom changes once the Cabinet has approved the plan.

Traditionally, the Japanese government has followed a balanced budget policy. The roots of this policy lie in a conservative view of what constitutes "sound" finance. This view developed in reaction to extravagant government spending and inflationary pressures felt during World War II and the immediate postwar period. A balanced budget was maintained until 1965, when national bonds were issued for the first time since the war. Despite the presence of those national bonds, which were issued periodically until the late 1970s, fiscal deficits did not start to pose serious problems until the mid-1970s.

Fiscal Policy in the 1970s

The gap between government expenditures and tax revenues, which corresponds roughly to the fiscal deficit, began to expand rapidly after the outbreak of the first oil-price shock in 1973. The situation then worsened throughout the rest of the 1970s.

What were the main causes of the sharp rise in fiscal deficits from 1975 onward? Asako, Ito, and Sakamato (1991) and Ishi and Ihori (1992) present useful descriptions of the rise and fall of Japanese deficits between 1975 and 1990. These authors attribute deficit increases in the second half of the 1970s to a combination of several factors, of which two are prominent. First, 1973—the year of the first oil-price shock—was also the year in which the Japanese government introduced new social security (welfare) programs. In the early 1970s, important institutional reforms of the social security system were carried out under the slogan "Construct a welfare state in Japan." Because they were indexed to various growth factors, the share of these programs relative to total government spending increased automatically during that decade. The introduction of social welfare programs coincided with rapid inflation caused by the first oil crisis and a switch to slower economic growth. Indeed, the growth rate of real GNP declined sharply, from 7.6 in 1973 to −0.6 percent in 1974, and from 5.5 percent in 1979 to 3.6 percent in 1980, a year after the second oil-price shock struck the Japanese economy. These experiences resulted in a sharp unanticipated reduction in revenue growth, which in turn contributed greatly to the increase in fiscal deficits during the early 1980s. It then became necessary to issue so-called "deficit bonds," bonds specifically offered to finance fiscal deficits.

Second, as a result of the economic summit of 1978, Germany and Japan tried to expand their economies to become "locomotives" for the rest of the world, at the urging of other Western countries, notably the United States. Japan adopted a set of highly stimulative fiscal policies that included increasing public investment. This unanticipated temporary increase in fiscal spending also contributed to the creation of fiscal deficits.

In sum, Japan's larger fiscal deficits resulted from a major burst of new spending on social welfare programs in the first half of the 1970s and on public investment in the second half of the same decade, as well as from a lack of tax revenues due to a slowdown of economic growth.

Fiscal Reconstruction in the 1980s

Because of the sharp increases in deficits in the mid-1970s, deficit reduction became one of the nation's most important economic objectives. The attempt to eliminate fiscal deficits was officially called "fiscal reconstruction."

At first, the government and the MOF attempted to raise tax revenues through a new value-added tax, called the "general consumption" tax. However, the strategy failed when this kind of tax was politically rejected in the general election of 1979. Following this defeat, the MOF changed its approach, applying constant pressure on each ministry and government agency to hold down expenditures when drawing up initial budget plans. In particular, limits were imposed on increases in spending for each ministry and agency. The ceiling was sharply tightened to 10 percent in 1980 and, in the last few years, has been lowered further to zero or negative rates of increase.

Another important step was the establishment of the Ad Hoc Council on Administrative Reform (Rincho) in 1981. Its mission was to review all government activities and make recommendations on rationalizing the government system. Rincho submitted five reports between 1981 and 1983 and recommended a number of important reforms to trim the bureaucracy. Among its major recommendations were to privatize three major public corporations, cut spending on public works, reduce the number of government employees, restrain social security benefits, and simplify certification and inspection procedures for manufactured products.

Although some of the proposals have never been implemented, the growth of government expenditure has indeed been restrained as a result of the policies that were adopted. Thus, general government expenditures excluding debt services did not grow much from fiscal year 1983 to fiscal year 1986. Under these circumstances, the government spending/GNP ratio decreased constantly in the first half of the 1980s, after a rapid rise in the 1970s. In addition, reform of health insurance in 1984 and of the social security system in 1985 also contributed greatly to reducing growth rates in social welfare spending. After 1980, the rising trend of fiscal deficits was reversed in terms of the bond dependency ratio (new bond issues relative to total expenditures). And debt-to-GDP ratios even fell roughly 7 percentage points from 1987 to 1991 (see the Tanzi and Fanizza paper, this volume), before the recent economic downturn.

Along with the severe spending constraints imposed by Rincho to achieve the goal of deficit reduction, the MOF began to fall back on various small measures to increase tax revenues. However, the MOF did not pursue major tax reforms of the kind that would greatly alter the basic tax structure until the late 1980s. After much trial and error, the value-added tax (VAT) was finally introduced in April 1989.

The Bubble Economy and Fiscal Reconstruction

A substantial tax increase was enacted in the second half of the 1980s and early 1990s, due mainly to the advent of the "bubble economy." One of the most remarkable phenomena in the second half of the 1980s, the "bubble economy" was chiefly caused by loose monetary policy. Excess money flowed into the stock and land markets, producing an abnormal hike in asset prices. During the period 1985 to 1990, the nominal (real) rate of economic growth was 6 (4.8) percent on average. Stock and land price hikes generated large tax revenues in the form of corporate, security transaction, and capital gains taxes. Tax revenues still fell short of government spending, but the general government balance, including accounts for social security funds, became positive for the period 1987 to 1992.

There is no doubt that this large, natural tax increase played a vital role in reducing accumulated deficits, which in turn achieved the MOF's target of fiscal reconstruction by 1991. The sharp rise in tax revenues, caused by the bubble phenomenon, looked like a "windfall."

However, after the bubble economy burst, tax revenues started to decline, reducing the fiscal balance in 1991.

PRIOR COMMITMENTS

Below I explain the types of prior commitments in the Japanese government's general account budget in terms of the functions or targets being served. Table 6.1 summarizes major expenditures between 1965 and 1993 in the general account, which includes the social security accounts.

Interest Payments on Government Debt

Government bond issues, which have become an important financing instrument, have increased in recent years. Originally these bonds were only used to finance construction projects; later some were issued specifically to finance fiscal deficits. Rapid accumulation of

Table 6.1 JAPAN'S GENERAL ACCOUNT BUDGET BY MAJOR EXPENDITURE PROGRAMS (RELATIVE TO GNP)

	1965	1970	1975	1980	1985	1990	1993
Debt services	0.07%	0.40%	0.67%	2.21%	3.18%	3.25%	3.17%
Local finance	2.18	2.28	2.84	2.73	3.02	3.49	3.22
General spending	8.86	8.22	10.2	12.8	9.78	8.42	8.22
Social security	1.58	1.57	2.53	3.42	2.97	2.66	2.71
Measures for the unemployed	0.20	0.12	0.11	0.16	0.12	0.08	0.07
Public health service	0.28	0.19	0.18	0.17	0.14	0.13	0.13
Social insurance	0.64	0.81	1.50	2.13	1.76	1.65	1.68
Social welfare	0.13	0.15	0.40	0.57	0.62	0.55	0.62
Public assistance	0.32	0.30	0.34	0.40	0.31	0.25	0.21
Public works	2.05	1.87	2.18	2.76	2.12	1.60	1.77
Public amenities	0.06	0.08	0.21	0.40	0.32	0.17	0.30
Improvement of conditions for agricultural production	0.06	0.25	0.27	0.37	0.29	0.22	0.24
Road improvement	0.88	0.78	0.72	0.79	0.61	0.41	0.52
Erosion and flood control	0.34	0.31	0.34	0.46	0.36	0.25	0.31
Education and science	1.43	1.28	1.77	1.86	1.50	1.17	1.18
National defense	0.92	0.78	0.90	0.92	0.98	0.95	0.94

Source: Ministry of Finance, *Budget Summary*, various years.

bonds has an undesirable effect on prior commitments, as suggested elsewhere in this volume by Professor Cordes, by dramatically increasing the size of interest payments and other debt services. In 1993 the share of interest payments and debt services relative to total government expenditures reached more than 20 percent. Debt service has become a very large prior commitment in recent years. Rapid growth of obligatory expenditures such as debt service crowds out general spending, naturally leading to rigidity in budget making.[2] In other words, the government has been losing the fiscal ability to cope with new social needs.

To restrain fiscal deficits, the MOF presents a medium-term fiscal plan each year. First, expenditures are extrapolated straightforwardly into the future by each expenditure item, assuming a continuation of current law and institutional structure. Under this current structure, total government spending is expected to rise over time, perhaps more than tax revenues, thus putting pressure on fiscal deficits. To reduce pressure on fiscal deficits in the future, two policy targets are introduced: one is to keep constant the level of construction bonds even as the economy expands, and the other to reduce steadily *new* issues of deficit bonds toward zero within three years. Since tax and nontax revenues in the future can be projected to grow at about the same rate as nominal income, future revenues can also be projected. The remaining expenditures-revenues gap then must be eliminated in the budgetary process either by enactment of expenditure cuts or revenue increases. The MOF has made effective use of this strategy and largely succeeded in containing demands for increased expenditures.

The successful efforts at deficit reduction in the 1980s can be seen most vividly in figure 6.1. When tax revenues as a share of GNP equal government spending as a share of GNP, the budget is in balance, as indicated by the 45 degree line. Although such balance has not been obtained over time, note the striking difference among periods. From 1965 to 1974, both tax and expenditure shares rise; from 1975 to 1980, expenditure shares rise at a much more rapid rate than tax shares. From 1981 to 1990, however, spending shares go down and tax shares go up, and substantial movement is made toward budgetary balance. From 1991 to 1994, however, the combined impact of an economic slowdown and some tax reduction mainly move the tax shares downward, while expenditure shares expand only modestly.

Social Security Expenditures

The social security budget represents the Japanese government's largest expenditure program, reflecting about 18 percent of the total ex-

Figure 6.1 JAPAN'S GOVERNMENT SPENDING AND TAX REVENUES, 1965–1994 (Relative to GNP)

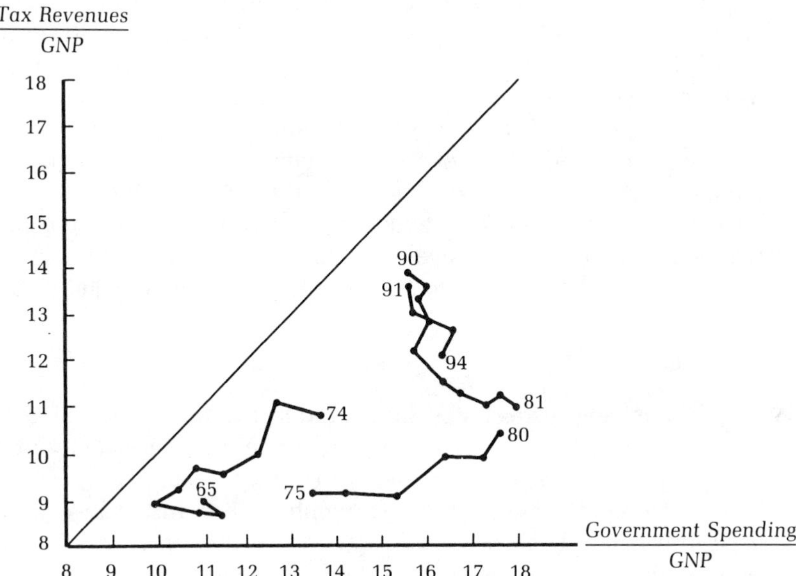

Source: Tax Bureau, Ministry of Finance, *Primary Statistics of Taxation*, various years.

penditure in the general account. The share of social security in the national budget increased considerably in the 1970s. However, the share has remained constant at about 18 percent since 1980. Social security expenditure is divided into five items: public assistance, social welfare, social insurance, public health services, and measures for the unemployed. Social insurance is the largest item, and its share of the total social security budget continued to increase until 1985. The share of social welfare is still increasing, while shares of the other items are decreasing.

Many people who find it difficult to support themselves financially and who require care, such as the aged, children, and the physically or mentally handicapped, must be supported by the public sector. The government provides various forms of support such as senior citizen homes, rehabilitation services, health visitor services, and special allowance payments. These expenditures, taken together, are classified as social welfare spending.

Social insurance is a public institution for mutual assistance supported by the receipts of compulsory contributions. These can be classified into four categories: medical insurance, public pensions, unemployment insurance, and workers' accident compensation insurance. Some medical insurance is subsidized by the government, depending on the financial statutes of the various programs. For example, National Health Insurance, whose recipients are mostly the aged and people on low incomes, is heavily subsidized by the government.

The Employees' Pension and the National Pension are Japan's two major public pension schemes. The government pays one-third of the basic pension benefit costs of these schemes. The reform of health insurance in 1984 and of the social security system in 1985 contributed greatly to reducing social security spending. However, considering the rapid growth of the aged population in the near future, more fiscal reforms will be needed to contain social security expenditures.

Public Works

Most of the expenditures for social capital formation are classified as public works expenses. Public works, the second largest item after social security, covers a wide variety of activities, its focus changing with the needs of the public. Recently emphasis has shifted away from road improvement toward measures aimed at improving living conditions such as sewage systems and housing programs.

The budget shares devoted to harbors and airports, improvement of basic conditions for agriculture, erosion and flood control, and forest roads and water supply for industrial use have changed little, even though the overall economic environment has changed drastically. This is because the share of each ministry's spending on public works has not changed for the last twenty years.

PRIOR COMMITMENTS AND THE "SUSTAINABILITY" PROBLEM

How does one measure an economy's capacity to finance fiscal deficits? What size of public debt can a capital market absorb if it is free of government intervention? Pressure in the capital market may hinder the finance of very large and persistent budget deficits and restrict the size of public debt. Attempts to issue more public debt may put sufficient pressure on real interest rates to destroy the stability of public debt dynamics. Essentially, the level of public debt must be kept within values that the capital market is willing to accept. If the level of public debt goes beyond these limits, it is deemed to be unsustainable by the capital market. As discussed in section 1 of the appendix to this chapter, the smaller the primary budget deficits and the higher the propensity to save, the growth rate of the economy, and the intergenerational transfer from the old to the young, the more likely that the sustainability problem will be alleviated.

Both increases in public spending and decreases in tax revenues (net of transfer payments) contribute to a rise in primary budget deficits (fiscal deficits excluding debt services), resulting in greater pressure on the sustainability problem. As already discussed, the main factors behind Japan's deficit reduction in the 1980s were a cut in public spending in the first half of the decade and a rise in tax revenues in the second half. In the 1990s it is expected that an increase in transfer payments due to aging as well as a decrease in tax revenues will contribute to higher primary deficits. It is very important to restrain this increasing trend in transfer payments, though this is by no means easy.

We consider two alternative ways to reduce primary deficits: increasing taxes and decreasing spending. In the Japanese fiscal system, the MOF, which represents government preferences, and the ruling party (RP), which reflects the majority of private preferences, cooperate to determine the budget. The bargaining game between the MOF and the RP is the most important process in formulating the budget. How difficult (or easy) is it to achieve fiscal reconstruction through such a bargaining process?

The model developed in section 2 of the appendix indicates that if deficits are due to an exogenous increase in public spending, it is rather easy to restore a balanced budget. On the other hand, if deficits are due to an exogenous increase in transfer payments or a decrease in tax revenues, it is not. The reasoning is as follows. Private agents always prefer small taxes net of transfer payments because they dislike a large net tax burden. However, they do not necessarily prefer a large level of government spending, because the benefit of public spending is spread across people and sometimes public activities crowd out private investment. The MOF likes to have a balanced budget at any level of spending. Thus, it is easier to reduce government spending than to raise taxes net of transfers. Since most of the deficits in the 1990s will be due to an increase in transfer payments, it will not be easy to return to a balanced budget in Japan.

To alleviate the sustainability problem, it will be necessary to reform the social security system, including health insurance and public pension programs. An independent organization outside the MOF-RP bargaining process, perhaps another "Rincho," endowed with strong powers, may be needed to restrain prior commitments.

Intergenerational Transfers

Although the Japanese public pension program is officially classified as a "funded" system, it is still at an early stage and may be regarded as a pay-as-you-go system. Over time, the government has increased benefit payments relative to contributions, turning the system into one that is less than fully funded. This tendency toward a pay-as-you-go system was already prevalent at the time of the 1973 reform, and is expected to continue to generate massive income transfers between generations.[3]

By definition, the pay-as-you-go public pension programs involve income transfers between generations. These transfers were especially notable in the start-up phase in 1973: the benefits were set at a relatively high level from the beginning and soon became inflation-indexed, while contributions started at a very low level. How much income does the present public pension program in Japan transfer between generations?

Table 6.2, taken from Takayama (1992), shows net average transfers through public pensions to the different cohorts by three types of households. As seen in the table, an enormous amount of income transfers from the young to the old will be involved in the public pension system. For example, the average amount of gross social security wealth (GSSW) to be received by a couple with one male wage earner born between 1925 and 1929 is 43 million *yen* at constant 1984 prices, while the present value of the couple's entire contributions to public pensions (social security contributions or SSC) amounts to only 7.8 million *yen*. Thus, through public pensions the couple enjoys a net average transfer of 35 million *yen* and a benefit/contribution ratio of 5.54.

Gross social security wealth declines with youth. In contrast, estimates of the present value of past and future contributions grow with youth. Because of these opposing movements of benefits and contributions, net transfers decline sharply for younger generations. For generations born after 1965, contributions to public pensions might turn out to be more than benefits eventually received.

To reduce the pressure from Japan's prior commitment to its pension system, it is desirable to switch from an unfunded to a funded system (Hatta and Oguchi 1992).[4] It would also seem useful to implement tax reform to raise consumption taxes and reduce income taxes. Since older generations do not pay much income tax, such tax reform would shift the tax burden from the young to the old (Ihori 1987), helping to reduce the pressure exerted by prior commitments.

Table 6.2 NET AVERAGE TRANSFERS THROUGH PUBLIC PENSIONS IN JAPAN (IN TEN THOUSAND YEN, BASED ON 1984 PRICES)

Birth Year[a]	Age in 1984	Category	Singles	Couples A[b]	Couples B[c]
1960–1964	20–24	GSSW[d](1)	3,184	3,024	4,027
		SSC[e](2)	2,072	2,417	3,600
		(1)-(2)	112	606	607
		(1)/(2)	1.05	1.25	1.17
1955–1959	25–29	GSSW(1)	2,281	3,294	4,577
		SSC(2)	1,968	2,359	3,478
		(1)-(2)	312	936	1,099
		(1)/(2)	1.16	1.40	1.32
1950–1954	30–34	GSSW(1)	2,357	3,492	4,563
		SSC(2)	1,744	2,080	2,914
		(1)-(2)	614	1,411	1,650
		(1)/(2)	1.35	1.68	1.57
1945–1949	35–39	GSSW(1)	2,283	3,643	4,627
		SSC(2)	1,359	1,827	2,495
		(1)-(2)	923	1,816	2,106
		(1)/(2)	1.68	1.99	1.84
1940–1944	40–44	GSSW(1)	2,245	3,806	4,627
		SSC(2)	1,143	1,542	2,072
		(1)-(2)	1,202	2,264	2,555
		(1)/(2)	2.05	2.47	2.23
1935–1939	45–49	GSSW(1)	2,425	3,959	4,614
		SSC(2)	932	1,266	1,655
		(1)-(2)	1,493	2,693	2,959
		(1)/(2)	2.60	3.13	2.79
1930–1934	50–54	GSSW(1)	2,572	4,141	4,780
		SSC(2)	712	1,003	1,361
		(1)-(2)	1,860	3,138	3,418
		(1)/(2)	3.61	4.13	3.51
1925–1929	55–59	GSSW(1)	2,530	4,316	4,947
		SSC(2)	508	780	1,076
		(1)-(2)	2,022	3,537	3,871
		(1)/(2)	4.98	5.54	4.60

Source: Takayama 1992.
a. The birth year and the age are for householders.
b. Couples A have one male earner.
c. Couples B have two earners.
d. GSSW is the present value of gross social security wealth.
e. SSC, social security contributions, is the present value of the past and future contributions to public pensions.

BEQUESTS IN JAPAN

Private intergenerational transfers from the old to the young reduce pressure on the sustainability problem. Bequests are a major form of such private intergenerational transfers. A number of studies have applied the methodology of Kotlikoff and Summers (1981) to the case of Japan to estimate shares of life cycle wealth and wealth due to intergenerational transfers. For example, Hayashi (1986) concludes that bequests from the old to the young are the main factor behind Japan's high saving rate. On the other hand, Horioka (1991) points out that the bulk of these bequests appear to be unintended or accidental. He argues that bequests often arise from risk aversion in the face of uncertainty about future medical expenses and the timing of death, or are motivated by implicit annuity contracts between the aged and their children or by strategic bequest motives—whereby the parent gives a bequest to offspring in exchange for a desirable action undertaken by the offspring. All of these patterns are consistent with the life cycle model.

A number of empirical studies shed light on the nature of the bequest motive in Japan (for example, Dekle 1990 and Ohtake 1991). Their findings suggest that bequests are generally intended. Japan's high level of private intergenerational transfers from the old to the young might be valuable in weakening the pressure caused by the expansion of Japanese government bonds.

As suggested earlier, a high economic growth rate could alleviate the sustainability pressure of prior commitments. It is also possible that items such as health care expenses and retirement benefits might grow more if economic growth is higher, thereby providing much less deficit relief than expected. It is therefore important to restrain social security expenditures. In earlier work (Ihori 1994) I examined the effect of bequest taxes on intergenerational transfers in an endogenous growth model. I found that the effect of the bequest motive on the growth rate is qualitatively the same in all three representative bequest motives (the altruistic model, the bequest-as-consumption model, and the bequest-as-exchange model). This means that transfers from the old to the young raise the rate of economic growth regardless of bequest motive. I also found that the impact of taxation of bequests is not necessarily the same in all of the three alternative bequest motives. However, when the bequest tax is initially high, further increasing it may well reduce the intergenerational transfer from the old to the young and, hence, reduce the rate of economic growth. Because of the steeply progressive estate tax structure in Japan, it is also useful to consider reducing those taxes in order to promote private transfers from the old to the young.

CONCLUSION

In the 1990s transfer payments due to aging, public pensions, and public debt are expected to have strong negative effects on Japan's debt level. It is useful to loosen the "yoke" of these prior commitments, because future windfall tax revenues cannot be expected as in an earlier period. Austerity measures that might be introduced include creating another "Rincho" to restrain such commitments, changing from an unfunded toward a funded pension system, raising consumption taxes while reducing income taxes, and reducing the progressivity of bequest taxes. These measures would help stimulate capital accumulation and economic growth in Japan.

Notes

1. The budget of Japan's national government includes the general account, special accounts, and the budgets of government-affiliated ministries and agencies. Of these, the general account is central to the budget process. Almost all national tax revenues except for local transfer taxes belong to the general account, as do revenues from new bond issues. The general account can greatly affect the entire fiscal system, although it reflects only a part of the whole budget. Government expenditures, excluding debt service and local finance, are referred to as general spending. Since the general account can be thought of as representing the entirety of Japan's fiscal activities, the size of its deficit is significant. Furthermore, because we are primarily interested in the fiscal policies adopted by Japan's Ministry of Finance, we focus on the budget in the general account of the national government.

2. The share of general spending as a proportion of total government expenditures declined from 79.8 percent in 1965 to 55.2 percent in 1993, while the share of debt service increased from 0.6 percent to 21.3 percent during the same period (Ministry of Finance, *Budget Summary*, various years).

3. In 1973 the replacement of the model benefit of the Employees' Pension was raised to 43 percent. An indexation provision for inflation was also introduced, and a number of other social security programs were improved or newly implemented.

4. Such a switch entails a transition problem. Initially, those starting to fund their plans end up paying for both their own retirement and that of the generation before them. See Hatta and Oguchi (1992), who investigated this problem in the Japanese pension system.

References

Asako, K., T. Ito, and K. Sakamoto. 1991. "The Rise and Fall of the Deficit in Japan." *Journal of the Japanese and International Economies* 5: 451–72.

Azariadis, C. 1993. *Intertemporal Macroeconomics*. Cambridge, Ma: Blackwell.

Dekle, R. 1990. "Do the Japanese Elderly Reduce Their Total Wealth? A New Look with Different Data." *Journal of the Japanese and International Economies* 4: 309–17.

Hatta, T., and N. Oguchi. 1992. "Changing the Japanese Social Security System from Pay as You Go to Actuarially Fair." In *Topics in the Economics of Aging*, ed. David Wise. Chicago: University of Chicago Press.

Hayashi, F. 1986. "Is Japan's Saving Rate So Apparently High?" *NBER Macroeconomics Annual* 1986: 147–210.

Horioka, C.Y. 1991. "Savings in Japan." Osaka University Discussion Paper No. 248.

Ihori, T. 1994. "Taxes on Capital Accumulation and Economic Growth." Photocopy.

________. 1987. "Tax Reform and Intergeneration Incidence." *Journal of Public Economics* 33: 377–87.

Ishi, H. 1993. *The Japanese Tax System*. Oxford, England: Clarendon Press.

Ishi, H., and T. Ihori. 1992. "How Have Fiscal Deficits Been Reduced in Japan?" Photocopy.

Kotlikoff, L.J., and L.H. Summers. 1981. "The Role of Intergenerational Transfers in Aggregate Capital Accumulation." *Journal of Political Economy* 89: 706–32.

Ohtake, F. 1991. "The Bequest Motive and the Saving/Labor Supply of the Aged." *Keizai Kenkyu* 42: 21–30 [in Japanese].

Samuelson, P. 1958. "An Exact Consumption Loan Model of Interest With or Without the Social Contrivance of Money." *Journal of Political Economy* 66: 467–82.

Takayama, N. 1992. *The Graying of Japan: An Economic Perspective of Public Pensions*. Tokyo, Japan: Kinokuniya.

APPENDIX 6.A

The Sustainability Problem

To define the concept of "sustainable" public debt and explore the determinants of its highest level, consider a simple pure-exchange two-period overlapping generations economy with constant population, à la Samuelson (1958) and Azariadis (1993, chapters 18 and 19). The per capita saving function of the young generation is portrayed by

$$s(r_{t+1}) = b_t, \tag{A1}$$

where r_{t+1} is the one-period interest rate on bonds maturing in time $t + 1$ and b_t is per capita public debt. It is assumed that savings increase with the rate of interest, i.e., $\partial s/\partial r > 0$. Then, from (A1) we have

$$r_{t+1} = r(b)_t, \tag{A1$'$}$$

The government budget constraint at time t+1 is given by

$$b_{t+1} = \frac{1 + r_{t+1}}{1 + n} b_t + g_{t+1} - \tau_{t+1} \tag{A2}$$

where g is per capita government spending, τ is per capita tax revenues, n is the rate of population growth, and b is per capita outstanding of public debt. Let us define the per capita primary deficit q as the difference between g and τ, and suppose for simplicity that $q = 0$. Then, substituting (A1)′ into (A2), we get

$$b_{t+1} = \frac{1 + r(b_t)}{1 + n} b_t. \tag{A3}$$

It can be shown that equation (A3) has two stationary solutions. One of them is an equilibrium with zero public debt and an interest rate equal to r(0). The other is the golden rule equilibrium with per capita public debt s(n) and an interest rate equal to the population growth rate n. The golden rule stock of public debt may be positive [$s(n) > 0$, the Samuelson case] or negative [$s(n) < 0$, the classical case], depending on the shape of the saving function.

Let us run a primary budget deficit initially at time 0, i.e., $q_0 = b_0 > 0$ but preserve primary budget balance ($q_t = 0$ for $t > 0$) thereafter. How big can initial debt b_0 be? In the Samuelson case, b_0 cannot exceed s(n). For, if $b_0 > s(n)$, then the interest rate needed to induce households voluntarily to hold b_0 would exceed the growth rate n in each period. Public debt would grow faster than the economy, with debt service surpassing in finite time the maximal flow of saving that the household sector is capable of producing. The government debt would no longer be held by the household and the government would go bankrupt. However, if $b_0 < s(n)$, public debt would grow more slowly than the economy and, over time, debt per capita would tend to become zero. For similar reasons, in the classical case, b_0 cannot exceed zero. Hence, the largest amount of per capita public debt that is consistent with competitive equilibrium b^* is either zero or $s(n)$, whichever is greater, that is, $b^* = \text{Max}\ [0, s(n)]$. As long as the outstanding stock of public debt is less than b^*, it is sustainable. As shown in Azariadis (1993), when the primary deficit q increases, $s(n)$ will be reduced.

Consider a simple overlapping generations model with per capita government spending g and lump sum taxes levied on the young generation τ_1 and on the old generation τ_2. Assuming for simplicity that the primary budget deficit is zero, we obtain

$$\tau_1 + \tau_2 = g.$$

The savings function is then given by

$$s_t = e_1 - \tau_1 - c_1' = \frac{1}{2}\left[e_1 - \tau_1 + \frac{e_2 - \tau_2}{1 + r_{t+1}}\right],$$

where e_1 and e_2 are endowments when young and old, respectively, and it is assumed that $e_1 > e_2$, $e_1 > \tau_1$, and $e_2 > g$.

The largest sustainable level of public debt b^* is given by

$$b^* = \text{Max}\left[0, \frac{e_1 - \tau_1 - (e_2 - \tau_2)}{2}\right].$$

It is clear that b^* is increasing with the first-period disposable income $(e_1 - \tau_1)$ and is decreasing with the second-period disposable income $(e_2 - \tau_2)$. An increase in τ_1, with a corresponding decrease in τ_2, which means an intergenerational transfer from the young to the old, reduces the golden rule stock of public debt.

A Bargaining Model of Fiscal Reconstruction

Suppose that both the Ministry of Finance (MOF) and the ruling party (RP) are concerned with taxes net of transfers (τ) and government spending (g), where τ and g are defined as a ratio of GNP. RP has the notion of optimal size of government deficit, which is positive and constant. This comes from a fiscal illusion: the RP expects that some of the tax burdens to finance a given level of spending may be transferred to future generations. The RP also believes that as long as the optimal deficit is realized, the smaller the values of τ and g the better. On the other hand, the MOF regards the balanced budget as the most desirable goal. It also believes that if a balanced budget is realized, the larger the values of τ and g, which is for the better.

For analytical convenience, let us assume that the initial equilibrium point is one of balanced budgets with relatively low levels of spending and taxes.

Let us examine several situations in which fiscal deficits occur. First, imagine an unanticipated increase in government spending, g. For example, in response to an unanticipated exogenous shock such as the oil-price crisis, government spending is forced to rise. If spending must be raised, what should the new level of τ be? For the RP, a point with a low level of τ is desirable, while for the MOF a point with a sufficiently high level of τ is desirable. If the bargaining power of the two groups is similar, the new equilibrium point is achieved somewhere between the two groups' preferred levels of τ.

Compared with the initial equilibrium, the level of government spending g is now high, while the level of tax revenues τ falls short at the new equilibrium, thus resulting in fiscal deficits. In other words, an unanticipated increase in government spending is to be financed by debt issuance.

Now consider the fiscal reconstruction process. If government spending can be adjusted flexibly, how will g and τ be changed? It is possible that a move from the new equilibrium back to the initial equilibrium is Pareto improving. During the fiscal reconstruction process, g is reduced substantially while τ does not decline much. Both groups gain and fiscal balance is restored. This process may be called the fiscal reconstruction movement without significant tax increases.

Next, suppose tax revenues are cut unexpectedly or, due to an unanticipated increase in social security programs, the MOF has to raise its transfer payments. For the RP a point with a relatively high level of g is desirable, while for the MOF a point with a low level of g is desirable. If the bargaining power of the MOF and the RP is almost the same, a new equilibrium point is reached somewhere between the two groups' desired levels of g. At the new equilibrium, government spending is likely to be about the same as the initial level while tax revenues (net of transfers) are reduced, resulting in fiscal deficits.

Let us investigate the fiscal reconstruction process when the size of tax revenues (net of transfer payments) is flexible. Interestingly, a move from the new equilibrium back to the initial equilibrium is not Pareto improving, because the MOF gains and the RP loses. For the MOF, an increase in τ for given g, which is consistent with this move, is desirable. For the RP, however, an increase in τ is not desirable for given g. Since the two groups' preferences conflict, it is difficult to implement fiscal reconstruction. This suggests that fiscal deficits cannot be easily reduced.

Chapter Seven

DEFICIT REDUCTION AROUND THE WORLD

Paul Posner and Barbara Bovbjerg

At the request of Senator Robert Kerrey, the U.S. Government Accounting Office (GAO) embarked on an examination of deficit reduction experiences in other countries. In earlier work on the long-range effects of fiscal deficits, GAO cited Organization of Economic Cooperation and Development (OECD) data suggesting that Australia, Germany, Japan, and the United Kingdom had successfully eliminated deficits in the 1980s.[1] Senator Kerrey asked what fiscal, economic, political, and public policymaking lessons the United States might learn from these countries' deficit reduction experiences, as well as those of Canada and Mexico. In addition to reviewing data provided by the OECD and the International Monetary Fund (IMF) on the fiscal deficits of our case study countries, we interviewed government policymakers, public policy critics, academicians, and journalists to better understand not only what deficit reduction took place, but how each country's deficit reduction strategies were formulated and implemented. An appendix provides individual country profiles that detail causes of and government responses to fiscal deficits, as well as government's financial balance, as a percentage of GDP, from 1980 to 1995.

INTRODUCTION

Deficit reduction is difficult in modern democracies. Some believe that deficits persist because the public perceives the benefits of achieving budget balance to be less compelling than the costs. The prospective benefits of prudent fiscal policy—lower interest rates, a larger pool of domestic savings to finance productive investment, and, ultimately, improved prospects for living standards in the future—are long-range and economy-wide. Decisionmakers and the electorate must balance these against the immediate and concentrated cost of expenditure cuts, increased taxes, and related reductions in public services and government transfers. Actions taken to achieve balance can therefore prove politically hazardous. Groups losing benefits can be readily mobilized against cutbacks, while members of the general public who will eventually benefit from long-term economic improvement only weakly perceive these advantages.

It is, therefore, hardly surprising that many OECD countries run deficits. The United States itself has a chronic history of budget deficits. Deficits have been reported in the federal, state, and local government sectors of the National Income and Product Accounts for all but 6 of the last 30 years and continuously since 1980. Moreover, cumulative deficits have vastly exceeded surpluses. The U.S. federal unified budget has been balanced only once over the last three decades, and the debt held by the public has grown from 41 percent to 52 percent of GDP.

More recently, the U.S. government's budget deficit rose from 2.8 percent of GDP in 1980, peaked at 6.3 percent in 1983, and registered 4 percent in 1990.[2] These continuous large shortfalls raised national debt levels from about $909 billion in 1980 to $3.2 trillion by 1990.

The U.S. Congress took action to reduce the deficit through the Budget Reconciliation Acts of 1990 and 1993. By imposing caps on discretionary spending and maintaining restraints on expansion of entitlements and tax benefits, the legislation has cut hundreds of billions of dollars from the deficit's expected levels in the 1990s. The Congressional Budget Office (CBO) now projects the deficit will be 2.5 percent of GDP in 1995.

Yet the deficit problem remains. CBO figures suggest that if no further action is taken, the deficit will once again resume its upward path after 1998, rising to 3.6 percent of GDP by 2005. Our work suggests that growing health care costs, the baby boom generation's eventual retirement, rising federal interest payments, and expected cyclical downturns will continue to exert upward pressure, making the problem even worse as the 21st century progresses (GAO 1992—see note 1). Eliminating the deficit and sustaining a surplus will be necessary to prepare for the nation's economic and demographic future, yet doing so will require fundamental policy changes of a sort not yet undertaken.

In this context, the elimination of deficits in some OECD countries in the 1980s—and their subsequent reappearance in some countries in the 1990s—is an important development. Exploring the reasons for other governments' fiscal successes, as well as failures, may help resolve this fiscal and political problem in the United States.

Of the six countries examined, Mexico overcame the largest fiscal deficit: in 1982, Mexico reported a general government deficit of 16.9 percent of GDP and by 1992 reported a surplus. Japan maintained a surplus for the longest period, from 1989 to 1993, as measured by OECD general government balance.[3] Canada's recent fiscal history most closely mirrors that of the United States, with deficits rarely dipping below 3 percent of GDP. Despite these differences in outcomes, certain themes regarding deficit reduction strategies cut across national borders.

For purposes of comparability among countries, one of the best measures of fiscal deficits and surpluses is that for the totality of government activity, or general government, from the United Nations' System of National Accounts (SNA). However, the general government fiscal balances may not be exact proxies for budget deficits as they are perceived in a particular country. In the case of a country with a unitary governmental system and a consolidated budget (covering all levels of government), the deficit may approximate the public sector borrowing requirement and not differ markedly from the SNA definition for general government. However, in some federal systems, the fiscal policy at the federal level may be perceived as completely separate from the fiscal policy at the state or local levels.[4]

Moreover, some countries such as Japan have large off-budget accounts for pensions, investment, or business-type activities. In these cases, political debate over fiscal policy can use data that substantially differ from those represented in the official SNA accounts. Although we display comparable data herein (see appendix 7.A), we focus our case study attention on the factors that are perceived as important in the formulation of public policy in each country. (It is important to note that in the appendix we use general government balances to define deficits, allowing us to make comparisons across governments. In contrast, any reference to deficits in the text refers to deficits as defined by each individual government.)

CAUSES OF THE DEFICITS

The causes of deficits are surprisingly similar across the six countries studied and have become more so as national economies have become more integrated.

Fiscal deficits of the 1980s were rooted in decisions made in the 1960s and early 1970s to create and expand public programs. Each of the six countries expanded public spending under the presumption that high economic growth rates would continue or resume. Japan and Germany also came under pressure from the G-7 countries to follow policies of fiscal stimulus during this period. By the time that economic growth rates slowed in the mid-1970s, many of these programs were entrenched and, consequently, contributed to fiscal imbalance.

Most of the countries visited reported that the sudden rise of oil prices in the 1970s precipitated recessions and contributed to or enhanced a slowdown in economic growth. These oil-dependent countries struggled to absorb the shock of higher prices while Mexico, an oil-producing country, became dependent on new-found wealth. The shock to growth patterns in both types of countries proved profound. Japan, the United Kingdom, Germany, and Australia reported continuous fiscal deficits after the mid-1970s; Mexico embarked on spending levels that proved unsustainable when oil revenues fluctuated.

Although Germany and Japan have requirements for a balanced budget, these do not appear to be effective barriers to deficits. In Japan, the Diet (the country's legislature) may only issue bonds if the funds are to be used for public construction, capital contribution, or loans. In Germany, investment expenditures are exempt from a balanced budget, and the balanced budget requirement can be waived if running a deficit is deemed to be necessary to stabilize prices, maintain a high level of employment, and achieve external balance. In both countries, deficits arose in the 1980s despite these measures.

IMPETUS FOR DEFICIT REDUCTION

What prompts governments to address fiscal deficits? Some observers suggest that governments will act only when markets refuse to continue financing a government's deficits. Yet of the six deficit-reducing countries studied, only Mexico faced this type of profound economic crisis—a loss of access to credit compounded by triple-digit inflation. Governments in the other five countries did not face such extreme external pressures, but appeared to act for other reasons.

A variety of economic, political, and cultural pressures led to the fiscal turning point in the other five countries. For example, Japan's culture places a high value on savings. Emerging concerns about debt levels, rising shares of the budget allocated to interest costs, and their effect on the government's ability to finance the nation's pension program in the long-term future were important in driving the government to action. In the United Kingdom, an election mandate to control inflation and reduce the size of government seemed to have provided the impetus. In Germany, fear of inflation and concern that rising interest payments were restricting the government's budgetary flexibility prompted deficit reduction efforts. Each of these countries responded to a threshold of concern that was unique and conditioned by history and traditions. Thus, an inflation rate triggering consensus in Germany about the need to control budget deficits would not necessarily do so in the United Kingdom.

Such pressures also had the effect of forcing some governments to change course. New governments of both the left and the right had to address the deficit even though they may not have campaigned on this issue. In several cases, governments campaigning for more public spending or tax cuts had to reverse themselves once in office. Although leaders explained this shift by pointing to worsening deficit trends, parties forming a government suddenly acquired a new constituency—the international credit markets—that rewarded different fiscal behavior than that promised during the heat of a campaign. The Australian Labor Party, for example, came to power without an expectation that deficit reduction would constitute a major policy initiative, only to find that its need for credibility abroad as an economic manager demanded such action. That government was also haunted by the specter of the economic failures of the previous Labor Party government and thus felt the need to "prove itself" with the Australian public. Most recently, the new Liberal Party government in Canada, after deemphasizing the deficit in the 1993 campaign, has now promoted deficit reduction to a higher priority. Once in office, the Liberals have emphasized Canada's stake in maintaining the confidence of the international credit markets in its currency and its ability to finance its debt.

Governments also came to realize that achieving their primary economic goals depended on reducing the deficit. In the United Kingdom, for instance, the Thatcher government campaigned as "supply siders" committed to strengthening the private sector and reducing the role of the public sector, but had to defer some of its policy changes when its commitment to reducing inflation caused deficit reduction to become a higher priority.

Most governments began deficit reduction during periods of slow economic growth or recession. Yet traditional macroeconomic thought suggests that stable economic growth over the course of the business cycle can best be promoted by a countercyclical fiscal policy. During times of robust economic growth, deficits should be reduced or eliminated to offset the buildup of inflationary pressures in the economy. Conversely, during economic downturns, deficits might very well be useful to stimulate growth and even jump-start the economy. Contrary to this prescription, some policymakers implemented deficit reduction policies during recessions or periods of slow economic growth. For example, the United Kingdom began its deficit reduction program during a recession in order to stem inflation and high interest rates. This action sparked controversy; 364 British economists wrote a letter to *The Times* (London) protesting the government's tight fiscal policies in the depths of a recession, arguing that the policies would deepen the economic trough.

As the economy improved in these countries, however, it became more difficult to maintain fiscal discipline. Some countries were able to sustain balance or surplus for several years, partly by maintaining expenditure controls instituted when the deficit was larger. But as the budget outlook improved due to successful deficit reduction and stronger economic growth, governments expanded programs or cut taxes in response to pent-up demands for social benefits or long-deferred political agendas. These actions may constrain these countries' capacity to respond through fiscal policy to future economic downturns.

ACTIONS TAKEN

In the 1980s, some countries were able to resolve their deficits through relatively incremental or marginal cuts, modification of benefit indexation schemes, or deferral of capital spending. Thanks to tax systems not fully indexed to inflation, these spending actions, coupled with revenue gains from economic recovery, were sufficient in some cases to resolve deficits. Other countries, however, instituted more fundamental reforms in government roles and responsibilities, most notably involving privatization and means testing of entitlements.

Actions such as shifting political responsibility for cuts to states or private entities and reducing capital spending were familiar budget responses that offered relatively easy, short-term fixes. Yet these strategies may, in fact, have only temporarily deferred spending pressures. Cutting capital spending, for example, may only result in greater spending needs in the future. Actions such as targeting spending cuts and de-indexing benefits were taken based on a longer term perspective and thus offered more permanent savings.

Few governments we visited significantly reduced their deficits as the result of tax reform, which tended to be revenue-neutral. Many allowed their income tax receipts to grow as a result of the worldwide economic growth in the 1980s. The natural revenue growth from an expanding economic base, together with tax brackets not fully indexed to inflation, allowed these governments to use revenues as major engines of deficit reduction without policy intervention.

Deficit reduction conferred the automatic dividend of lowering interest payments on the debt, both by reducing the growth of the debt itself and, in some cases, by contributing to lower interest rates. In Mexico, for example, interest payments were reduced from nearly 20 percent of GDP in 1987 to 3.9 percent of GDP in 1992 as a result of restructuring and debt repayment. Over this period, reduced interest payments were responsible for 15.7 percentage points of the total public expenditure reduction of 18.7 percentage points of GDP.

Imposing Limits on Government Spending

All six governments studied used some form of spending limit or target to control aggregate spending. These overall limits were a departure from the budgeting approaches of the past in that they imposed a top-down limit on central government spending. There was wide variation in the nature of the spending limits, ranging from nominal limits in Japan, the United Kingdom, and Canada, to broad fiscal goals in Germany, Australia, and Mexico. Although the nature and effectiveness of these limits varied, each represented a multi-year approach that sought to reduce real overall spending by examining both discretionary and mandatory programs.

In the United Kingdom, the government used planning totals to manage its budget and to ensure that overall spending did not exceed a ceiling. The planning total covered the majority of the budget, excluding interest and social security spending growth resulting from a downturn in the economy. The government attempted to stay within the planning totals, and if spending in one area grew faster than predicted, would reduce spending in other areas to stay under the limit. For example, health spending was protected but total spending had to remain below the planning total. As a result of these limits, annual real growth in public expenditures in the United Kingdom averaged only 1.3 percent during the 1980s, representing a significant drop from 3.3 percent during the 1970s.

The Japanese government used spending limits extensively by imposing ceilings, and sometimes negative ceilings, on portions of the budget. In 1982 the government imposed a ceiling of zero percent nominal growth over the previous year's budget. In 1984 the ceilings for current expenditures were lowered to minus 10 percent and the ceiling for investment was lowered to minus 5 percent. Ceilings on current expenditures remained at minus 10 percent throughout the rest of the 1980s and up to this writing. As in the United Kingdom, certain programs were exempted from cuts, but overall spending limits had to be met. Spending was thus held relatively constant as a percentage of GDP throughout the 1980s.

Other countries' governments used broad fiscal policy goals, rather than actual spending limits, to reduce spending. In Germany the goal was to hold the growth in spending at all levels of government to 3 percent each year during much of the 1980s. The Australian government had a goal of reducing overall spending as a percentage of gross domestic product, but only applied strict limits to the 10 percent of its budget associated with administrative costs. It required federal agencies to reduce these costs each year in exchange for greater management flexibility.

The Canadian government established spending limits in the early 1990s which stated that non-interest spending through 1995, including mandatory spending, could not exceed levels projected in 1991. The legislation stipulated that if program expenditure rose above its projected level for economic or policy reasons, the increase had to be offset by reductions elsewhere in the budget. However, some analysts question the effectiveness of these limits, arguing that the ceilings were too high and did not force constraint. Several experts suggest that the spending limits enacted in the early 1990s may not be renewed by the new government.

Restraining Social Program Spending

Spending for social services was restrained in several countries by making changes in the way benefits were adjusted for inflation and reducing or eliminating benefits for upper income recipients. By moving away from the universality of some benefits, governments were able to realize savings and maintain or increase benefits to those in greatest financial need. In addition to increased targeting, some governments achieved savings through changes in large demand-led programs. Although these changes often produced only minimal short-term savings, they will result in significant long-term savings.

Decisions to increase targeting affected education, health, pensions, unemployment, family assistance, and industrial subsidies. In Australia, reductions were made in all these areas. In Germany, modification of statutory benefits included a cut in children's benefits, conversion of financial aid for students from grants to loans, and limits on the adjustment of social assistance rates.

Pension commitments were modified in most of the countries by making changes to indexing provisions or the means-testing of benefits. For example, in Germany increases in pensions were postponed by six months; in the United Kingdom pensions were indexed to prices rather than wages, and some limited means-testing was introduced.

Australia's approach to means- and asset-testing benefit programs deserves particular mention. In the 1980s, Australia moved away from universality in its pension and child assistance programs. The government's deficit reduction strategy relied in part on targeting spending for such public benefits to needier (i.e., not middle and upper income) groups. As one official told us, "Welfare should be welfare." This significant shift in public priorities may have special relevance to the United States, where concern about entitlement benefits is growing.

Shifting Political Responsibility for Cuts

Some countries found it politically attractive to shift costs to other levels of government or to the private sector. The governments of Australia and Canada reduced aid to lower levels of government, thereby shifting some of the tough budget decisions down to the states or provinces.

Privatization also represented a common deficit reduction strategy, although the degree to which it contributed to improved fiscal balance varied greatly from one country to another. In Mexico privatization contributed in two ways: by providing one-time revenue that was reserved for debt repayment, and by removing subsidized activities from the public budget. The United Kingdom pursued privatization to a great extent in the 1980s, reflecting the Conservative Party government's political philosophy of downsizing government and pursuing economic efficiency. Canada and Japan also pursued privatization, although apparently more as a means to improve economic efficiency than to save government money in the short run. Although most countries changed management practices for efficiency gains, these changes were not meant to contribute significantly to deficit reduction.

Reducing Capital Spending

Capital spending was also an easy target for deficit reduction measures. Reductions in capital spending occurred at the central government level and at lower levels of government as a result of central funding cuts. For example, Mexico reduced capital spending by half between 1982 and 1988. In Germany, capital spending by all levels of government declined by 5.5 percent a year between 1981 and 1984. Australia also made significant reductions in capital spending as part of its deficit reduction strategy.

Revising Methods of Indexation

Some countries modified or eliminated the linkage of program benefits to inflation as a way to reduce spending. In the United Kingdom, this indexation of benefits was shifted from wage to price changes. At the time of the change, it made little difference in benefits because wages and prices were growing at the same pace, but based on historical experience policymakers expected prices to grow more slowly. Their predictions proved accurate, and the shift saved several billion pounds over the long term. Canada modified its indexing scheme for some benefit and transfer programs to the growth in GDP minus 3 percentage points.

Unlike the United States, most of the countries studied had nonindexed tax systems that provided a significant fiscal boost when their economies picked up and that substantially contributed to the attainment of budget balance or surplus. As budget balance or surplus was achieved, the fiscal dividend arising from bracket creep was sometimes given back to the taxpayers in the form of occasional tax cuts. Conservative governments in two countries—Australia in the 1970s and the United Kingdom in the 1980s—instituted some indexation of their income tax and allowance systems, but subsequently suspended some provisions as the revenue impact of indexing became more apparent. In Canada tax rates were fully indexed in the mid-1970s, but in 1985 indexation was modified so that now adjustments only take place when inflation exceeds 3 percent.

Enacting Tax Reform

Most of the countries studied enacted some form of tax reform during the deficit reduction period, but these changes were largely revenue-neutral. Many of the reforms were characterized by base-broadening to finance broad rate reductions or by a shift from income to consumption taxes. In some countries, income tax reductions offset increases in or the creation of consumption taxes. For example, Japan reduced income tax rates in exchange for instituting a 3 percent value added tax (VAT). Others, such as Mexico, also financed tax rate reductions with increased tax enforcement. Few countries intended such tax changes to contribute to deficit reduction in the short run; ministries of finance favored the changes for efficiency and longer run performance improvements and as an inducement for broader public support of fiscal austerity.

ACHIEVING POLITICAL AGREEMENT

During the period when these countries undertook fiscal austerity measures, governments in the five countries that balanced their budgets were re-elected, some several times. Although the relationship between these fiscal policies and re-election is unclear, successful deficit reduction did not represent the electoral threat that some might expect.

Political Strategies

For a period of time, governments in most of these countries turned fiscal austerity into a seemingly unassailable political virtue. The governing party defined the deficit as a principal public agenda item. Once this occurred, opposition parties had little choice but to frame their policies in deficit reduction terms. For example, the Australian Labor Government of the mid- and late 1980s aggressively attacked the budget deficit, forcing the conservative opposition to engage in something of a bidding war over whose policy alternatives promised the greatest amount of deficit reduction.

The governments of Germany and Japan achieved similar success in defining priorities, skillfully employing their countries' cultural predispositions toward saving and fiscal responsibility to emphasize the need for fiscal restraint. This created a situation where groups opposing cuts had to propose other, offsetting savings to meet fiscal goals.

Governments in many of these countries engaged in some form of consensus building to achieve political and popular support for their fiscal policies. This was especially noteworthy in Australia, Germany, and Mexico. In these countries, key business and labor interest groups affected by deficit reduction and instrumental to achieving economic reform were brought into the decisionmaking process. Governments reached agreement with these groups by offering incentives or convincing them that these actions would be to their advantage. Clearly identifying the expected economic and fiscal benefits of deficit reduction was also an important factor in bringing these groups to the table.

Consensus was not as easy to achieve in Canada. During the 1980s the Canadian government, like the U.S. government, struggled with the lack of consensus on how to reduce budget deficits. In the absence of consensus, interest groups were sometimes able to defeat the government's deficit reduction plans. For example, when the Canadian prime minister attempted to limit indexation of old age pensions, he was rebuffed by outraged senior citizens.

Governments in these countries also advocated deficit reduction as critical to achieving broader economic and political goals. Most governments were able to convince the public that sacrifice in the form of deficit reduction would be rewarded with short- and medium-term economic gain manifested in lower inflation and improved prospects for financing future commitments. The Japanese government, utilizing the country's predisposition toward saving and fiscal responsibility, focused on the long run to develop a sense of consensus. It emphasized the problem of growing budgetary inflexibility and the importance of building an operating surplus to finance the needs of future retirees. The government of Mexico successfully argued for deficit reduction as a response to a national economic crisis and as a way to restore the credit market's faith in the country's currency and debt.

Strategies to Soften the Pain of Fiscal Austerity

The strategies used to reduce the deficit also helped promote political support and defuse or mollify potential political opposition. In some countries, the government made the pain of expenditure reduction palatable to affected groups through trade-offs. In Australia, unions agreed to economic reforms in exchange for increased health care coverage and tax reductions. Although this agreement imposed a significant fiscal cost on the government, the government gained union support for its broader economic and fiscal reforms that included targeting social benefits, as well as the real wage reductions necessary to improve Australia's economic outlook. The Mexican government also engaged in an economy-wide trade-off of lower real wages to avoid massive layoffs. In addition, President Salinas introduced a program of infrastructure grants to extremely poor areas to ease the adjustment costs of economic reform. In both Australia and Mexico, the willingness of involved parties to make trade-offs seemed to stem from the conviction that doing nothing to bring down the deficit would be the worst possible policy choice.

Countries used a variety of other strategies to defer, obscure, or shift the political pain associated with deficit reduction. Officials told us that cuts in capital spending for new projects were easier to make than cuts in operating programs or subsidies on which current beneficiaries had come to depend. As mentioned, reductions in assistance to states enabled the national government, in effect, to transfer to the states the political burden of deciding how to allocate cuts. The devolution of responsibilities to the private sector through privatization shed public sector burdens and responsibilities.

Some countries adopted longer term strategies that delayed the real pain associated with deficit reduction. In these cases, policies were adopted that did not significantly cut current benefits or beneficiaries but rather phased in reductions affecting future beneficiaries. This kind of strategy gives future beneficiaries time to adjust their plans without unduly disrupting the lives of current program clientele who depend on the program. This approach is particularly important when cutting subsidies that have been, in effect, capitalized in the value of property or other asset holdings. For example, the United Kingdom established a ceiling on home mortgage interest deductions at a time when most taxpayers' deductions were far below the ceiling. Inflation, however, has now made the ceiling an effective cap on the deduction, without any subsequent action on the part of policymakers. More recently, several countries have begun to explore ways of reforming their pension systems, including privatizing the system or increasing the age of eligibility. These reforms will certainly have an impact on future generations of retirees.

Many countries asked for equal sacrifice from all major groups or agencies through some kind of across-the-board cuts or targets. Groups or agencies may be more likely to acquiesce to deficit reduction if they do not feel unfairly disadvantaged in relation to their competitors. While these kinds of cuts promoted a perception of horizontal equity, other strategies appealed to vertical equity notions by targeting cuts to wealthier groups. For instance, Australia means-tested pensions and other benefits that were previously available to all, while Canada instituted a provision to "clawback" pensions received by wealthier taxpayers.

Finally, most countries relied on elasticities embedded in the revenue and/or the spending sides of budgets to take advantage of favorable economic trends, without taking further policy actions. Most notably, this involved the absence of indexation of revenues, which enabled countries to reap major fiscal dividends from economic growth and inflation. But countries were not entirely passive in this regard, as many adjusted indexing provisions for spending programs downward to reduce automatic spending increases when inflation accelerated.

BUDGET PROCESS ACTIONS

Budget process reform also played a part in the deficit reduction story of some of the countries studied, as both a fiscal and a political strategy. For example, the Australian government used management and budget reforms to implement deficit reduction and to maintain budget discipline during the 1980s. Management reforms such as the Financial Management Improvement Program were coupled with budgetary reforms that centralized budget decisions and made them more transparent, not only to strengthen leaders' fiscal control, but also to demonstrate the government's commitment to sharing in the sacrifice expected of the public.

However, reforms alone did not guarantee successful deficit reduction. The Canadian government sought to reduce public spending and improve quality of public services by launching reforms during the 1980s in the areas of performance planning, accountability, and resource flexibility. Although the central government had some success in reducing program spending as a percentage of GDP between 1984 and 1990, it could not reduce its budget deficit below 3 percent of GDP.

Political will, rather than budget reforms in and of themselves, produced the most effective deficit reduction strategies. Although reforms in some countries unquestionably aided governments in controlling, implementing, and tracking their budget and policy decisions, most governments took action rather than rely on automatic mechanisms to make the tough budget choices.

EPILOGUE

Four of the five nations achieving balance or surplus have returned to budget deficits as of this writing—Japan, Germany, the United Kingdom, and Australia. In all instances, at least some of the deficit has resulted from cyclical economic downturn. Mexico, the sole government of the six currently in fiscal balance, plans further fiscal austerity measures as part of its response to the *peso* crisis that began in December 1994.

It is clearly difficult to sustain fiscal balance in many of these countries. As progress is made, the urgency of fiscal restraint dissipates and budget decisionmakers become more vulnerable to pent-up demands for new spending or revenue reductions. In Australia, election year initiatives in the early 1990s seem to have adversely affected structural balance. In the United Kingdom, recent deficits can be attributed to both election year initiatives and to tax cuts premised on an overly optimistic assessment of fiscal stability. In Germany, unification expenses have overwhelmed fiscal balance.

This apparent retreat from fiscal discipline typically occurred during or after periods of strong economic growth that benefited the budget beyond the structural improvements already achieved. These cyclical dividends from economic growth made governments' fiscal positions appear better than warranted by their fundamental structural balance. Political leaders, faced with apparent fiscal prosperity and the easing of previous economic concerns, made budgetary decisions that reduced the structural progress previously achieved. These actions once again contradicted traditional macroeconomic thinking, which calls for fiscal contraction during periods of economic growth. In the face of apparent fiscal progress, it is difficult for leaders to sustain austerity over a prolonged period of time. Demands and needs that are delayed or deferred during periods of fiscal austerity reemerge on the public agenda, and leaders have a more difficult time legitimizing constraint once budgets and the economy appear to be healthy.

Nevertheless, the countries studied are surely better off fiscally and economically than if they had not reached balance. Their debt levels would be higher today if current deficits were added to bases not already reduced by several years of austerity. In addition, some economists believe that these countries may still experience improvements in long-run economic growth that would not have occurred otherwise, thanks to the earlier increases in savings and investment documented in this paper.

Notes

1. U.S. Government Accounting Office (GAO). 1992. "Budget Policy: Prompt Action Necessary to Avert Long-Term Damage to the Economy." GAO/OCG-92-2. June 5.

2. Congressional Budget Office, various years. *The Economic and Budget Outlook.* Washington, D.C.

3. Japan, like the United States, does not use the OECD definition of deficit in developing its fiscal and budgetary policies. As a consequence, OECD figures may depict a somewhat different view of Japan's fiscal condition than might official Japanese measures. For the purposes of consistency across case study countries, we use the OECD definition, which is general government financial balances (all levels of government combined including social security trust funds)—revenues minus expenditures.

4. This may be most prevalent in the United States because state and local borrowing is done entirely separately from federal borrowing. The federal government usually bears no contingent liability for debt repayment of other levels of government.

APPENDIX 7.A

Australia

General government deficits (all levels of government) were entrenched for at least 35 years before surplus was achieved in 1988–1989. At its height in 1983, the deficit reached 4 percent.

Primary Causes of Fiscal Deficit

- Recession caused cyclical spending increase and revenue reduction;
- Fiscal stimulus and health care programs of the new Labor Government increased expenditures.

Impetus for Dealing with Deficit

- Fall in commodity prices (current account deficit increased from 3.7 percent of GDP to 5.5 percent between 1983 and 1986);
- Rapid increase in Australia's foreign indebtedness;
- Major depreciation in the Australian dollar during 1985 and 1986;
- Concerns over international competitiveness;
- New Labor Government's desire for credibility.

Government Actions

Expenditures

- Significantly reduced budget outlays over four consecutive budgets from 1986 to 1989, primarily in the areas of education, health, social security, and welfare;
- Targeted programs to the needy;

- Reduced transfer payments to states;
- Reduced capital spending;
- Reduced subsidies to some industries;
- Implemented budget process reform;
- Required annual "efficiency dividend" of government departments.

Revenues

- Sold assets;
- Enforced fringe benefit tax;
- Reduced tax expenditures;
- Left taxes unindexed;
- Periodically cut tax rates;
- Defeated proposed value added tax.

METHODS OF ACHIEVING AGREEMENT

- The government held a National Economic Summit in 1983 to form a plan to address economic problems;
- The government made trade-offs with unions including providing health care coverage and other social spending (the "social wage") in exchange for reduced real wages;
- The government raised public concern over the country's economic future (e.g., the Treasurer characterized Australia as a potential "banana republic");
- A sub-unit of the full cabinet, called the Expenditure Review Committee, made decisions on tough budget cuts;
- The government presented reductions in social spending as a method to better target the needy (e.g., by proclaiming no more unemployment checks for 16-year-olds);
- The government turned expenditure restraint into a political virtue.

Canada

Canada began running general government deficits (all levels of government) in 1975, which grew to 6.9 percent of GDP by 1983. The government was able to reduce the deficit to 2.5 percent of GDP in 1988, but it increased again to 6.8 percent in 1993.

PRIMARY CAUSES OF FISCAL DEFICIT

- Drop in productivity and economic growth in the 1970s and 1980s;
- High real interest rates and high inflation in the 1980s;
- Indexation of personal income taxes and social benefits in 1973.

Figure 7.A.1 GOVERNMENT FINANCIAL BALANCES—AUSTRALIA (ALL LEVELS OF GOVERNMENT)

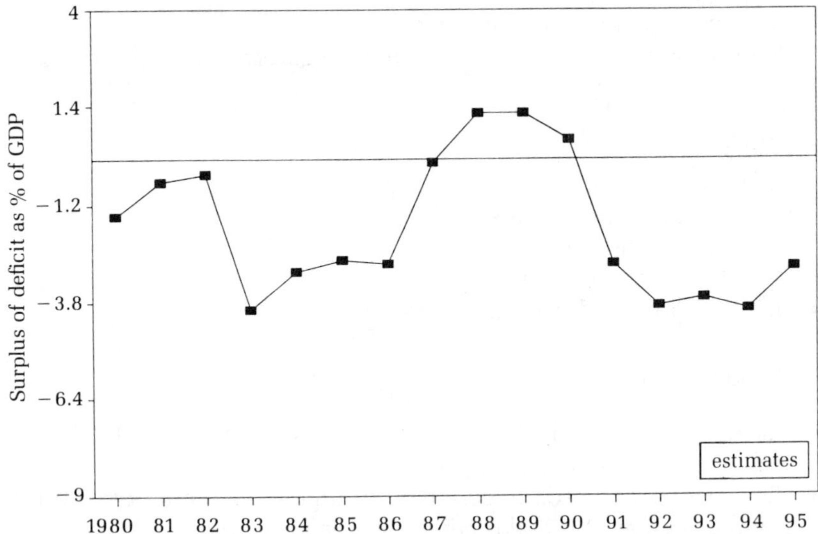

Source: OECD. 1994 *Economic Outlook* #56. Organization for Economic Cooperation and Development, Paris, France, Dec., p. A32.

IMPETUS FOR DEALING WITH DEFICIT

- Growing size of interest payments;
- Growing size of foreign debt and concern over financing debt on the international market.

GOVERNMENT ACTIONS

Expenditures

- Deleted overlapping and duplicate functions, cut large grants, and reduced overhead;
- Placed limits on total program spending;
- Froze wages of public employees;
- Capped welfare subsidies to the three wealthiest provinces;
- Required Canadian seniors to repay 15 cents of their Old-Age Security pensions for every dollar above a certain threshold;
- Limited the indexation of a major transfer program to the provinces to the growth in GDP minus 3 percentage points.

Revenues

- Limited income tax indexation to the growth in GDP minus 3 percentage points;
- Broadened the tax base, closed tax loopholes, and reduced the number of tax brackets;
- Introduced a revenue-neutral Goods and Services Tax of 7 percent.

Methods of Achieving Agreement

- The Progressive Conservative Party had a strong mandate when it took office in 1984 and immediately outlined a strategy to reduce the deficit. It did not, however, successfully build consensus nor sustain a long-term strategy.

Federal Republic of Germany

In 1982–1983 a new coalition government began taking steps to reduce public sector deficits. The general government deficit (all levels

Figure 7.A.2 GOVERNMENT FINANCIAL BALANCES—CANADA (ALL LEVELS OF GOVERNMENT)

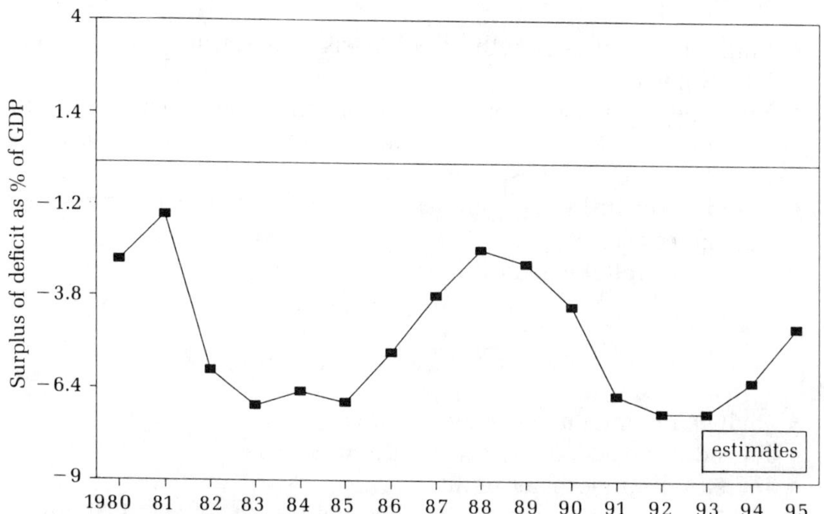

Source: OECD. 1994 *Economic Outlook* #56. Organization for Economic Cooperation and Development, Paris, France, Dec., p. A32.

of government) was reduced from almost 4 percent of GDP in 1981 to balance in 1989. During this time government expenditures fell from nearly 50 percent to 45 percent of GDP.

Primary Causes of Fiscal Deficit

- Recessions triggered by the oil crises of 1973–1974 and 1979–1980 resulted in cyclical spending increase and revenue reduction;
- Government based budget estimates on exaggerated growth expectations;
- Government significantly expanded the public sector in the 1970s.

Impetus for Dealing with Deficit

- Inflation hit a post-war high of about 6 percent;
- The Deutsche Mark dropped in relation to the U.S. dollar;
- Unemployment topped the psychological barrier of 1 million;
- In 1982 a new coalition government promised fiscal restraint;
- A constitutional balanced budget requirement did not preclude deficits.

Government Actions

Expenditures

- Limited spending growth by all levels of government to no more than 3 percent;
- Modified statutory benefits by cutting children's benefits, converting financial aid for students from grants to loans, and limiting the adjustment of social assistance rates;
- Hired fewer full-time civil servants and limited or deferred their pay increases;
- Reduced capital expenditures;
- Reduced personnel expenditures.

Revenues

- Reduced numerous tax expenditures;
- Raised value added and other indirect taxes;
- Increased Bundesbank profits;
- Achieved privatization proceeds and/or savings of about 10 billion DM between 1982 and 1989;
- Raised social security taxes;

Figure 7.A.3 GOVERNMENT FINANCIAL BALANCES—GERMANY (ALL LEVELS OF GOVERNMENT)

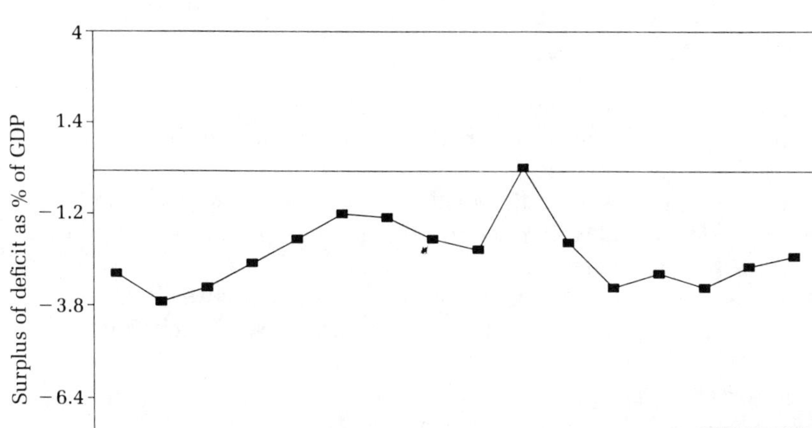

Source: OECD. *1994 Economic Outlook* #56. Organization for Economic Cooperation and Development, Paris, France, Dec., p. A32.

- Kept income taxes unindexed;
- Reduced tax rates in three stages.

Methods of Achieving Agreement

- The government capitalized on the general public's fear of inflation;
- The government built consensus through the open German budget process and the requirement that the budget must pass through Parliament's upper house, which comprised representatives of the state governments;
- The government recommended sustained budget deficit reduction policies through the Financial Planning Council, which represents federal, state, and local finance ministries as well as the central bank.

Japan

Japan ran a general government deficit (all levels of government) between 1975 and 1986, which peaked at 5.5 percent of GDP. Japan's budget was in surplus from 1987 through 1993, but returned to deficit in 1994.

PRIMARY CAUSES OF FISCAL DEFICIT

- Moderation in economic growth: real average annual rate of 12.1 percent in the 1960s, and real average annual rate of 3.8 percent from 1974 to 1985.
- Disruption in oil supplies in 1973 and subsequent recession;
- Expanded social welfare commitments made in the belief that high growth would continue;
- Increased spending, undertaken in conjunction with Germany and the United States, in an attempt to boost the world economy.

IMPETUS FOR DEALING WITH DEFICIT

- Growing interest payments;
- Future impact of social security.

GOVERNMENT ACTIONS

Expenditures

- Placed across-the-board limits on the growth of certain government expenditures;
- Reduced a limited number of civil servants;
- Implemented a 10 percent medical insurance copayment.

Revenues

- Began taxing interest income in 1987;
- Implemented a 3 percent value added tax in 1989 in exchange for income tax cuts;
- Kept income taxes unindexed; strong economic growth and high asset prices in the late 1980s and early 1990s resulted in buoyant tax revenues.

METHODS OF ACHIEVING AGREEMENT

- The influential Ministry of Finance took the strong position that deficits were detrimental for Japan and promoted deficit reduction as a virtue;
- The business community supported the government's deficit reduction policies because of certain mutual goals including efficiency and privatization.

Figure 7.A.4 GOVERNMENT FINANCIAL BALANCES—JAPAN (ALL LEVELS OF GOVERNMENT)

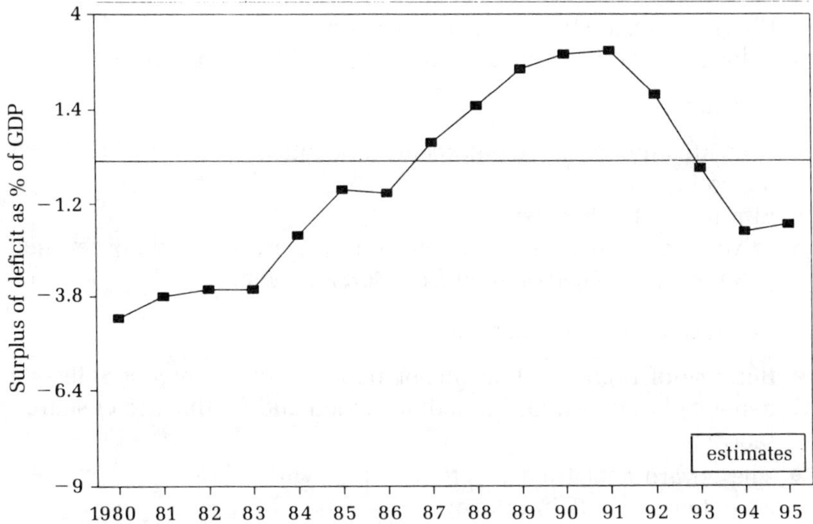

Source: OECD. 1994 *Economic Outlook* #56. Organization for Economic Cooperation and Development, Paris, France, Dec., p. A32.

Mexico

Mexico's general government deficits (all levels of government) were not significant until they exploded in the early 1980s, reaching 16.9 percent of GDP in 1982. The deficit was slashed in half in 1983 but rose again to 16 percent in 1987. Mexico reached a surplus in 1992.

Primary Causes of Fiscal Deficit

- Growth of revenues did not keep pace with increased spending to promote investment and protect jobs;
- Expectations of continued high oil revenues;
- High interest rates.

Impetus for Dealing with Deficit

- Lost access to world credit markets;
- Triple digit inflation.

GOVERNMENT ACTIONS

Expenditures

- Eliminated investment and maintenance;
- Allowed inflation to make real cuts in public sector wages.

Revenues

- Dramatically increased enforcement of both corporate and personal tax collections;
- Eliminated tax breaks;
- Privatized the majority of public enterprises, with bulk of revenue (6.3 percent of GDP) gained from 1989 to 1992.

METHODS OF ACHIEVING AGREEMENT

- Because of high inflation, major political and economic interests perceived the need for immediate action and for the idea of shared sacrifice;
- The government tried to protect employment levels, and workers accepted pay cuts in return;

Figure 7.A.5 PUBLIC SECTOR BORROWING REQUIREMENT (PSBR) MEXICO

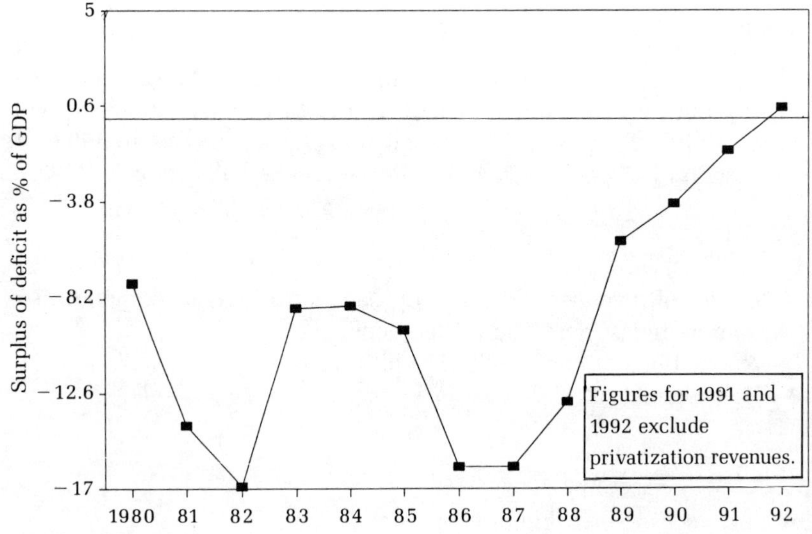

Source: Banco de Mexico.

Figure 7.A.6 GOVERNMENT FINANCIAL BALANCES—UNITED KINGDOM (ALL LEVELS OF GOVERNMENT)

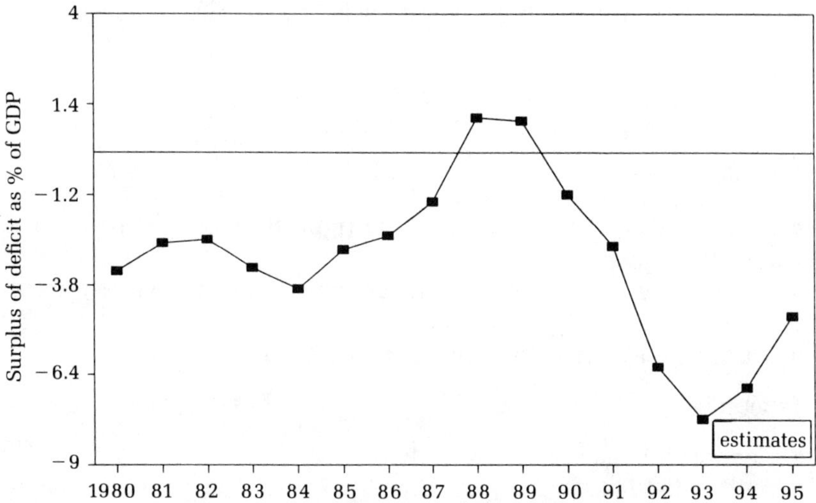

Source: OECD. 1994 *Economic Outlook* #56. Organization for Economic Cooperation and Development, Paris, France, Dec., p. A32.

- The government and the private sector agreed on economic targets in a public pact;
- The government met deficit reduction and economic targets to gain credibility.

United Kingdom

The United Kingdom had persistent general government deficits (all levels of government) of 3 to 4 percent of GDP through the 1970s and 1980s. The government reduced the deficit in the mid-1980s and ran a surplus in 1988 and 1989. The United Kingdom has surged back into a high deficit, which is currently over 7 percent of GDP.

Primary Causes of Fiscal Deficit

- Continuing social spending commitments made in the 1970s;
- Election commitments to major increases in public sector wages;
- Cyclical spending increase and revenue reduction from a deep recession.

IMPETUS FOR DEALING WITH DEFICIT

- High inflation;
- 1979 election mandate for lower spending and taxing and for privatization;
- 1976 sterling crisis.

GOVERNMENT ACTIONS

Expenditures

- Controlled overall growth through tight, three-year expenditure growth targets;
- Changed the base for public pension indexation from wages growth to price growth, a generally lower base;
- Made no major structural program changes/eliminations.

Revenues

- Conduced large-scale privatization;
- Shifted the tax burden from direct to indirect taxes with a small net gain in revenue;

Figure 7.A.7 GOVERNMENT FINANCIAL BALANCES—UNITED STATES (ALL LEVELS OF GOVERNMENT)

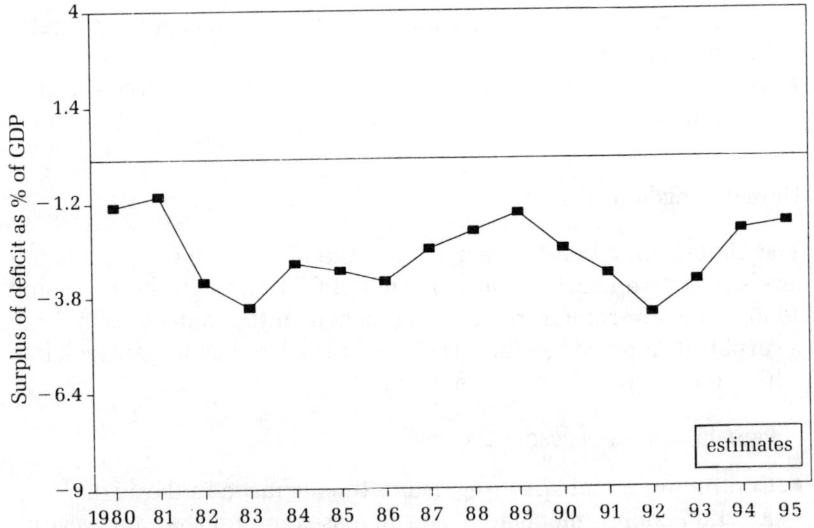

Source: OECD. 1994 *Economic Outlook* #56. Organization for Economic Cooperation and Development, Paris, France, Dec., p. A32.

- Gained strong revenue growth from economic growth; it was commonly perceived (by both the government and private sectors) that the economy had shifted onto a higher growth path;
- Shifted timing for corporation tax depreciation allowances, closed some tax loopholes, and temporarily suspended indexation of some tax allowances;
- Benefited from substantial oil revenue until 1986, when oil prices collapsed.

Methods of Achieving Agreement

- The government stuck to deficit reduction, privatization, and focus on consumption rather than on income taxes, in accordance with its election mandate;
- Public medium-term financial plans helped the Treasury pressure ministers to keep to restricted growth targets and "spread the pain" among departments;
- The government timed actions to cause little immediate pain but future fiscal gains.

COMMENTS ON "THE YOKE OF PRIOR COMMITMENTS"

COMMENT BY YUTAKA KOSAI

I am very impressed by the high-quality analytical rigor and the policy relevance of the papers in this volume. The authors of these papers are collectively playing the role of Cassandra, warning about an imminent fiscal crisis in the advanced nations due to population aging, increased prior commitments, and saving-investment imbalances.

I share with conference organizers the view that, because of the populist tendencies of today's well-developed democracies and welfare states, fiscal discipline is often overlooked. Instead of a wholesale surrender to or denial of these populist tendencies, we should estimate the risks involved and design remedies for them.

Prior commitments such as entitlements or long-term plans for public investment deprive fiscal structures of flexibility and help aggravate fiscal imbalances. However, prior commitments provide beneficiaries with assurance of continued support and assist those concerned in planning for the future. Prior commitments reduce uncertainty and should be valued in the aggregate after counterbalancing costs with benefits.

Prior commitments are similar to long-term labor contracts. Employers are obliged to employ workers with whom they have signed contracts despite changes in the former's situation. This diminishes the risk of unemployment for the employee, but may increase employers' risk of profit squeeze. Still, as long as firms are less risk-averse than employees, or as long as firms are in a position to reduce risks by having access to capital markets, long-term labor contracts can be welfare-augmenting.

Prior commitments are also like long-term borrowing. Firms are obliged to pay interest, however widely profits fluctuate, but they can avoid risk by refusing to renew the debt. Prior commitments resemble capital outlay. Portfolio selection is equally important when investing in human capital, in financial assets, and in institutional arrangements.

Having said that, we must recognize that, compared to capital market transactions, fiscal precommitments involve greater danger of departing from equilibrium. Like other public goods, fiscal prior commitments are faced with issues such as fiscal illusion, free riders, and political vested interests. In contrasts to market decisions, budget constraints on prior commitments do not work, because expenditure decisions are made independent of revenue decisions.

Some remedies are suggested by these considerations. First, fiscal precommitments can be privatized and replaced by security provided through market mechanisms such as the financial or insurance markets. Second, in cases where privatization is inappropriate, precommitments on the expenditure side should be accompanied by simultaneous precommitments on the revenue side in order to attain balance of costs and benefits, and to avoid an increase in future budgetary deficits. This method requires "earmarked" taxation and breaks with the traditional principle of unitary budgets. I believe that current budgets are sufficiently large and diverse to allow for this kind of decisionmaking. Of course, revenue-side precommitments also bring about rigidities in the fiscal allocation. Schemes such as "sunset" legislation and periodical recalculations and reviews might also limit these precommitments.

Finally, to cope with an environment different from that in which original precommitments were made, a system of flexible readjustment should be introduced. Perhaps precommitments should be made not in absolute terms, but in proportion to important variables that affect the capabilities or the desirability of keeping the commitments made in previous times. Credibility of prior commitments can be enhanced by increased flexibility built into the original commitments themselves.

The new fiscal order must be compatible with the realities of the economic, political, and social order of the day. The issue should be addressed from a wider perspective than that of fiscal management in the narrow sense.

COMMENT BY YASUSHI IWAMOTO

In my comments I will point out some problems in comparing the extent of non-discretionary expenditure in the Japanese and U.S. budgets, and discuss ways to reduce Japan's budget deficits.

The Cordes and Ihori papers make it possible for us to compare the status of Japanese and U.S. non-discretionary expenditures. Although the two countries share many common problems, we must recognize that simply comparing numbers can be misleading. First, the degree of acceptance of the concept of "discretionary" is very different in the two countries. This concept is widely used in the United States in official budget documents; in Japan, however, the Ministry of Finance has not sorted expenditures, and Japanese economists and the media pay less attention to these issues. Second, some discretionary expenditure programs are difficult to change because groups that benefit from such expenditures resist change. The division between non-discretionary and discretionary, therefore, is imperfect. Finally, while Cordes examines the federal government budget, Ihori investigates the general accounts. These two cannot be easily compared because the central government plays somewhat different roles in the two countries.

The three papers in Part Two of this volume discuss measures to reduce budget deficits or increase fiscal austerity. Let me focus on Ihori's proposal for actions that should be taken in Japan. I basically agree with his recommendations, except for the cut in the inheritance tax. In my opinion, a cut in the inheritance tax is not likely to contribute to economic growth in Japan. The inheritance tax is mostly irrelevant for average income households and is confined mainly to wealthy people with large inheritances. A noticeable characteristic of Japanese household saving is that every income class contributes to national saving. It is difficult to empirically prove that the inheritance tax affects the saving level of Japanese households. It may have a greater impact on saving in countries such as the United States, where saving is more concentrated among high-income groups.

The top priority of reforming Japan's fiscal system should be reform of the social security system. The Japanese social security system does not have enough funds to cover future increases in benefits due to population aging. A worse problem is that this fact has not been widely recognized. Our program initially started as a fully funded system. In 1975, however, the legislation was changed to increase social security benefits, and some people began to receive benefits in excess of their contributions. Since the 1975 reform did not increase the social security contributions rate, benefits have been paid from the contributions of the working-age population. Although Japan's social security fund current has a large surplus, keeping current levels of contributions constant would eventually cause the collapse of the whole system.

Unfortunately, people ignore the necessary reform of social security system by looking only at the surplus currently running in the social security fund—a misleading measure of the financial status of the social security system. Population structure also has a serious impact on the financial condition of other activities of government, due to the fact that benefits and contributions do not match at each household life stage. Given this mismatch, the increasing ratio of the elderly will worsen the government budget. There are two choices for public financial policy. One is to try to keep the budget balanced. The other is to balance the benefits and contributions of each generation. The choice can be determined by evaluating the imbalances caused by each policy. The first choice creates intergenerational imbalances of lifetime burdens, causing the younger generation to bear heavier burdens as the population ages. Under the latter policy, changes in population structure would create a budget deficit or surplus, but the budget would eventually balance in the long term. Unfortunately, our society is mainly focused on the first choice, because we prefer to avoid possible political struggles that come from levying a considerably higher burden on the younger generation. However, much attention should be paid to the latter choice, because it provides one means of dealing with longer term problems.

COMMENT BY HIROSHI SHIBUYA

I would like to comment on the theme of prior commitments from the point of view of its connection to taxpayers. Professor Cordes's paper states that under conditions in which taxes cannot be raised, the only means of achieving fiscal restructuring is to restrain prior commitments. However, the long-term trend in the United States—in terms of the burden on taxpayers—is that the portion of fiscal expenditures that can be covered by general revenues such as income taxes is shrinking, while the portion of social insurance covered by social security taxes is increasing.

Taxpayers are demanding reductions in taxes paid to general revenues, yet they accept higher contributions to social security programs, where future benefits are linked to current tax contributions. A typical example can be seen in the tax policies of the Reagan administration, which lowered income taxes while raising social security taxes.

As Professor Cordes states, taxpayers do not wish to pay higher taxes. But at the same they demand general tax reductions, they may support tax increases to pay for entitlement programs when there seems to be a link between future benefits and current costs. Therefore, we should not overlook the possibility of fiscal restructuring, especially with regard to social security, where the relationship between cost and contribution is close and the proportionate share of fiscal resources is growing.

I also wonder if this mode of thinking can be applied to other countries as well. In the case of Japan, fiscal restructuring enabled the general government to show a surplus. The main reason, of course, was that the central government reduced its deficit, but it is also important to note that the social security fund, especially the pension system, increased its surplus. Once again, we can trace a historical pattern of taxpayers demanding expansion of social security systems because costs correspond closely to benefits.

Professor Ihori posits a separation between government and social insurance in Japan. But in the United States, social security is usually included in the federal budget, a factor that must be considered when comparing these two countries. The "government disbursements of social insurance" referred to by Professor Ihori are actually transfers from the central government's general accounts to special social insurance accounts. Disbursements from general accounts were reduced and individual tax rates lowered (or at least tax raises were avoided), but a portion of social insurance funding was simply shifted from income taxes to social security contributions.

Japan's social insurance system is segmented into separate occupational and regional schemes. Prior to the tax reform of the 1980s, the pension system was deteriorating because of maturity, leading the government to transfer funds from its general account. At the same time that financial restructuring was being implemented, the pension system was also being reformed. The result was fiscal adjustments occurring through intra-scheme transfers within the social security system. In short, social insurance contributions replaced general revenues as the source of new funds for the deteriorating systems within the financial structure. These are the real "reductions" in central government expenditures on social insurance described in Professor Ihori's paper.

One clear lesson is that restraining the "size of the public sector as a whole" necessitates thinking in terms of separating "general accounts" from "social insurance that can be paid from social insurance contributions." One reason is that it is much easier for taxpayers to accept contributing to social insurance than it is for them to accept paying income taxes. This is because such contributions are clearly used for social insurance and clearly linked to benefits.

The scale and composition of the general accounts should be determined on the premise that taxpayers permit a certain level of tax burdens going toward general revenues. Similarly, we must think about the links between payments and benefits when determining the scale and composition of social insurance. It is highly likely that social insurance will continue to grow relatively larger while the income tax burden will continue to be restrained.

Part Three

FISCAL POLICY AND WORLDWIDE SAVING AND INVESTMENT

Chapter Eight

FISCAL POLICY, GLOBAL SAVING AND INVESTMENT, AND ECONOMIC GROWTH

Masahiro Kawai and Yusuke Onitsuka

This paper examines the impact of fiscal policy on saving, investment, and economic growth from a global perspective. Fiscal policy consists of changes in government purchases, transfer payments, subsidies, taxes, and borrowing from the private sector. In both conventional theory and actual policy implementation, fiscal policy is an instrument for (a) providing public goods that cannot be adequately supplied by the private market, (b) redistributing income across people of differing age, income, job status, and health, and (c) stabilizing macroeconomic fluctuations of real output and inflation. The government clearly plays a positive role in these activities. However, once government activity becomes excessive, the large size of government can be detrimental to economic efficiency and growth.

In this paper, we examine cross-section data from 19 OECD countries and attempt to uncover empirical relationships between various fiscal and key macroeconomic variables. We attempt to measure econometrically the impact of budget deficits on private capital formation, the current account, and macroeconomic performance variables, and we explain why government has grown so much and why budget deficits have persisted over time in many OECD countries. Finally, we speculate about future fiscal developments in the industrialized countries and the impacts of these developments on developing and transitional economies.

CORRELATIONS AMONG SAVING, INVESTMENT, AND THE CURRENT ACCOUNT

First, we examine empirical relationships among saving, investment, and the current account, as well as statistical correlations between fiscal and key macroeconomic variables. We use a sample of 19 OECD countries for the period 1980–1993. The variables in each country are averaged over a 14-year period to abstract from the effects of business cycle fluctuations (14 years may be regarded as long enough to average out business cycles).[1]

Table 8.1 summarizes the data and their cross-country correlation coefficients. The variables reported are net saving, net fixed capital formation (or net fixed investment), and the saving and investment balance (S-I balance for short), all defined as a percentage of nominal GDP. Net saving and net fixed investment are for the national economy as a whole as well as for the private sector. The current account is roughly the same as a country's national net lending, or S-I balance. Current receipts, total outlays, current transfers to households, financial balances, and structural financial balances, again all relative to GDP, are for the general government sector. The general government consists of the federal, state, and local governments as well as social security funds.[2] The private sector consists of firms and households. The right-hand section of panel A, table 8.1, also shows the performance of key macroeconomic variables for 19 OECD countries. Key macroeconomic variables include the growth rate of real GDP, the rate of inflation of GDP deflators, the unemployment rate, and the real long-term interest rate.

Correlations Between Saving and Investment

A large literature now exists on the positive correlations between saving and investment in time-series and cross-country data. Our data set confirms these positive correlations. As shown in table 8.1, panel B (column 1 down), national net saving and net fixed capital formation, as a ratio of GDP, are highly and positively correlated with each other, with a correlation coefficient of 0.88. This correlation is somewhat lower (0.72) for private net saving and net fixed investment (column 4 down). Many economists have noted the pervasiveness of this positive saving-investment correlation in OECD countries (Feldstein and Horioka 1980; Obstfeld 1986; and Tesar 1991).

Feldstein and Horioka (1980) first interpreted this correlation as indicating a lack of international capital mobility, while others have subsequently argued that, even with perfect capital mobility, the positive correlation between saving and investment can result from a government's intentional or unintentional policy to target the current account (Bayoumi 1990) or from technology shocks that affect saving and investment in the same direction (Obstfeld 1986; Tesar 1991; and Baxter and Crucini 1993). The lower correlation between private saving and investment may support the view that government behavior is partly responsible for the observed high correlation of national saving and investment. However, the private saving-investment correlation is still high, which may be the result of imperfect capital mobility and the presence of exogenous shocks causing both private saving and investment to move in the same direction.

Saving-Investment Balances: Private and Government

The second empirical relationship seen in table 8.1, panel B (column 6 down), is a strong negative correlation of minus 0.82 between the private S-I balance (net lending) and the government S-I balance (financial balance). The correlation is somewhat lower (in absolute value) at minus 0.68 when the structural financial balance is used. Similar negative correlations (not shown) are also found in the time-series data. This negative correlation mirrors the positive saving-investment correlation for the national economy as a whole.

There are three possible reasons for the negative correlation between private and government S-I balances. The first concerns government policy. Two policy alternatives for S-I balances are available to governments. A government can adopt a macroeconomic policy to target the current account directly. In this case, it controls its own S-I balance to offset changes in private S-I balances and maintain a target balance in the current account. Alternatively, a government can adopt countercyclical fiscal policy to stabilize fluctuations in real output and inflation. When the economy goes through business cycles, economic expansions tend to be associated with worsening private S-I balances, and economic contractions with improving private S-I balances. Government attempts to stabilize the business-cycle fluctuations through countercyclical fiscal policy tend to improve the fiscal balance in booms, due to cyclically induced rises in taxes and falls in expenditures. These same attempts, when implemented at a downturn, worsen the fiscal balance due to cyclically induced declines in taxes and rises in expenditures. Either way, a government can adjust its S-I balances to offset changes in private S-I balances. However, because these government policy actions are tied to cyclical aspects of the economy, it is unlikely that they explain our data, which are supposed to represent averages over business cycles.

A second possible factor behind the negative correlation between private and government S-I balances focuses on the effects of different trends in economic growth rates. Table 8.1, panel B, very weakly suggests that countries with rapid economic growth on average tend to

Table 8.1 SAVING, INVESTMENT, AND SAVING AND INVESTMENT (S-I) BALANCES OF THE MAJOR OECD COUNTRIES AND THEIR MACROECONOMIC PERFORMANCE

	PANEL A Average for the Period 1980–1993 (%)														
	National Saving and Investment (As a Percentage of Nominal GDP)			Private Saving and Investment (As a Percentage of Nominal GDP)			General Government Budget (As a Percentage of Nominal GDP)					Macroeconomic Performance (Percentage)			
	Net Saving	Net Fixed Capital Formation	Current Account	Net Saving	Net Fixed Capital Formation	Net Lending (S-I Balance)	Current Receipts	Total Outlays	Current Transfers to Households	Financial Balances	Structural Financial Balances	Real GDP Growth Rate	Inflation Rate (GDP Deflator)	Unemployment Rate	Real Long-term Interest Rate
Country/Period	1980–92	1980–92	1980–93	1980–92	1980–92	1980–92	1980–93	1980–93	1980–92	1980–93	1980–93	1980–93	1980–93	1980–93	1980–93
United States	4.0	5.1	−1.7	7.5	4.8	2.2	30.6	33.3	11.6	−2.8	−4.8	2.2	4.7	7.1	5.0
Japan	18.5	15.7	2.2	13.2	11.0	2.7	31.7	32.2	11.6	−0.5	−0.1	3.6	1.9	2.4	4.4
Germany	10.1	7.9	1.5	9.0	6.1	4.0	45.0	47.4	19.5	−2.3	−2.1	2.1	3.3	6.9	4.3
France	7.8	8.0	−0.5	8.2	6.6	1.6	48.2	50.6	23.4	−2.5	−2.0	1.9	5.9	9.4	5.0
Italy	9.1	8.9	−1.1	16.0	6.9	8.8	39.5	50.2	18.0	−10.7	−11.1	2.0	10.2	10.6	3.6
United Kingdom	4.3	5.9	−0.7	5.1	5.0	1.2	39.5	42.3	14.1	−2.7	−2.1	1.7	6.9	8.9	3.9
Canada	7.2	9.5	−2.3	10.4	8.5	2.7	39.9	44.8	12.6	−5.0	−4.5	2.3	4.7	9.6	6.3
Australia	3.9	8.0	−4.4	4.4	7.5	−2.9	33.5	35.1	11.0	−1.6	−1.2	2.9	6.6	8.1	6.0
Austria	12.1	11.5	−0.2	10.3	8.7	2.6	47.4	50.2	20.4	−2.9	−2.0	2.0	4.0	3.3	4.1
Belgium	8.2	8.3	0.8	13.9	6.3	8.7	51.1	59.4	26.8	−8.4	−8.3	1.8	4.2	10.8	5.9
Denmark	6.5	8.6	−1.5	7.2	7.1	0.3	56.8	59.5	19.6	−2.7	−2.0	1.7	5.2	9.5	7.3
Finland	6.8	9.4	−2.6	1.9	7.0	−5.1	47.3	45.8	16.7	1.5	0.6	1.7	6.2	6.5	6.0
Greece	8.4	10.7	−3.8	15.9	7.4	NA	31.6	42.3	14.0	−10.7	−10.0	1.5	17.8	7.0	NA
Ireland	8.0	10.7	−2.6	12.9	8.4	3.9	40.4	47.6	17.9	−7.2	−6.5	3.8	6.4	14.7	5.6
Netherlands	12.5	9.2	2.5	13.7	7.6	7.4	51.8	56.4	30.6	−4.6	−3.3	1.8	2.4	8.7	5.8
Norway	11.3	10.0	1.4	4.8	8.0	−3.2	89.1	50.6	17.5	3.5	−3.7	2.6	5.7	3.6	5.8
Portugal	19.6	22.1	−3.1	25.3	22.8	1.6	38.4	44.3	12.1	−5.9	−5.8	2.4	16.8	6.7	−0.2
Spain	9.1	10.0	−1.4	10.0	8.2	3.4	35.3	39.9	15.8	−4.6	−3.5	2.4	9.0	18.1	4.8
Sweden	4.3	6.6	−1.6	4.2	5.2	−0.3	59.9	62.3	20.7	−2.4	−3.1	1.2	7.3	3.1	4.3

PANEL B Cross-Country Correlation Coefficient Matrices

	National Saving and Investment (As a Percentage of Nominal GDP)			Private Saving and Investment (As a Percentage of Nominal GDP)			General Government Budget (As a Percentage of Nominal GDP)					Macroeconomic Performance (Percentage)			
	Net Saving	Net Fixed Capital Formation	Current Account	Net Saving	Net Fixed Capital Formation	Net Lending (S-I Balance)	Current Receipts	Total Outlays	Current Transfers to Households	Financial Balances	Structural Financial Balances	Real GDP Growth Rate	Inflation Rate (GDP Deflator)	Unemployment Rate	Real Long-term Interest Rate
Country/Period	Col. 1	Col. 2	Col. 3	Col. 4	Col. 5	Col. 6	Col. 7	Col. 8	Col. 9	Col. 10	Col. 11	Col. 12	Col. 13	Col. 14	Col. 15
Column 1	1.00														
Column 2	0.88	1.00													
Column 3	0.39	−0.06	1.00												
Column 4	0.69	0.73	−0.01	1.00											
Column 5	0.78	0.95	−0.17	0.72	1.00										
Column 6	0.22	0.01	0.43	0.62	−0.03	1.00									
Column 7	0.00	−0.14	0.41	−0.34	−0.14	−0.27	1.00								
Column 8	−0.11	−0.19	0.26	−0.04	−0.18	0.23	0.66	1.00							
Column 9	−0.01	−0.26	0.55	0.00	−0.29	0.46	0.47	0.80	1.00						
Column 10	−0.01	−0.10	0.27	−0.69	−0.10	−0.82	0.47	−0.13	−0.12	1.00					
Column 11	0.00	−0.06	0.21	−0.61	−0.08	−0.687	0.14	−0.16	−0.06	0.86	1.00				
Column 12	0.39	0.40	0.04	0.19	0.33	−0.01	−0.21	−0.53	−0.40	0.13	0.12	1.00			
Column 13	0.13	0.43	−0.63	0.52	0.48	−0.09	−0.25	−0.12	−0.36	−0.51	−0.56	−0.20	1.00		
Column 14	−0.26	−0.17	−0.23	0.15	−0.10	0.39	−0.30	−0.01	0.11	−0.47	−0.32	0.14	0.12	1.00	
Column 15	−0.56	−0.64	0.08	−0.64	−0.71	−0.14	0.27	0.20	0.27	0.25	0.23	−0.04	−0.71	0.19	1.00

Source: OECD 1994; and IMF 1995.

have a favorable fiscal balance and stronger private investment than saving. This is because in countries with persistently rapid economic growth, tax receipts tend to be smaller relative to GDP than in countries with persistently slow growth, while government outlays tend to be even smaller. In addition, the private saving ratio tends to be high and the investment ratio even higher due to vigorous economic activity. Conversely, countries with persistently slow economic growth generally have a less favorable fiscal balance and weaker private investment than saving. This is because in slowly growing economies, tax receipts tend to be large relative to GDP while government outlays tend to be even larger. At the same time, the private saving ratio is generally low and the investment ratio even lower.

A third possible reason for the negative correlation between private and government S-I balances focuses on private sector behavior. When the government cuts taxes or raises expenditures, causing its fiscal balance to deteriorate, people in the private sector may anticipate higher future tax obligations. They increase saving to prepare for the future, thus inducing their S-I balances to improve. On the other hand, when the government raises taxes or reduces expenditures, causing the fiscal balance to improve, people may anticipate lighter future tax burdens. They increase consumption, thereby inducing their S-I balances to deteriorate.

Unlike the first possible explanation for the negative correlation between private and government S-I balances, the second and third do not depend on the cyclical nature of the economy. The third explanation does, however, assume that households have perfect or quasi-perfect foresight. The realism of this assumption, with its long time horizon and its underlying Barro-Ricardo view of rational consumers endowed with operative bequest motives, is open to question and requires further empirical study.[3]

The negative correlation between government and private S-I balances implies that an increase in the government budget deficit may not, by itself, lead to a deterioration in a country's current account. However, this is an issue that should be resolved empirically.

Budget Deficits, Government Size, and Macroeconomic Performance

The correlation coefficients between fiscal policy (the general government's current receipts, outlays, transfers to households, financial balances, and structural financial balances) and key macroeconomic variables are also shown in table 8.1, panel B, columns 7 to 15 down. Key macroeconomic variables examined include the growth rate of real GDP, the rate of inflation, the unemployment rate, and the real long-term interest rate.

The growth rate of real GDP is negatively correlated with the size of the government, as measured by total current receipts, total outlays, and current transfers to households, while it is less (in absolute value) correlated with the fiscal balance. The negative correlation is strongest (minus 0.53) for total outlays, which include government consumption, investment, subsidies, and current transfers to households. The negative correlation with current transfers to households, which include unemployment compensation, early retirement benefits, and social welfare payments, is weaker but still high (in absolute value) at minus 0.40. This negative correlation suggests that countries with big governments tend to experience slow economic growth, and that countries with small governments tend to experience rapid economic growth.

As also shown in the table (panel B, column 10 down), the rate of inflation is negatively correlated with the fiscal balance, the correlation coefficient being minus 0.51 (or minus 0.56 when the structural fiscal balance is used). This means that countries with large budget deficits tend to experience high inflation and countries with budget surpluses or small deficits tend to experience low inflation.[4]

The unemployment rate tends to be negatively correlated (minus 0.47 to minus 0.32) with the fiscal balance (panel B, column 10 down). This means that countries with high unemployment tend to have large budget deficits and countries with low unemployment tend to have small budget deficits.

Finally, real long-term interest rates are positively correlated with government size but the degree of correlation is not very large (0.20 to 0.27 as shown in columns 7 to 9 down). The interest rates are not negatively correlated with the fiscal balance. However, strong negative correlations exist between real interest rates and investment or saving. That is, countries with high real interest rates tend to have low investment and low saving, and vice versa. The negative correlation with real interest rates is slightly stronger if private saving and investment rather than national saving and investment is used.

FISCAL POLICY, CAPITAL SHORTAGE, AND ECONOMIC GROWTH

Below, we investigate the impact of budget deficits and government size on capital formation, current accounts, and macroeconomic performance including real economic activity and inflation.

Budget Deficits and Private Capital Formation

When a government's current receipts fall short of its outlays, budget deficits emerge. Budget deficits imply that a government spends more than it saves, eating up private saving that would otherwise be available for productive investment. Hence, "capital shortage" may occur with large budget deficits.

As seen in table 8.1 (panel B, column 4 down), there exists a strong negative correlation between private net saving and the fiscal balance (a correlation coefficient of minus 0.69 to minus 0.61), which suggests that a large deficit tends to be associated with low private saving.[5] However, the correlation between private net fixed capital formation and the fiscal balance is insignificant (minus 0.10 to minus 0.08), appearing to suggest that budget deficits do not have a strong negative impact on private investment. But to examine the effect of budget deficits on private investment one must control for country-specific factors affecting private investment, such as private saving.

For this purpose we have estimated private net fixed capital formation by using private net saving and government structural fiscal balances, all measured as a ratio of GDP, over a cross-section sample of 19 countries. The regression result not only confirms the Feldstein and Horioka (1980) finding, that private net investment and saving are highly positively correlated in cross-country data, but also shows that the fiscal balance has a significantly positive impact on private capital accumulation. We find that a 1 percentage point increase in the structural budget deficit (a negative of the structural financial balance relative to GDP) leads to a 0.7 to 0.8 percentage point decline in private investment (as a ratio of GDP).[6] The budget deficit indeed eats up financial resources that could otherwise be channeled into private productive capital formation. In this sense, the budget deficit directly crowds out private investment, producing a "capital shortage."

Fiscal Policy and the Current Account

What is the effect of budget deficits on a country's current account? Our earlier discussion indicates that an increase in the budget deficit is associated with an offsetting increase in the private S-I balance. Hence, the budget deficit does not directly cause current account deficits. Theoretically, whether the budget deficit causes current account deficits, thereby producing "twin deficits," is also ambiguous; it depends on how the budget deficits are financed (Frenkel and Razin

1987; and Kawai and Maccini 1995) and how private saving responds to a change in budget deficits.

To examine the question econometrically, we have estimated the current account by using private net saving, private net investment, and the structural fiscal balance, all measured as a proportion of GDP. The estimation equation is a modified version specified by Sachs (1981).

The regression result demonstrates that private saving has a positive impact and private investment has a negative impact on the current account. In addition, the structural fiscal balance has a significantly positive influence on the current account. We find that a 1 percentage point increase in the structural budget deficit (relative to GDP) reduces the current account (as a ratio of GDP) by a 0.6 percentage point. Hence, our sample data suggest that a budget deficit tends to produce "twin deficits."

Government Size and Macroeconomic Performance

The next question concerns the impacts of budget deficits and government size on macroeconomic performance. Three measures of government size may be considered, all relative to GDP—current receipts, total outlays, and current transfers to households. In preliminary investigations we find that the total outlays-to-GDP ratio affects macroeconomic variables more strongly than the other two measures. Therefore, here we only report the results based on government size as defined by total outlays.

We estimate the macroeconomic performance variables, such as the growth rate of real GDP, the inflation rate of GDP deflators, and the unemployment rate, by using the government's structural fiscal balance and total outlays, both relative to GDP. We also include country-specific factors to explain the macro performance variables; the factors chosen depend on the type of macroeconomic performance variable.[7]

Our OLS regression results demonstrate that the growth rate of real GDP does not depend on the fiscal balance but is inversely affected by government size. A 1 percentage point rise in the total outlays-to-GDP ratio reduces the real growth rate by 0.04 of a percentage point.[8] On the other hand, the rates of inflation and unemployment do not depend on the size of the government but are inversely affected by the fiscal balance. A 1 percentage point increase in the structural budget deficit-to-GDP ratio raises the inflation rate by 0.3 of a percentage point and the unemployment rate by 0.4 of a percentage point. Thus, an increase in government size is not conducive to economic growth, and an increase in the budget deficit worsens both inflation and unemployment. These results are consistent with the pro-market view that to secure better macroeconomic performance, it is necessary to avoid excessive expansion of government activity and large structural budget deficits.

It may be argued that causal links between government size and structural budget deficits on the one hand, and macroeconomic performance on the other, may not be a one-way street running from the former to the latter (Saunders and Klau 1985). Differing macroeconomic performances across OECD countries may also be the cause of cross-country variations in government activity and budget deficits. It is possible that economies experiencing persistently slow growth, high inflation, and structurally high unemployment may be forced to resort to various types of government programs such as purchases of goods and services, transfer payments, and subsidies, to cope with macroeconomic difficulties. Furthermore, as economic performance deteriorates in many OECD countries, the spending required by prior commitments may rise despite the fact that future economic prospects are not as bright as when the commitments were originally legislated. These tendencies may increase government size and exacerbate budget deficits. Thus, there may be a two-way link between fiscal policy and macroeconomic performance.[9]

THE POLITICAL ECONOMY OF FISCAL POLICY

So far we have tried to uncover empirical relationships among fiscal and key macroeconomic variables, using cross-country data. We find that countries with large structural budget deficits tend to have low private investment, less favorable current account positions, and high rates of inflation and unemployment, while countries with big governments tend to have low economic growth. This suggests that it is important to contain government size and structural budget deficits in order to promote private capital formation, economic growth, disinflation, and employment.

Below we examine the political economy aspects of the growth of government and the persistence of budget deficits over the last 25 years.

The Size of Government

Figure 8.1 plots the size of general government, as measured by its total outlays-to-GDP ratio, for the United States, Japan, Sweden, OECD-Europe, and the weighted average of all OECD countries (OECD-Total for short). The figure shows that government outlays grew continuously after the first oil-price shock in 1973, and that the growth slowed in the 1980s before rising again in the early 1990s. Slower growth in real output after 1973 failed to contain public spending,

Figure 8.1 GENERAL GOVERNMENT TOTAL OUTLAYS (RELATIVE TO GDP) FOR 1970–1993

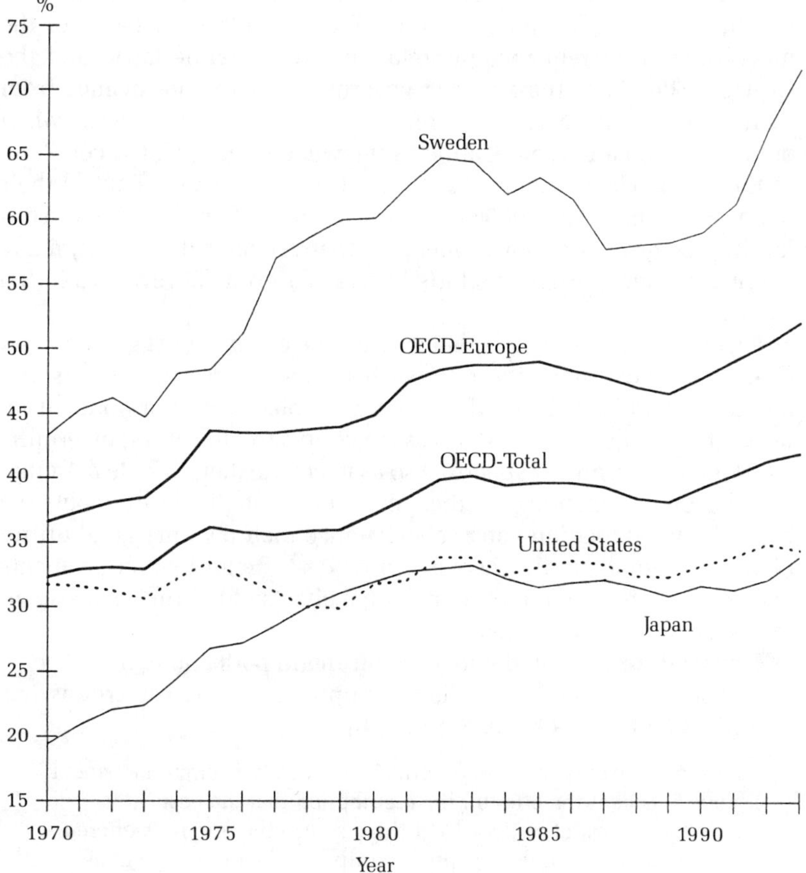

Source: OECD. *Economic Outlook*, various issues, Paris: OECD.

leading to a visible increase in the government outlays-to-GDP ratio. Particularly rapid increases were observed in OECD-Europe and especially in Sweden, which has the biggest government (as a share of GDP) among the OECD countries. The total outlays-to-GDP ratio for OECD-Europe rose from 37 percent in 1970 to 45 percent in 1980, and then to 52 percent in 1993. The ratio in Japan—the OECD country with the smallest government—also grew sharply during the 1970s, from 19 percent in 1970 to 32 percent in 1980, reaching 34 percent in 1993 after remaining flat in the 1980s. The Japanese government, though still small, is now of comparable size to that of the United States, which, like most OECD governments, has grown gradually but persistently over the past 25 years.

Figure 8.2 depicts the current receipts-to-GDP ratio. Sweden again has the biggest government among OECD countries in terms of the magnitude of current receipts relative to GDP, while Japan and the United States have the smallest governments. A major change from figure 8.1 is that government receipts rose persistently, even when outlays peaked and then declined somewhat in many OECD countries in the 1980s. Hence, some OECD countries were able to control their budget deficits in the 1980s but were not entirely successful in containing the growth of government on the revenue side. In fact, many countries made conscious efforts to raise government revenues in the 1980s.

There are various models that explain the expansion of government. One model postulates the rational behavior of pressure groups and median voters (recall that the "median" voter may tip a policy from minority to majority status). Pressure groups (rent-seekers) determine the level of government spending so as to equate their private marginal benefits due to spending to their marginal costs, including lobbying costs. Rational median voters also balance their own marginal utility of various benefits with their marginal cost, including tax payments and other costs due to the disincentive effects of the higher marginal tax rates on the national economy.

A second, related model focuses on the imperfections of the political process in relation to the assumptions of interest groups. As described by Lindbeck (1993, pp. 7–8):

> "When one particular group of citizens in society is offered a benefit, it tends to accept the offer on the assumption that the costs are borne mainly by the rest of society. Next time, some other group is offered a benefit, which it happily accepts according to the same type of assumption about who pays the costs—and so on, period after period. In the end almost everyone may, in fact, be accountable for the costs of

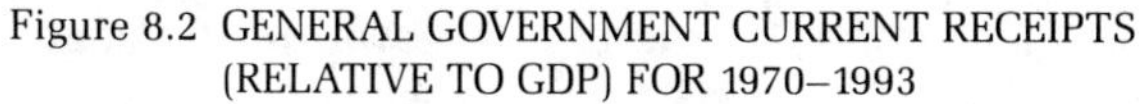

Figure 8.2 GENERAL GOVERNMENT CURRENT RECEIPTS (RELATIVE TO GDP) FOR 1970–1993

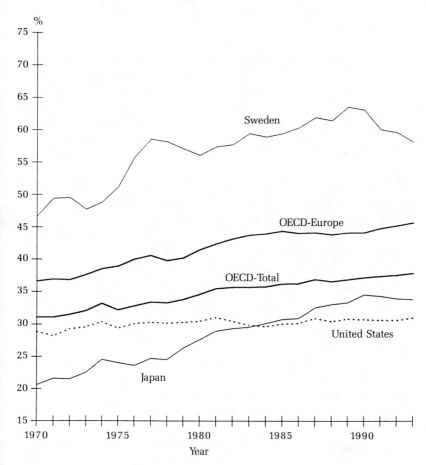

Source: OECD. *Economic Outlook*, various issues, Paris: OECD.

each other's benefits, and (nearly) all citizens may end up as losers because of the disincentive effects on the national economy."

Finally, a model of political business cycles attributes the secular growth of government to business cycles. When negative shocks hit the economy and raise the unemployment rate, as in the case of the 1973 oil-price shock, the government and the ruling party come under political pressure to increase government spending to reduce unemployment and stabilize the economy. This pressure is particularly difficult to resist before an election. An increase in government spending may lead to economic recovery and eventually cause an overheating of the economy. With lower unemployment, higher inflation, and larger budget deficits, the government comes under pressure to reduce spending or raise taxes in order to restore the fiscal balance. A contractionary fiscal policy, although usually not sufficient to balance the budget, reverses the employment situation, and the government once again comes under pressure to expand fiscally in time for the next election. This process may tend to increase government size, because the government is usually incapable of returning to the lower level of spending (relative to GDP) that prevailed prior to the fiscal expansion. Each fiscal expansion tends to create various pressure groups which strongly resist attempts to cut back the gains they have made.

It is possible that a lax budgetary process lies behind the weak political processes described above.[10] Failure of political coordination is of key importance here. It is extremely difficult for the government, voters, and pressure groups to simultaneously decide on all budget items in a cooperative fashion.

The expected rise in the proportion of the aged population in many OECD countries will increase political pressure for higher spending in the form of social security and welfare payments. This pressure will appear over and above the constant demand for increases in many other types of social services provided by the government, including income maintenance, health, and education. As a result, government activity in the economy is bound to grow steadily unless conscious efforts are made to contain it. The growth of government distorts the work incentives of private agents and increases inefficiencies in resource allocation, resulting in slower economic growth.

Budget Deficits

Figure 8.3 plots the budget deficit as a percentage of GDP for the United States, Japan, Sweden, OECD-Europe, and the weighted average of all OECD countries (OECD-Total). Unlike government size, there has been no clear tendency for budget deficits to rise since the mid-1970s. There was a sudden and sharp increase in the budget deficits for OECD-Total after 1973, clearly linked to the sudden slowdown in real output growth and a corresponding increase in unemployment. Average budget deficits stayed at a high level until the latter part of the 1980s, when they improved significantly before deteriorating once again. The U.S. budget deficit was reduced in the late 1970s but widened again in the 1980s. In contrast, in the late 1970s Japan's fiscal

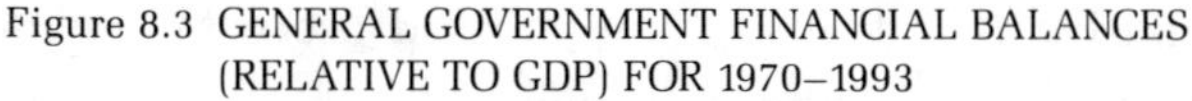

Figure 8.3 GENERAL GOVERNMENT FINANCIAL BALANCES (RELATIVE TO GDP) FOR 1970–1993

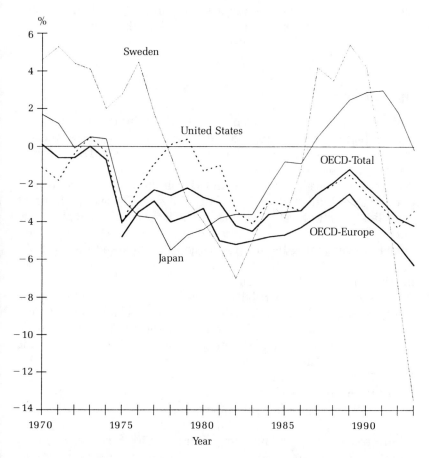

Source: OECD. *Economic Outlook*, various issues, Paris: OECD.

balance improved significantly from a large deficit and turned into surplus in the second half of the 1980s, though the surplus started to shrink in the beginning of the 1990s due to the severe recession.

When spending by OECD governments rose markedly in the first half of the 1970s, taxes could not be raised and, legislatively, government services could not be cut back immediately. (Note, however, the more automatic revenue increases detected by Posner and Bovbjerg, chapter 7 of this volume.) Tax increases were politically unpopular and risky for ruling parties and cutting back on other government programs was equally difficult due to the political processes mentioned earlier.[11] Accumulated public debt increases debt service obligations, which themselves are a source of budget deficits. Hence, there is a tendency for budget deficits to develop absent a political mechanism to check the budgetary process and impose fiscal discipline.

Japan's Experience

Two key factors have provided a fiscal disciplining mechanism in Japan. The first is a fiscal consolidation program that was adopted in the early 1980s and maintained for more than ten years. This program was initiated by the Nakasone administration and made effective under the strong leadership of Toshio Dokoh, head of the Provisional Council for Administrative Reform (Rinji Gyosei Chosakai). The fiscal consolidation effort was a response to the large deficits and mounting public debts that emerged as a result of the drastic fiscal expansion aimed at overcoming the deep recession that followed the 1973 oil-price shock and reducing the large current account surplus under pressure from the United States.

The second factor contributing to Japan's fiscal discipline is the Ministry of Finance (MOF). With its stubborn balanced-budget ideology, the MOF has played a key role in providing an effective disciplining mechanism by coordinating various political and economic interests during the budgetary process. In the budget planning stage, the MOF negotiates with individual ministries, which represent the political and economic demands of respective interest groups, over the allocation of government resources. The MOF coordinates conflicts between private and social interests, thus avoiding coordination failure problems among interest groups. The MOF has been able to play this coordinating role for most of the postwar period under the political system dominated until recently by the Liberal Democratic Party.

The fiscal consolidation program, together with the MOF's role as fiscal disciplinarian and budget coordinator, has prevented not only an "overshooting" of the welfare state but also excessive budget deficits. The country's fiscal balance moved from deep in the red in the late 1970s to far into the black in the second half of the 1980s. However, it is too soon to judge if this fiscal consolidation is permanent. It may be a temporary response to the rapid accumulation of public debts in the late 1970s and early 1980s. Given that the Japanese political system is clearly headed toward multi-party coalition governments, it may become increasingly difficult to contain structural budget deficits and control the size of public debts.

CURRENT ACCOUNTS AND GLOBAL SAVING AND INVESTMENT

Below we speculate about what will happen to saving, investment, and the current account of the OECD countries. The development of saving and investment in these countries has important implications for economic growth in developing countries and the transitional economies of the former Eastern Bloc nations.

Factors Affecting Saving

At least three factors contribute to the reduction of national saving: population aging, secular slowdown of economic growth, and growing impatience of individuals toward income allocation over time or saving for the future.

First, as the proportion of the elderly in the population rises, a country's propensity to save generally declines. This happens because the elderly simply consume more, intergenerational income transfers from the young to the old reduce the national saving rate, and mounting pressure to expand social security and welfare programs results in a decline in government saving. To the extent that a decline in government saving is not fully offset by a rise in private saving, national saving will decline.

Second, a slowdown of economic growth tends to reduce saving. It is true that intertemporal optimization theory suggests that a fully anticipated fall in future output growth encourages private saving today: saving rises today because (expected) total wealth available for lifetime consumption declines and, hence, consumption in each period is lower while output today is still high. Theory also suggests that an unanticipated fall in output today discourages private saving: saving declines today because the fall in consumption in each period induced by a decline in total wealth is not as large as a fall in output today. Thus the net effect of an economic slowdown on saving is uncertain because of these two offsetting factors. The evidence suggests that a permanent slowdown of real output reduces private saving (Bosworth 1993). This is a robust empirical result observed in many countries.[12]

A slowdown of economic growth tends to reduce government saving as well. Most programs, including social security and welfare schemes, are often based on the assumption that the economy will continue to grow at the historically achieved pace. When actual rates of economic growth fall short of those anticipated rates, government spending does not fall and may even rise. Since slower economic growth reduces tax revenues, government saving tends to decline. Because the growth rate is more likely to fall than to rise in many OECD countries in the future, pressure to reduce government saving will probably increase.[13]

Finally, as people grow accustomed to a high and rising level of affluence, measured by, say, per capita consumption, there is a general tendency for the saving rate to fall. People become less patient, in that they prefer to consume sooner rather than later, as they take for granted a high and increasing standard of living. Many OECD countries, including Japan and the United States, appear to be showing such a tendency, although it is difficult to isolate this factor empirically from those mentioned above.

On the other hand, several offsetting factors can contribute to higher saving. For instance, a further reduction in military spending, reflecting the end of the cold war, could be significant for the United States. A "peace dividend" may accrue in the form of greater net saving on the part of the government. The improved longevity of the population could also raise the saving rate. As people's life expectancy rises, they must consume less when young or postpone retirement to prepare for life after retirement. This stimulates saving. In addition, as people realize that the levels of social security and welfare payments the government promises them are too high to balance the fiscal budget, they may protect themselves by increasing private saving to cope with future uncertainties. Nonetheless, these offsetting factors will probably not be strong enough to prevent a fall in saving in many OECD countries.

Factors Affecting Investment

It is harder to predict what will happen to investment. If the anticipated slow growth of many OECD countries is correct, their investment may not rise sharply. In any case, the expected persistence of budget deficits is not conducive to capital accumulation. But rapid technological progress raises the marginal products of capital and labor and encourages productive investment. Maintaining a market environment that is friendly to innovation and technological improvement is the most important way to promote capital investment.

Even if it is difficult to contain the growth of government spending, it is possible to change the composition of spending in order to stimulate capital accumulation. For example, favorable tax treatments for capital investment and R&D activities are more productive than spending on transfer payments to households. The key factor influencing a country's investment is its ability to shift expenditures away from unproductive spending toward spending for productive purposes.

World Current Accounts

Table 8.2 reports the current accounts of the industrialized and developing countries from 1980 to 1993. This type of data has the serious problem that the world current account, which should sum up to zero in theory, sums up to a large negative number in practice. This problem implies uncertainty about whether the industrialized countries which recorded current account deficits in the 1980s and early 1990s did indeed run current account deficits. Although it is not possible to resolve this difficult problem here, we can say with some confidence that the industrialized countries do not appear to have provided large amounts of capital to the developing countries and former socialist economies in recent years. In the first half of the 1980s, the United States experienced large structural budget deficits and, after a recession, rapid economic growth, which helped the current account to deteriorate. Huge U.S. current account deficits of 100 to 150 billion dollars per annum were largely offset in the 1980s by the pool of net saving from Japan and West Germany. However, this offset effect now appears to be vanishing.

Two decades or so from now, Japan's saving rate is likely to decline substantially due to a rapid change in its demographic composition, which will reduce its current account surplus or make it into the red. As seen in table 8.2, Germany's current account turned into deficits in the early 1990s because of a drastic fiscal expansion following the unification of East and West Germany, which turned the European Union (EU) as a whole into a deficit area. This situation may be reversed as the eastern part of unified Germany implements the adjustment necessary for its economic transformation. However, Germany and other EU countries will also come under the kinds of pressures, mentioned earlier, which eventually raise fiscal and current account deficits—a scenario likely to exacerbate global capital shortage.

Table 8.2 CURRENT ACCOUNT BALANCE OF THE INDUSTRIALIZED DEVELOPING COUNTRIES, 1980–1993 (Millions of U.S. Dollars)

	1980	1981	1982	1983	1984	1985	1986	1987	1988	1989	1990	1991	1992	1993
Industrialized Countries	-64,672	-27,795	-31,115	-24,572	-53,327	-60,622	-31,718	-60,799	-55,922	-82,197	-117,798	-34,170	-46,186	-5,208
G7 Countries	-31,556	-264	-9,300	-14,689	-54,926	-58,377	-26,110	-54,025	-49,827	-60,666	-94,681	-24,335	-35,500	-13,458
United States	2,250	5.051	-11,420	-43,650	-98,760	-121,700	-147,460	-163,395	-126,670	-101,190	-90,462	-8,320	-66,380	-109,247
Japan	-10,750	4,770	6,850	20,800	35,000	49,170	85,831	87,020	79,610	56,990	35,870	72,905	117,640	131,470
Germany	-13,759	-3,343	5,009	5,437	9,599	17,023	40,080	46,283	50,764	57,696	45,793	-18,775	-22,121	-21,393
Canada	-1,534	-5,740	1,573	1,706	1,218	-2,279	-8,190	-8,754	-12,564	-19,735	-22,172	-25,343	-23,012	-19,601
France	-4,208	-4,811	-12,082	-5,166	-876	-35	2,430	-4,446	-4,795	-5,661	-15,236	-7,030	4,337	10,201
Italy	-10,417	-10,318	-7,155	892	-2,941	-3,865	2,534	-2,429	-6,600	-11,900	-16,827	-24,060	-27,908	11,176
United Kingdom	6,862	14,127	7,895	5,292	1,834	3,309	-1,335	-8,304	-29,572	-36,866	-31,647	-13,712	-18,056	-16,064
Other Industrialized Countries	-33,116	-27,531	-21,785	-9,883	1,599	-2,245	-5,608	-6,774	-6,095	-21,531	-23,117	-9,835	-10,686	8,250
Developing Countries	29,574	-49,946	-82,281	-57,787	-29,169	-23,817	-42,438	-1,182	-12,037	-6,911	-3,760	-83,427	-68,351	-109,720
Africa	-1,219	-22,121	-21,475	-12,140	-5,915	1,002	-5,255	-3,163	-7,297	-5,015	738	-1,894	-4,726	-8,652
Asia	-15,156	-20,378	-17,254	-15,157	-4,988	-13,926	3,784	21,360	9,828	1,644	-40.2	-3,321	-6,317	-25,737
NIEs	-10,491	-8,498	-4,252	167	4,972	8,786	21,286	27,707	24,493	20,216	10,350	5,596	3,483	4,860
ASEAN-Four	-1,260	-7,717	-13,140	-15,480	-6,930	-4,108	-2,833	-365	-1,632	-4,804	-13,883	-17,049	-11,763	-14,336
China	-2,475	2,104	5,823	4,487	2,509	-11,417	-7,034	300	-3,802	-4,317	11,998	13,272	6,401	-11,609
Europe	-11,914	-8,681	-2,465	-1,762	769	98	-2,224	1,205	8.066	3,896	-7,842	-3,006	-4,456	-13,853
Middle East	88,108	43,528	504	-20,454	-18,025	-8,710	-21,651	-10,420	-12,818	-1,515	5,120	-59,064	-20,755	-20,600
Western Hemisphere	-30,245	-42,295	-41,592	-8,275	-1,011	-2,280	-17,092	-10,164	-9,816	-5,925	-1,373	-16,141	-32,098	-40,878
All Countries	-35,079	-77,741	-113,396	-82,359	-82,496	-84,438	-74,155	-61,980	-67,958	-89,108	-121,557	-117,597	-114,536	-114,928

Source: IMF 1995; and Asian Development Bank 1994.

Note: Asian NIEs (newly industrializing companies) in the table include Korea, Taiwan, Hong Kong, and Singapore. Hong Kong's data are proxied by trade balances. ASEAN-Four includes Malaysia, Thailand, Indonesia, and the Philippines.

However, there are some positive factors in the world economy that will help to relieve capital shortage. The most noteworthy is the rapid growth of the East Asian economies, which has increased both saving and investment in the region. What is significant is that saving has grown more rapidly than investment, making the East Asian developing region, particularly the newly industrializing economies (NIEs) encompassing Korea, Taiwan, Hong Kong, and Singapore, a surplus area. Transfer of East Asian saving to the rest of the world may alleviate the capital shortage problem, helping to prevent real interest rates from rising on a global scale and the rate of world economic growth from slowing down significantly.

CONCLUSION

This paper has analyzed data from the OECD countries and assessed the implications of increasing government size and widening budget deficits for capital accumulation and economic growth. Though our empirical findings are provisional, they show that a rise in structural budget deficits tends to be associated with lower private capital formation, high inflation, and high unemployment, and that large government is associated with slow economic growth. Because a persistent budget deficit means that less saving is available to the private sector for productive capital formation, and lower investment results in only smaller fruits to be enjoyed in the future, governments must make every effort to reduce structural budget deficits. Given the possible detrimental effect of government size on the economy, governments should not make themselves excessively large.

One of the implications of the slower growth likely in OECD countries in the future is that only limited amounts of saving will be available for developing countries and economies in transition. Hence, these growing, capital-poor countries may also have a low rate of growth, making it difficult to achieve political stability and full integration into an open world trading system. The most urgent task for many OECD countries is to trim unproductive and inefficient government spending and reduce structural budget deficits. This will promote capital accumulation globally and enhance the prospects for better economic performance.

Notes

1. When statistics are not available for the entire sample period, the necessary data are obtained by averaging statistics over the period for which they are available.

2. Our definition of government is that of general government in national accounts and does not include off-budget activities or public enterprises.

3. The Barro-Ricardo view of rational consumers endowed with operative bequest motives holds that when there is a cut in lump-sum taxes today, consumers increase saving as if they themselves would have to pay for the tax increase in the future, which will be necessary to balance the government budget over time. Essentially, the consumers who care about the taxes their children (or their children's children) will have to pay in the future leave private savings for their children to help them pay the tax bills.

4. The rate of inflation is also negatively correlated with the current account, with the correlation coefficient of minus 0.63 (table 8.1, panel B, column 3 down). That is, high-inflation countries tend to have large current account deficits while low-inflation countries do not.

5. This is one of the important factors underlying the Barro-Ricardo explanation for the negative correlation between the private and government S-I balances.

6. To account for possible simultaneity bias due to the endogeneity of the right-hand side variables, the 2SLS (two-stage least squares) estimation method is used in addition to the OLS (ordinary least squares) method. The OLS and 2SLS regression results in this and other parts of the paper are available from the authors upon request.

7. In addition to general government total outlays and structural financial balances (both relative to GDP), we use national net fixed investment (relative to GDP) to explain the growth rate of real GDP, the growth rate of money supplies to explain the inflation rate, and the rate of increase in real wages to explain the unemployment rate.

8. Our result that the level of government size has a negative impact on the economic growth rate is consistent with those of both Landau (1983) and Ram (1986). However, Ram claims that a better specification is to use the change in, rather than the level of, government spending (as a ratio of output). The rationale for our specification is that it is the accumulated value of government outlays that affect real output and, thus, that the growth rate of real output should depend on the level of government outlays (as a proportion of GDP).

9. The 2SLS regression of the macroeconomic performance variables on structural budget deficits and government size yields less satisfactory results than the OLS regression.

10. Roubini and Sachs (1989a) separate the movement of the government expenditure-to-output ratio into three parts and identify factors affecting each: a long-run target level, a partial adjustment part, and an unanticipated cyclical part. They find that the long-run target level is affected by political and institutional characteristics of the economy. For example, countries with multi-party coalitions more dependent on the pressures of interest groups and those with strong political demands for income transfer payments tend to have large governments.

11. Roubini and Sachs (1989b) examined the economic and political forces leading to large budget deficits in the OECD countries. Their empirical study supports the view that there is a tendency for larger deficits to emerge in countries with weaker governments, where weakness is indicated by a short average tenure of government and by the pressure of many political parties within ruling coalition governments.

12. The theoretical interpretation of the empirical result is that people tend to regard economic growth (or decline), even if persistent over a long time period, as temporary, and thus increase (or decrease) saving accordingly.

13. It is observed that economic growth is positively correlated with the country's saving; see the cross-country correlation between national net saving and the growth rate in table 8.1, panel B, column 1 down, which is 0.39. This implies that a slowdown of economic growth in many OECD countries is likely associated with a decline in national saving.

References

Asian Development Bank. 1994. *Key Indicators of Developing Asian and Pacific Countries.*

Baxter, Marrianne, and Mario J. Crucini. 1993. "Explaining Saving-Investment Correlations." *American Economic Review* 83 (June): 450–72.

Bayoumi, Tamim. 1990. "Saving-Investment Correlations: Immobile Capital, Government Policy or Endogenous Behavior?" *IMF Staff Papers* 37 (June): 360–87.

Bosworth, Barry P. 1993. *Saving and Investment in a Global Economy*. Washington, D.C.: The Brookings Institution.

Feldstein, Martin S., and Charles Y. Horioka. 1980. "Domestic Saving and International Capital Flows." *Economic Journal* 90 (June): 314–29.

Frenkel, Jacob A., and Assaf Razin. 1987. *Fiscal Policies and the World Economy*. Cambridge, Ma., and London: The MIT Press.

IMF (International Monetary Fund). 1995. *International Financial Statistics Yearbook 1994*. January. Washington, D.C.: IMF.

Kawai, Masahiro, and Louis J. Maccini. 1995. "Twin Deficits vs. Unpleasant Fiscal Arithmetic in a Small Open Economy." *Journal of Money, Credit, and Banking* forthcoming.

Landau, Daniel. 1983. "Government Expenditure and Economic Growth: A Cross-Country Study." *Southern Economic Journal* 49 (January): 783–92.

Lindbeck, Assar. 1993. "Overshooting, Reform and Retreat of the Welfare State." Seminar Paper No. 552 (October), Institute for International Economic Studies.

Obstfeld, Maurice. 1986. "Capital Mobility in the World Economy." *Carnegie-Rochester Conference Series on Public Policy* 24 (Spring): 55–103.

OECD. 1994. *Economic Outlook*, vol. 56. December. Paris: Organization for Economic Cooperation and Development.

Ram, Rati. 1986. "Government Size and Economic Growth: A New Framework and Some Evidence from Cross-Section and Time-Series Data." *American Economic Review* 76 (March): 191–203.

Roubini, Nouriel, and Jeffrey D. Sachs. 1989a. "Fiscal Policy." *Economic Policy* 4 (April): 99–132.

———. 1989b. "Political and Economic Determinants of Budget Deficits in the Industrial Democracies." *European Economic Review* 33 (May): 903–38.

Sachs, Jeffrey D. 1981. "The Current Account and Macroeconomic Adjustment in the 1970s." *Brookings Papers on Economic Activity* 1 (April): 201–68.

Saunders, Peter, and Friedrich Klau. 1985. "The Role of the Public Sector: Causes and Consequences of the Growth of Government." *OECD Economic Studies* No. 4 (Spring): 5–239.

Tesar, Linda L. 1991. "Savings, Investment and International Capital Flows." *Journal of International Economics* 31 (August): 55–78.

APPENDIX 8.A

This appendix explains and summarizes the regression equations used to obtain econometric evidence reported in the main text.

Private Net Fixed Investment

The first regression is that for private net fixed investment:

$$(I^P/Y)_j = \alpha + \beta(S^P/Y)_j + \gamma(SFB/Y)_j + u_j,$$

where $(I^P/Y)_j$ is private net fixed capital formation relative to GDP; $(S^P/Y)_j$ is private net saving relative to GDP; $(SFB/Y)_j$ is the government's structural financial balance relative to GDP; and j refers to a cross-section observation of country j (= 1, 2, . . ., 19). All variables are averaged data for the 1980–1993 period.

The OLS regression yields

$$\underset{(1.049)}{\alpha = 3.262}, \quad \underset{(0.114)}{\beta = 0.745}, \quad \underset{(0.200)}{\gamma = 0.704}, \quad R^2\text{-adjusted} = 0.69,$$

where numbers in the parentheses are the estimated standard errors. To take account of possible simultaneity bias due to the endogeneity of the right-hand side variables, the 2SLS estimation is also run by using the average data for the 1970–1979 period of the growth rate of real GDP, national net fixed capital formation (relative to GDP), national net saving (relative to GDP), and general government financial balances (relative to GDP), as instrumental variables. The result is

$$\underset{(1.085)}{\alpha = 3.985}, \quad \underset{(0.140)}{\beta = 0.715}, \quad \underset{(0.304)}{\gamma = 0.808}, \quad R^2\text{-adjusted} = 0.68.$$

Hence, a rise in the structural fiscal deficit, or a decline in $(SFB/Y)_j$, reduces private net fixed investment.

The Current Account

The next regression equation is that for the current account:

$$(X/Y)_j = \alpha + \beta(S^P/Y)_j + \gamma(I^P/Y)_j + \delta(SFB/Y)_j + u_j,$$

where $(X/Y)_j$ is the current account relative to GDP and the right-hand side variables are defined above. The OLS regression yields

$$\underset{(1.083)}{\alpha = 0.849}, \ \underset{(0.178)}{\beta = 0.463}, \ \underset{(0.204)}{\gamma = -0.532}, \ \underset{(0.217)}{\delta = 0.574}, \ R^2\text{-adjusted} = 0.23.$$

The 2SLS regression with the same instrumental variables as above yields

$$\underset{(1.376)}{\alpha = 0.480}, \ \underset{(0.222)}{\beta = 0.435}, \ \underset{(0.269)}{\gamma = -0.420}, \ \underset{(0.325)}{\delta = 0.637}, \ R^2\text{-adjusted} = 0.17.$$

The results clearly indicate that a rise in the structural fiscal deficit causes the current account to deteriorate.

Macroeconomic Performance Variables

The last type of regression equation is the following:

$$MP_j = \alpha + \beta Z_j + \gamma(SFB/Y)_j + \delta(TO/Y)_j + u_j,$$

where MP_j is the macroeconomic performance variable; Z_j is a set of country-specific factors affecting the macroeconomic performance; $(SFB/Y)_j$ is the government's structural financial balance relative to GDP; and $(TO/Y)_j$ is the government's total outlays relative to GDP. As country-specific factors, we choose the growth rate of population and national fixed capital formation relative to GDP for the real growth rate equation, the growth rate of money supplies (money plus quasi-money) for the inflation rate equation, and the rate of change in real wages (nominal wages divided by wholesale price indices) for the unemployment rate equation. It turns out that population growth is never a statistically significant variable in the real growth rate equation and, hence, it was dropped from the final equation. The data for population, money supplies, nominal wages, and wholesale price indices are taken from IMF, *International Financial Statistics*, various issues. When 2SLS regressions are run, we use the left-hand side and right-hand side variables, MP_j, Z_j, $(FB/Y)_j$, and $(TO/Y)_j$, all averages for the 1970–1979 period, as instrumental variables.

The OLS and 2SLS estimation results are summarized as follows:

(a) The Growth Rate of Real GDP:

OLS:
$$\alpha = \underset{(0.892)}{3.343},\ \beta = \underset{(0.036)}{0.056},\ \gamma = \underset{(0.043)}{0.013},\ \delta = \underset{(0.016)}{-0.035},\ R^2\text{-adjusted} = 0.26.$$

$$\text{OLS: } \alpha = \underset{(0.866)}{3.343},\ \beta = \underset{(0.035)}{0.055},\ \delta = \underset{(0.015)}{-0.036},\ R^2\text{-adjusted} = 0.30.$$

$$\text{2SLS: } \alpha = \underset{(0.973)}{2.176},\ \beta = \underset{(0.038)}{0.081},\ \delta = \underset{(0.017)}{-0.017},\ R^2\text{-adjusted} = 0.22.$$

(b) The Inflation Rate of GDP Deflators:

OLS:
$$\alpha = \underset{(2.950)}{-3.892},\ \beta = \underset{(0.118)}{0.826},\ \gamma = \underset{(0.151)}{-0.331},\ \delta = \underset{(0.053)}{0.017},\ R^2\text{-adjusted} = 0.82.$$

$$\text{OLS: } \alpha = \underset{(1.116)}{-3.004},\ \beta = \underset{(0.108)}{0.813},\ \gamma = \underset{(0.140)}{-0.345},\ R^2\text{-adjusted} = 0.82.$$

$$\text{2SLS: } \alpha = \underset{(1.427)}{-3.556},\ \beta = \underset{(0.142)}{0.961},\ \gamma = \underset{(0.194)}{-0.102},\ R^2\text{-adjusted} = 0.79.$$

(c) The Unemployment Rate:

OLS:
$$\alpha = \underset{(5.895)}{5.666},\ \beta = \underset{(0.885)}{0.685},\ \gamma = \underset{(0.298)}{-0.398},\ \delta = \underset{(0.110)}{-0.019},\ R^2\text{-adjusted} = -0.03.$$

$$\text{OLS: } \alpha = \underset{(2.620)}{4.764},\ \beta = \underset{(0.852)}{0.702},\ \gamma = \underset{(0.285)}{-0.389},\ R^2\text{-adjusted} = 0.33.$$

$$\text{2SLS: } \alpha = \underset{(4.381)}{-1.784},\ \beta = \underset{(1.755)}{3.002},\ \gamma = \underset{(0.479)}{-0.606},\ R^2\text{-adjusted} = -0.33.$$

The OLS estimation results indicate that government size affects the growth rate of real GDP and that structural fiscal balance affects the inflation and unemployment rates, though the last effect is not statistically significant. It turns out that the 2SLS estimation results are less satisfactory.

Chapter Nine

DEFICITS, TAX POLICY, AND SAVING

Mark Robson

As discussed in other papers in this volume, many OECD countries have found themselves facing uncomfortably large budget deficits since the late 1980s. These deficits have not been caused by a fall in the overall level of taxation. As can be seen in table 9.1, total revenues as a percent of GDP levels have gone up slightly between 1986 and 1992, although there have been shifts among sources of taxation. The increase in government deficits arose instead from higher public expenditure mainly due to increased transfer payments associated with high unemployment and an aging population.

The size of budget deficits affects the level and allocation of national saving. The ratio of gross national saving to GDP in the 1980s for each OECD country was typically several percentage points below levels of the 1960s and early 1970s (table 9.2). Although economic theory has little to say about whether the level of savings can be too low in the long term, there is widespread agreement among policymakers that a worldwide decline in saving *could* have far-reaching implications for future well-being. The fall in total saving in OECD countries comes at a time when increased demands for global savings arise from the need for investment to transform the former centrally planned economies into market economies, to replace public sector infrastructure, and to attain environmental objectives. Concerns about a possible worldwide shortage of capital are continuing into the 1990s, as noted at the annual International Monetary Fund meeting in Madrid in October 1994, stimulating interest in policy measures aimed at promoting private saving.

The need to finance higher government expenditure may affect total national saving in several ways, the net effect of which may be difficult to predict. When issuing additional debt, governments compete with private deposit takers to attract investors, leading to a rise in nominal yields and a fall in bond prices. This has already occurred, following the many new bond issues put out by European governments. However, the net effect on government revenue depends not only on

Table 9.1 SOURCES OF GENERAL GOVERNMENT REVENUES, 1986 AND 1992 (AS A PERCENTAGE OF NOMINAL GDP)

	Income and Profits		Social Security		Payroll		Property		Goods and Services		Others		Total	
Country	1986	1992	1986	1992	1986	1992	1986	1992	1986	1992	1986	1992	1986	1992
United States	12.2	12.2	8.6	8.8	—	—	3.0	3.3	5.1	5.0	—	—	28.9	29.3
Japan	13.2	12.5	8.6	9.7	—	—	3.1	3.1	3.8	4.1	0.1	0.1	28.8	29.5
Germany	13.0	12.7	14.0	15.2	—	—	1.1	1.1	9.5	10.6	—	—	37.5	39.6
France	8.0	7.6	18.9	19.5	0.9	0.9	2.1	2.2	13.0	11.7	1.3	1.8	44.2	43.7
Italy	13.7	16.6	12.4	13.3	0.2	0.1	1.0	1.0	8.9	11.4	—	—	36.2	42.4
United Kingdom	14.9	12.7	7.0	6.3	—	—	5.0	2.8	12.1	12.1	—	1.3	39.0	35.2
Canada	15.2	16.4	4.5	6.0	—	—	3.1	4.0	9.8	9.5	0.4	0.5	33.2	36.4
Unweighted average "G7" countries	12.9	13.0	10.6	11.3	0.2	0.1	2.6	2.5	8.9	9.2	0.3	0.5	**35.4**	**36.6**
Unweighted average OECD countries	14.7	14.3	9.3	9.9	0.4	0.3	1.8	2.0	11.5	11.8	0.3	0.4	**38.1**	**38.7**

Source: Revenue statistics of OECD member countries, 1987; and Revenue statistics of OECD member countries, 1993.

Table 9.2 GROSS SAVING AMONG OECD COUNTRIES (AS A PERCENTAGE OF GDP)

	Average in the 1960s	Average in the 1970s	Average in the 1980s	Average 1990–1992	Change Between the Average in the 1980s and: Average in the 1960s	Average in the 1970s
Australia						
National *of which*	24.7	24.1	20.6	17.9	−4.1	−3.5
Public	—	2.8	1.9	—	—	−0.9
Household	—	13.2	10.9	—	—	−2.3
Corporate	—	8.1	7.7	—	—	−0.4
Austria						
National *of which*	27.7	28.0	24.3	25.8	−3.4	−3.7
Public	7.2	6.2	2.7	2.5	−4.5	−3.5
Household	5.4	6.2	6.4	8.4	1.0	0.2
Corporate	15.1	15.6	15.2	14.9	0.1	−0.4
Belgium						
National *of which*	22.4	23.1	16.9	21.3	−5.5	−6.2
Public	1.2	0.0	−6.0	−4.3	−7.2	−6.0
Household	9.8	15.1	13.1	15.3	3.3	−2.0
Corporate	11.4	8.1	9.7	10.3	−1.7	1.6
Canada						
National *of which*	21.9	22.9	20.7	15.4	−1.2	−2.2
Public	3.6	2.7	−1.4	−3.1	−5.0	−4.1
Household	7.8	10.4	12.2	10.7	4.4	1.8
Corporate	10.5	9.7	9.9	7.8	−0.6	0.2

Table 9.2 GROSS SAVING AMONG OECD COUNTRIES (AS A PERCENTAGE OF GDP) (*Continued*)

	Average in the 1960s	Average in the 1970s	Average in the 1980s	Average 1990–1992	Change Between the Average in the 1980s and: Average in the 1960s	Average in the 1970s
Denmark						
National *of which*	23.3	20.9	15.4	18.6	−7.9	−5.5
Public	—	5.4	0.4	−0.1	—	−5.0
Household	—	—	—	—	—	—
Corporate	—	—	—	—	—	—
Finland						
National *of which*	25.4	26.7	24.2	17.3	−1.2	−2.5
Public	7.3	9.0	7.3	3.6	0.0	−1.7
Household	6.4	7.3	7.6	8.2	1.2	0.3
Corporate	11.6	10.3	9.3	5.4	−2.3	−1.0
France						
National *of which*	26.2	25.8	20.5	20.7	−5.7	−5.3
Public	—	3.6	1.4	1.2	—	−2.2
Household	—	13.6	10.2	8.7	—	−3.4
Corporate	—	8.5	8.7	10.6	—	0.2
Germany						
National *of which*	27.3	24.3	22.3	23.5	−5.0	−2.0
Public	6.2	3.8	1.9	1.3	−4.3	−1.9
Household	6.9	8.7	7.9	8.3	1.0	−0.8
Corporate	14.2	11.8	12.5	13.8	−1.7	0.7
Greece						
National *of which*	19.2	25.8	17.7	14.9	−1.5	−8.1
Public	3.9	2.3	−6.9	−10.9	−10.8	−9.2
Household	9.3	16.0	15.8	17.1	6.5	−0.2
Corporate	6.0	7.5	8.7	8.7	2.7	1.2

Iceland						
National *of which*	25.4	24.8	18.7	15.4	−6.7	−6.1
Public	—	5.6	6.6	2.7	—	1.0
Household	—	—	—	—	—	—
Corporate	—	—	—	—	—	—
Ireland						
National *of which*	18.4	21.3	18.4	25.0	0.0	−2.9
Public	—	−1.4	−5.7	—	—	−3.7
Household	—	—	—	—	—	—
Corporate	—	22.7	24.1	—	—	1.4
Italy						
National *of which*	28.1	25.9	22.0	18.7	−6.1	−3.9
Public	2.1	−5.1	−6.4	—	−8.5	−1.3
Household	—	27.1	22.3	—	—	−4.8
Corporate	—	4.0	6.1	—	—	2.1
Japan						
National *of which*	34.5	35.3	31.7	34.3	−2.9	−3.7
Public	6.2	4.8	4.9	9.0	−1.3	−0.1
Household	13.3	17.9	15.3	13.7	2.0	−2.6
Corporate	14.9	12.3	11.2	11.2	−3.7	−1.1
Netherlands						
National *of which*	27.6	24.9	23.1	24.9	−4.5	−1.8
Public	4.6	3.3	−0.2	−0.5	−4.8	−3.5
Household	—	9.5	9.4	12.2	—	−0.1
Corporate	—	11.6	13.4	13.3	—	1.8
New Zealand						
National *of which*	21.2	22.2	20.1	18.1	−1.1	−2.1
Public	—	—	—	—	—	—
Household	—	—	—	—	—	—
Corporate	—	—	—	—	—	—

Table 9.2 GROSS SAVING AMONG OECD COUNTRIES (AS A PERCENTAGE OF GDP) (*Continued*)

					Change Between the Average in the 1980s and:	
	Average in the 1960s	Average in the 1970s	Average in the 1980s	Average 1990–1992	Average in the 1960s	Average in the 1970s
Norway						
National *of which*	27.4	26.8	27.7	23.5	0.3	0.9
Public	6.5	7.9	8.6	—	2.1	0.7
Household	—	5.9	4.1	—	—	−1.8
Corporate	—	12.7	15.0	—	—	2.3
Portugal						
National *of which*	23.1	26.0	24.3	25.9	1.2	−1.7
Public	—	−0.4	−1.7	—	—	−1.3
Household	—	—	25.4	—	—	—
Corporate	—	—	0.6	—	—	—
Spain						
National *of which*	24.7	25.5	21.1	20.9	−3.6	−4.4
Public	—	—	0.4	—	—	—
Household	—	—	8.6	—	—	—
Corporate	—	—	11.9	—	—	—
Sweden						
National *of which*	24.0	21.1	17.7	16.5	−6.3	−3.4
Public	—	—	2.1	—	—	—
Household	—	—	3.1	—	—	—
Corporate	—	—	11.9	—	—	—

Switzerland						
National *of which*	29.4	28.6	28.5	30.2	−0.9	−0.1
Public	4.5	3.9	3.6	1.2	−0.9	−0.3
Household	7.9	8.9	9.1	—	1.2	0.2
Corporate	17.1	15.9	15.8	—	−1.3	−0.1
Turkey						
National *of which*	14.8	17.1	19.3	19.8	4.5	2.2
Public	—	—	—	—	—	—
Household	—	—	—	—	—	—
Corporate	—	—	—	—	—	—
United Kingdom						
National *of which*	18.4	17.9	16.6	13.8	−1.8	−1.3
Public	3.6	2.6	0.5	−0.1	−3.1	−2.1
Public	5.4	6.2	6.2	7.1	0.8	0.0
Corporate	1.7	9.2	10.1	6.7	8.4	0.9
United States						
National *of which*	19.9	19.6	17.7	15.1	−2.2	−1.9
Public	1.9	0.4	−1.9	−2.9	−3.8	−2.5
Household	9.3	10.7	10.6	9.1	1.3	−0.1
Corporate	8.7	8.5	9.0	8.9	0.3	0.5

Source: OECD *National Accounts*, various years.

changes in saving/consumption behavior but also on the structure of the tax system.

The purpose of this paper is to explore the implications of tax policy for both public saving (reduction of government deficits, by repayment of reduction of planned borrowing) and private saving (mainly by households, since this is the dominant sector). In particular, can shifts in tax policy create enough private saving to overcome large public deficits or dissaving? Much of this paper is based on an extensive study by the OECD Committee on Fiscal Affairs (OECD 1994b).

DEFICITS AND SAVING

The connection between the two objectives of seeking to reduce government deficits and raising the level of saving is a complicated one, particularly when tax policy is one of the instruments being considered. The need to reduce a deficit often implies that taxes must increase. There are only three significant sources of tax revenue in OECD countries: labor income, consumption, and capital income. To date, it has not been possible for any country to generate significant revenues from new taxes on energy or raw materials.

At times of high unemployment, increasing the burden of tax on labor income, particularly at lower earnings levels, may be counterproductive if labor markets are inefficient (OECD 1994a, chapter 9). Increasing taxes on consumption may adversely affect demand, prolonging recession. Increasing taxes on capital income might reduce the level of private saving even further.

At the household level, many individuals find that after enforced early retirement, serious illness, or loss of employment, their private resources may be insufficient to maintain accustomed living standards and they may have to rely on state benefits that are often intended to meet only basic needs. Given continuing levels of high unemployment, this has become a chronic problem and has raised important concerns about how to balance the composition of saving between, for instance, long-term contractual plans and liquid investments. It may be little consolation to a household head who is suddenly unemployed that he or she will benefit from a generous pension—in cases where retirement age is a long way off, available savings are not readily available, and it is not possible to borrow against future pension rights.

THE TAXATION OF CAPITAL INCOME AND ITS EFFECT ON SAVING

In many countries investment income was taxed in the past at very high effective rates, particularly while exchange controls were in force, so that investment outside the country of residence was tightly restricted. When macroeconomic policy focused on stimulating demand, saving was often effectively discouraged. In some cases, investment income was taxed at higher progressive rates than labor income, on the grounds of redistribution (equating investment incomes with greater ability to pay) or because labor income was considered exposed to greater risk (e.g., from unemployment). At the same time, long-term saving associated with provision for old age was granted generous tax privileges. With the abolition of exchange controls and the opening up of financial markets and opportunities for overseas investment, however, there has been a tendency to reduce effective tax rates on many non-retirement types of saving.

For many OECD countries, new foreign investment opportunities have led to dramatic increases in gross cross-border flows over a short period. Table 9.3 shows gross inflows and outflows of direct investment for 1986, 1989, and 1991. Most smaller countries have experienced dramatic changes since opening up their markets. Although there are almost no reliable data on flows of portfolio investment, it seems likely—both on *a priori* grounds and in light of certain countries' experiences—that the location of portfolio investment is highly sensitive to changes in domestic tax policy.

New budget expenditures require new sources of tax revenue or borrowing, or both. Higher tax rates on domestic saving may produce some revenue but drive mobile capital abroad, reducing funds for domestic investment and making taxes more difficult to collect. If taxes, in fact, discourage saving, there may be adverse effects on capital formation. Many countries have responded to this dilemma by willingly reducing or eliminating taxes on saving in various forms. Countries that wish to continue to raise tax revenues from investment income (for example, Belgium and Germany), whether by withholding taxes at source or by imposing a general income tax, have found it very difficult to do so in the face of tax competition from other countries and information constraints. The allocation of savings among assets by households is likely to be influenced by the fact that in all countries certain forms of saving receive more favorable tax treatment than others, whether due to deliberate policy or simply because the

Table 9.3 GROSS CROSS-BORDER DIRECT INVESTMENT FLOWS OF OECD COUNTRIES: 1986, 1989, AND 1991 (MILLIONS OF U.S. DOLLARS)

	1986		1989		1991	
Country	Outflow	Inflow	Outflow	Inflow	Outflow	Inflow
Australia	3,419	3,457	2,831	7,289	2,026	4,763
Austria	313	182	855	578	1,288	359
Belgium/Luxembourg[a]	1,627	631	6,114	6,731	6,068	8,923
Canada	4,066	990	4,603	2,027	3,840	5,141
Denmark	646	161	2,027	1,084	1,851	1,530
Finland	810	340	3,106	488	1,064	−247
France[a]	5,230	2,749	18,137	9,552	20,529	11,073
Germany[a]	9,621	1,191	14,538	7,126	22,334	3,178
Greece	N/A	471	N/A	752	N/A	1,135
Iceland[a]	2	8	8	−27	10	35
Ireland	N/A	−43	N/A	85	N/A	97
Italy[a]	2,661	−15	2,003	2,529	6,672	2,542
Japan[a]	14,480	226	44,130	−1,054	30,726	1,368
Netherlands	3,147	1,861	11,538	6,367	11,976	5,058
New Zealand	87	390	135	434	528	1,724
Norway	1,605	1,023	1,352	1,511	1,842	−379
Portugal	−2	242	85	1,740	474	2,451
Spain[a]	457	3,442	1,470	8,424	3,571	10,422
Sweden	3,707	939	9,738	1,523	6,751	5,727
Switzerland	1,461	1,778	7,852	2,254	4,502	1,996
Turkey	N/A	125	56	663	53	783
United Kingdom	17,119	8,557	35,191	30,369	17,865	21,141
United States	18,679	36,145	30,167	69,010	28,197	12,619
TOTAL	89,135	64,850	195,936	159,455	172,167	101,439

Source: *OECD International Direct Investment Statistics Yearbook 1993*, compiled from national statistics.
a. Reinvested earnings not included in national statistics.

more mobile forms of saving (such as financial capital that can be invested abroad) are hard to tax. While tax relief for specific types of saving might possibly stimulate the overall level of saving, it may do so at the expense of an efficient allocation of saving, particularly when restrictions are placed on the manner in which tax-preferred savings can be invested and the extent to which they can be invested abroad. Conversely, countries may use certain forms of tax relief specifically to attract savings from abroad. In addition to efficiency considerations, questions arise concerning the implications of various types of relief for equity, administrative simplicity, and transparency of countries' tax systems.

The purpose of a recent OECD report (1994b) was to consider the available evidence to answer the following questions:

- Does taxation actually affect the level of national saving?
- What principles should govern tax policy toward household saving?
- To what extent does taxation affect the composition of household saving?
- What tax incentives are offered to encourage different types of saving?
- What can we say about the effects of the tax incentives used?
- What alternative non-tax measures are used in OECD countries and what are their advantages?
- What is the cost of tax incentives to various types of saving in terms of tax revenue forgone?
- To what extent does the interaction between OECD countries' tax systems affect the global allocation of saving?
- How might the tax treatment of saving be changed in OECD member countries in order to improve the national and global allocation of saving in a way that benefits all countries?

In considering government budget deficits, the first question above—does taxation affect the level of national saving?—is conceptually the most important. There are three possible answers to this question. First, assuming that pre-tax rates of return to households remain constant (as in a small, open economy), if the government cuts taxes on capital income in the hope of stimulating saving, households might simply hold consumption constant, reinvesting their additional after-tax capital income. National saving would thus remian constant because the fall in tax revenue (public saving) would exactly equal the increase in household net assets (private saving). Second, households might increase consumption, spending at least a part of their additional after-tax income. As long as households did not spend all their additional post-tax income, national saving would fall while household saving would rise. Finally, attracted by the higher after-tax yield, households might choose to consume less, saving more of their labor income, resulting in a rise in national saving.

The findings of a majority of empirical studies suggest that the last of these three scenarios is the least likely. The principal effect of tax cuts on capital income is to transfer assets from the government to the private sector, with an increase in the government deficit at best matched by an increase in household saving. However, it is difficult to generalize across all types of capital tax cuts; for instance, if the tax cuts were selective by type of savings asset, the effect of tax reductions might cause shifting of assets more than anything else.

This general conclusion is confirmed by Gylfason (1993), who summarizes the results of 24 empirical studies between 1967 and 1992, including those by Hall (1988), and Blinder. As a summary of about half the studies, Gylfason quotes Blinder's view that ". . . there is *zero* evidence that tax incentives that enhance the rate of return on saving actually boost the national saving rate. *None*. *No* evidence. Economists now accept that as a consensus view." These studies cited by Gylfason and the OECD (1994b) report that claim to find a positive relationship between tax rates and saving find only a modest relationship: each percentage point increase in the after-tax rate of return typically results in a 0.5 to 0.7 percentage point increase in the ratio of aggregate saving to GNP. These studies include Wright (1967, 1969); Juster and Wachtel (1972); Boskin (1978); Gylfason (1981); Mankiw, Rotemberg, and Summers (1985); and Barro (1992). Even if one accepted these latter, minority results, abolishing capital income taxes entirely would make only a small dent in currently observed government deficits.

THE EFFECTS OF TAX POLICY ON HOUSEHOLD SAVING

The OECD (1994b) report concludes that there is no clear evidence of significant tax effects on household saving. Whether tax incentives make a difference to overall levels of household saving in a particular country at a given time depends on many other factors including wealth effects, expected inflation, the availability of public and private pension schemes, and consumer credit.

When considering tax effects on the *composition* of household saving, however, the empirical evidence is striking. The literature is relatively small, due primarily to the lack of data sets of good quality, but shows that there are two well-known ways in which taxes may affect portfolio composition. First, differences in effective tax rates may lead to some portfolio specialization. That is, households facing lower marginal tax rates may hold a greater proportion of more heavily taxed assets than those facing higher tax rates, which hold a greater proportion of tax-exempt or tax-privileged assets. Second, taxes affect the trade-off between risk and return, although their impact on demand for risky assets is theoretically ambiguous. For example, Feldstein (1976, p. 648) led the way with his study of 1962 Federal Reserve Board data for the United States, concluding that, "The personal income tax has a very powerful effect on individuals' demands for portfolio assets, after adjusting for the effects of net worth, age, sex, and the ratio of human to non-human capital." However, there was a major technical defect in his study: in considering the decision to hold observed amounts of particular assets, Feldstein excluded all households not holding those assets, inducing sample selection bias and ignoring the "spillover" effect. This last refers to the fact that the proportion of an individual's wealth invested in a particular asset depends on the combination of assets in the portfolio.

In the early 1980s there appeared a series of studies based on large micro-data sets that used Heckman's (1979) procedure to overcome the limitations of Feldstein's study. The most important of these works are those by Dicks-Mireaux and King (1983) using 1977 data for Canada; King and Leape (1984) using 1978 data for the United States; Hubbard (1985) using 1979 data from a different source for the United States; and Agell and Edin (1990) using 1979 data for Sweden. Each study used a wide variety of explanatory variables but all found qualitatively similar and significant effects of the tax rate on portfolio composition. It is evident from the data used by these studies that in all countries most households choose to hold only a small number of available types of savings assets. The first stage in the model used for each of these four studies, therefore, is for each household to decide whether to hold a particular asset at all—a discrete choice that will depend on information and transaction costs, and on constraints on negative holdings (e.g., short-selling) of many assets, as discussed in Auerbach and King (1983). The second stage is the choice of how much of an asset to hold.

Each of the studies cited finds strong effects of taxes on the decision concerning whether to hold an asset (that is, the first stage). The influence of taxation on the decision concerning how much to invest in a particular asset (the second stage) is less clear cut. Indeed, almost all of the first stage estimates are statistically significant, suggesting the importance of taxes. However, few of the estimates, apart from the Canadian case, find any significant relationship between tax rates and the proportion of each particular asset in total net assets.

Not all the results in these studies are easy to explain in terms of a simple theory of household behavior, and since each data set is very heterogeneous, analysis of subgroups might give a richer picture. It is also clear that each country's tax system (for example, interest deductibility and other means of sheltering taxable income) and other institutional features are important, as discussed in detail for the United States by Steuerle (1985, 1990). However, given this heterogeneity, the fact that tax rate effects are so significant is impressive.

One would expect the principal effect of introducing new tax incentives for specific types of saving to be a displacement from other forms of saving, particularly if other close saving substitutes are not readily available. The efficiency cost could thus be high unless such special schemes are carefully targeted, which may be very difficult given the complications of trying to decide what is "new" saving. Even if an increase in short-run saving is achieved, this will not be carried over into the medium term, to the extent that planned saving is simply brought forward to take advantage of the reliefs. This is indeed what Steuerle (1990) finds in many cases, and, of course, *a fortiori* such "saving" does not translate into new investment.

However, there is some recent evidence that tax concessions *may* have a significant effect in stimulating overall household saving in particular circumstances. To be compatible with the previous result—little connection between consumption and the rate of tax return—this would have to mean that the mechanism involved was rather different or that special features applied. Indeed, "Registered Retirement Savings Plans" in Canada and "Section 401(k)" plans in the United States (Kusko, Poterba, and Wilcox 1994) both involve generous tax concessions to saving for retirement, but are also associated with high-profile information campaigns and matching employer contributions. The effect that these plans have on savers may be due not simply to the enhanced rate of return but to a "something for nothing" attitude—an opportunity too good to miss in a situation where there are no close saving substitutes.

TAX NEUTRALITY IN THEORY AND PRACTICE

As an alternative approach to *ad hoc* tax concessions that distort household saving decisions, a desire for neutrality in the taxation of saving has led many economists to argue for a pure comprehensive income tax (CIT) or expenditure tax (ET) treatment. By comprehensively treating all saving alike, distortions among assets would disappear, even while the tax base was converted from income to consumption. Few countries come even close to these idealized forms, but two other approaches that have many of the attractions of the ideals while being easier to operate have already been applied. These two approaches are tax-free savings accounts and flat rate taxes on investment income. Under the ET and tax-free savings account principles, interest income is not taxed; under the CIT principles, interest income (unless saved) is taxed at the same rate as labor income; and under the flat rate tax concept, interest income is taxed at a single, positive rate determined independently of taxes on labor income.

Causes of Variation

The OECD (1994b) report describes the tax regime for five basic assets: bank deposits, government bonds, direct share purchases, pensions, and owner-occupied housing. Tax rates turn out to vary dramatically both within and across OECD countries. Taxes affect three points at which tax may be assessed: acquisition of the asset, the holding period, and asset disposal. At the first of these steps, the main issues are whether the cost is deductible from the income tax base, whether any transaction taxes are payable, and whether the interest cost of borrowing to finance acquisition is tax-deductible. Over the holding period, the obvious question is whether income arising is subject to withholding tax and, if so, whether the tax is final (often at the taxpayer's option, so that the withholding tax rate is an upper bound) or creditable against income tax at progressive rates. In some countries it is also necessary to consider the treatment of accruals of gain (or, conceivably, changes in market value). On disposal there are several possibilities. The tax base may be the whole disposal proceeds or just the gain over cost (in each case possibly modified to take account of inflation); or the taxable amount may be added to income and taxed at normal rates or subject to a special tax at lower rates or at a flat rate. The "normal" tax regimes for each of these assets vary greatly across OECD countries, although in some cases there are clear modes.

The tax treatment of pensions and owner-occupied housing in OECD countries has traditionally been much more generous than other forms of household saving, because these assets are associated with provision for old age. While it seems clear that many countries are concerned about the disparity of tax treatment of different forms of saving, politically it has been very difficult to increase effective tax rates on such long-term investments. In the case of pensions, almost all countries permit deduction from income tax of contributions to approved pension plans, most of which are exempt from tax on their income. In addition to these exemptions, amounts withdrawn at pensionable age (as lump sums or annuities) are often tax-free or taxed at especially low rates.

At first sight, tax treatment of housing is often as generous as that for pensions, although for different reasons. In several countries, interest is tax deductible on borrowing for house purchase and seven countries allow some form of relief for capital cost. Where imputed income—that is, the rent saving that is achieved by owning housing—is taxed on the owner-occupier, the value assessed is below market rental value, and most countries that tax capital gains on disposal of assets exempt much of the gain, at least on first homes. However, high transaction taxes and local property taxes significantly increase the tax burden on housing, bringing it closer in line with the tax burden on other assets.

There appears to be no clear trend in the taxation of savings in recent years. Many countries have reduced tax rates, lowering, in particular, withholding taxes on interest at source, or have introduced flat rate or tax-free schemes for particular kinds of saving. However, some countries (Austria, Germany, and Italy) have introduced or increased certain withholding taxes and many have removed or restricted exemptions or tax deductions for interest expenses.

Denmark, Finland, Norway, and Sweden have moved their tax systems toward flat rate taxes on capital income, to greater or lesser extents, although in 1994 Denmark proposed to move back in the direction of a CIT as a result of lower levels of inflation. Radical reforms have also been put into effect in Ireland and Portugal to reduce differences in the taxation of different types of saving. Germany, Ireland, and Italy have shown interest in using withholding taxes to limit evasion of tax on capital income. It is apparent that pressures driving change in the taxation of savings differ in intensity across OECD countries.

Variation by Country

Using the well-known King-Fullerton methodological framework (King and Fullerton 1984), it is in principle not difficult to calculate marginal effective tax rates for each of these assets in each country. In the OECD (1994b) report this has been done for two hypothetical individuals: the "average production worker" (APW), whose situation is examined in an annual OECD publication (1994c), and a "top rate taxpayer," liable at the top marginal rates of each relevant tax, thus representing an upper bound. The results, calculated using tax and actual inflation rates as of January 1993, are shown in table 9.4.

As seen in that table, in most countries the tax burden on bank deposits and on government bonds issued at par does not differ greatly, but in some countries (Greece, Italy, Turkey) special provisions result in significantly lower tax burden on government bonds. Furthermore, in most countries bonds issued at a significant discount at par are taxed more lightly, because gains are taxed at lower rates than interest income. However, looking first at the position of the APW, tax rates on bank deposits at rates of inflation are generally very high compared to tax rates on labor income (not shown).

In the case of direct share purchases, although it is not obvious from this table, the tax rates levied at the personal level are generally much lower than the rates on interest income. Many differences are due to alternative integration systems—with lower overall taxes usually in countries that try to avoid taxing income twice at both the corporate and personal levels. As shown in table 9.4, for pensions, the four different cases reflect treatment of premiums paid (tax deductible or not) and pension payments received. Negative tax rates can be achieved by an average production worker in 12 countries.

The case of housing is slightly different because it is the asset for which most savers borrow. For comparability, the figures presented in table 9.4 assume a marginal purchase financed entirely by equity. Without debt, tax rates for housing are in most cases noticeably lower than those for interest income (not shown), reflecting zero or low income taxes on imputed income, and capital gains exempt or taxed at lower effective rates than income (Germany actually has very negative rates overall).

In the last ten years most countries have enacted major reforms in the taxation of capital income. Many have reduced marginal income tax rates or introduced flat rate taxes. However, effective marginal rates on interest income remain disconcertingly high (not shown), particularly compared to saving in the form of pension funds or owner-occupied housing. Effective tax rates on direct holdings of shares are also generally high if corporate and personal taxes are taken into account.

Governments concerned about both a wide dispersion of tax rates across assets and high marginal tax rates on more liquid forms of saving could have reacted in several different ways. They might have indexed capital income to inflation or introduced separate, lower schedules of marginal rates or further reduced flat rate taxes. Instead, many have followed variations on one particular theme, namely introducing special tax thresholds, below which the effective tax rate is zero.

SPECIAL INCENTIVE SCHEMES TO ENCOURAGE HOUSEHOLD SAVING

As seen above, bank deposits, bonds, and direct share purchases are generally taxed more heavily than pensions and housing, and the tax burden on interest rises dramatically with the level of inflation. In the

Table 9.4 MARGINAL EFFECTIVE TAX RATES BY ASSET, PERSONAL TAX RATE: AVERAGE PRODUCTION WORKER (APW) CASE, AND TOP RATE

			Government Bonds							
	Bank Deposits		Deep Discount Short Term		Deep Discount Long Term		Issued at Par		Direct Share Purchases	
Country	APW	Top Rate	APW	Top Rate	APW	Top Rate	APW	Top Rate	APW	Top Rate
Australia	42.8	52.3	41.6	51.1	40.7	50.1	41.6	51.1	37.3	45.9
Austria	39.3	39.3	43.7	50.1	32.2	32.5	40.1	40.1	6.9	31.1
Belgium	15.5	15.5	18.3	18.3	15.4	15.4	18.3	18.3	10.6	10.6
Canada	57.8	69.3	46.2	65.9	46.2	64.5	57.8	69.3	13.8	48.2
Denmark	67.6	95.1	54.1	80.3	54.1	80.3	67.6	95.1	18.6	44.6
Finland	28.2	28.2	29.6	29.6	28.4	28.4	28.2	28.2	29.0	48.4
France	38.8	83.9	20.7	55.7	20.7	54.9	25.9	55.3	10.0	68.3
Germany	53.6	107.3	42.9	87.9	42.9	87.9	53.6	107.3	9.7	28.0
Greece	52.8	52.8	0.0	0.0	0.0	0.0	0.0	0.0	0.0	0.0
Iceland	0.0	0.0	0.0	0.0	0.0	0.0	0.0	0.0	3.3	67.7
Ireland	39.1	69.6	31.3	55.7	31.3	55.7	39.1	69.6	34.7	42.0
Italy	56.9	56.9	19.0	19.0	19.0	19.0	23.7	23.7	11.8	17.4
Japan	25.1	25.1	25.2	25.2	24.0	24.0	25.7	25.7	10.7	15.7
Luxembourg	0.0	97.7	0.0	80.2	0.0	80.2	0.0	97.7	10.2	28.2
Netherlands	57.1	104.9	45.7	87.3	45.7	87.3	57.1	104.9	12.8	36.5
New Zealand	30.2	41.5	30.2	41.5	29.2	40.3	30.2	41.5	8.0	11.0
Norway	41.7	67.0	41.7	67.4	40.2	66.3	41.7	67.0	21.3	42.5
Portugal	51.0	51.0	40.8	40.8	40.8	40.8	51.0	51.0	7.2	7.2
Spain	49.6	118.1	49.6	118.2	47.3	114.8	49.6	118.1	21.6	57.2
Sweden	56.9	104.7	56.9	92.0	54.6	90.1	56.9	91.3	40.8	80.2
Switzerland	36.4	74.0	32.1	62.6	29.7	60.2	39.3	76.9	7.7	16.9
Turkey	89.1	89.1	7.1	7.1	1.4	1.4	6.3	6.3	1.6	1.6
United Kingdom	33.4	53.4	33.4	53.4	32.3	51.9	33.4	53.4	10.0	37.6
United States	36.9	75.2	27.0	67.0	25.5	59.8	24.6	64.9	29.0	48.7

Table 9.4 MARGINAL EFFECTIVE TAX RATES BY ASSET, PERSONAL TAX RATE (*Continued*)

	Pensions								Owner-Occupied Housing Financed Entirely by Equity			
	Deductible Premiums				Nondeductible Premiums							
	Standard Tax Payout		Lower Tax Payout		Standard Tax Payout		Lower Tax Payout		No Local Taxes		With Local Property Taxes	
Country	APW	Top Rate	APW	Top Rate	APW	Top Rate	APW	Top Rate	APW	Top Rate	APW	Top Rate
Australia	−7.9	−30.6	−33.0	−55.9	25.8	25.8	14.2	14.2	6.2	6.2	26.9	26.9
Austria	−12.5	−21.4	−16.3	−28.5	11.9	18.9	8.2	11.9	9.7	15.2	11.8	18.3
Belgium	52.4	60.8	−24.3	−49.1	n.a.	n.a.	n.a.	n.a.	26.7	26.7	35.9	35.9
Canada	0.0	0.0	−36.0	−41.2	n.a.	n.a.	n.a.	n.a.	2.1	2.1	12.4	12.4
Denmark	15.6	15.6	−35.3	−76.9	n.a.	n.a.	n.a.	n.a.	27.7	51.3	38.0	61.6
Finland	31.6	31.6	n.a.	n.a.	n.a.	n.a.	n.a.	n.a.	11.4	29.1	n.a.	n.a.
France	0.0	30.3	−10.0	−6.1	43.8	152.7	34.0	118.4	16.5	47.5	22.7	53.7
Germany	0.0	0.0	−21.4	n.a.	n.a.	0.0	n.a.	n.a.	−18.8	−37.4	−14.4	−32.8
Greece	n.a.	n.a.	n.a.	n.a.	n.a.	n.a.	n.a.	n.a.	57.0	116.3	n.a.	n.a.
Iceland	n.a.	n.a.	n.a.	n.a.	73.4	73.4	n.a.	n.a.	1.4	48.7	9.7	56.9
Ireland	−10.4	−27.2	−42.2	−58.6	n.a.	n.a.	n.a.	n.a.	11.4	41.0	n.a.	n.a.
Italy	n.a.	n.a.	n.a.	n.a.	n.a.	n.a.	n.a.	n.a.	16.1	19.5	27.0	30.4
Japan	n.a.	n.a.	n.a.	n.a.	17.9	49.7	8.7	22.8	20.8	22.4	38.2	39.7
Luxembourg	0.0	0.0	−27.4	−62.4	22.6	42.3	10.9	19.6	16.3	16.5	31.8	32.0
Netherlands	0.0	0.0	−36.0	n.a.	41.1	70.5	20.5	n.a.	25.5	42.8	32.3	49.6
New Zealand	n.a.	n.a.	n.a.	n.a.	56.2	56.2	37.9	37.9	0.0	0.0	n.a.	n.a.
Norway	34.9	33.7	n.a.	n.a.	45.5	45.5	n.a.	n.a.	9.5	15.6	42.5	17.6
Portugal	−6.6	−12.8	−34.4	−62.5	33.5	57.9	6.1	9.9	10.3	20.7	33.1	43.4
Spain	0.0	0.0	n.a.	n.a.	39.0	111.9	n.a.	n.a.	21.0	52.7	33.4	65.1
Sweden	17.9	17.9	n.a.	n.a.	17.9	17.9	n.a.	n.a.	23.8	61.0	46.5	83.7
Switzerland	1.4	1.4	n.a.	n.a.	35.4	78.6	n.a.	n.a.	17.2	32.3	19.3	34.4
Turkey	n.a.	n.a.	n.a.	n.a.	n.a.	n.a.	n.a.	n.a.	26.9	26.9	34.6	34.6
United Kingdom	−10.2	−20.7	n.a.	−41.8	26.6	26.6	n.a.	n.a.	2.4	2.4	n.a.	n.a.
United States	0.0	0.0	n.a.	n.a.	n.a.	n.a.	n.a.	n.a.	0.0	0.0	18.4	12.8

absence of indexation provisions, many countries in recent years have introduced special tax incentives to encourage saving in forms that would otherwise be relatively heavily taxed. The motive may not be solely to encourage household saving; several countries cite the encouragement of wider share ownership as a reason for granting tax concessions for dividends and capital gains on equities.

Tax Relief for Interest Income

Because the effective tax rate on interest income is very high even when inflation is at modest levels, many countries now tax interest on bank deposits or government bonds at flat rates. These flat rates are below the progressive marginal income tax rates that apply to earned income. This course is of greater benefit to investors with higher marginal rates of tax and higher incomes. A small number of countries, therefore, have instead adopted limited exemption schemes.

In France, interest payable on a "PEP" (*plan d'épargne populaire*) is exempt from tax. Interest on some other types of accounts is also exempt up to a ceiling, such as the first savings deposit account and accounts for industrial development. In the United Kingdom, "TESSAs" (tax-exempt special saving accounts) were introduced in January 1991. Interest is free from tax provided that the deposit remains in a designated account for five years. A simpler approach, adopted by the Netherlands, is to exempt a fixed amount of interest income from all sources.

For many years, some countries have operated similar schemes whereby the deposit is earmarked for specific purpose such as house purchase. However, since this form of subsidy benefits only taxpayers, non-tax incentives may be used to provide a flat rate benefit—either univerally, instead of tax relief, or exclusively to non-taxpayers, alongside tax relief (see discussion below).

Tax Relief for Investment in Shares

Several schemes allow privileged treatment of investment in shares in order to encourage issues of new equity to individuals and to widen share ownership. The first kind of scheme gives tax relief on purchases of shares, up to the full purchase price including transaction costs, and operates in many countries according to conditions on the shares themselves. Usually only newly issued equity in approved, domestic resident companies qualifies.

Many countries that tax long-term capital gains exempt from tax some shares, subject to various ceilings and conditions. A small number of countries that subject dividends to income tax allow special tax exemptions up to a ceiling. Very similar schemes have operated in the United Kingdom since 1986 (personal equity plans) and in France since 1992 (*plans d'épargne en actions*). In each case, subject to annual limits on the amount that can be invested, the income and any capital gains from the investment are exempt from tax, with the dividend imputation credit being refunded by the government. Some other countries have an exemption or lower tax rate limit that applies to the amount of annual dividends received rather than to the amount of the investment.

Non-tax Incentives

Non-tax incentives take many different forms that vary across OECD countries. These incentives are usually made available in the place of tax relief, so that the benefit to all individuals—taxpayers or not—is at the same marginal rate. Occasionally a non-tax incentive may operate alongside tax relief, providing a subsidy to non-taxpayers only, usually at the lowest positive rate of tax.

In general, threshold schemes that have proven popular as a means of relieving interest income from a high effective tax rate may not be able to ensure that each taxpayer benefits from only one threshold (that is, does not open several accounts), although it is too early to judge the level of successful enforcement. Clearly, such schemes cannot encourage saving by non-taxpayers. If interest rates offered under these special schemes fall somewhat, non-taxpayers could even be discouraged from saving. Moreover, because of the low level of the thresholds, these schemes are unlikely to be of great interest to very high income individuals.

INTERNATIONAL ISSUES

Although the principal source of capital for OECD countries remains domestic savings rather than investment by foreigners, this trend has weakened since the early 1980s, particularly within the European Community. There are specific reasons for this change, including large public sector deficits, especially in the United States. But many countries have removed capital controls, allowing financial markets to become more globally integrated.

If in international capital markets capital income would be taxed only by residence of owners, the taxation of saving would not affect the level of investment. German investors, for instance, would be indifferent to the effects of the British tax system on its own residents; these German investors, therefore, would be influenced primarily by the rate of return available on the British investment. Very different results follow if taxation of capital income occurs at the country of source, rather than the country of the residence of the owner. In that case, international investors will demand that the same after-tax rate of return be available no matter the country of source in which they place their saving. Taxation of saving then would tend to increase domestic interest rates and reduce domestic investment.

In simple models, the world is better off with integrated capital markets. Trade in capital goods is made easier for those both buying and selling that capital. Nonetheless, it is possible for some countries to try to use the tax system to collect more than a "fair" share of total taxes or to attract saving from abroad—at least as long as the other countries do not reciprocate. Even without these discriminatory tax measures, true neutrality in the ways that capital is allocated among countries may not be achievable because of conflicting claims among countries on the allocation of international investment.

A pressing issue at present is that much interest income may be escaping tax altogether, as a result of deposits being placed with banks overseas, which is exacerbating the budget deficits of several countries as well as raising issues of horizontal equity among different taxpayers. Many OECD countries have no withholding tax on interest, and many of those that do, exempt non-resident individuals under domestic law or treaty arrangements, thereby attracting savings from abroad. Because of practical limitations on the operation of exchange of information arrangements, much of this income may not be declared or reported to the tax authorities in the country of residence. This is certainly suggested by recent Belgian and German experiences with withholding taxes on interest, and has prompted calls for a general withholding tax at the OECD level on most payments of interest to individuals. These two countries, respectively, had to reduce and withdraw withholding taxes on interest to stem the flight of cash deposits to neighboring countries with no domestic withholding tax applied to non-residents. If a common withholding tax were introduced and, as a matter either of law or practice, was final, then the source basis of taxation would apply. It is apparent that the possibility of coordination, combining the threat of withholding taxes with improved exchange of information, should be reconsidered.

CONCLUSION

There is no clear evidence that the level of taxation, along with other factors affecting the rate of return, *does* affect the level of household saving. Some research claims to find a positive relationship, and some a negative one; most studies have concluded that there is no discernible or only a moderate effect. At first this might seem surprising; certainly the enthusiasm for cuts in taxes on capital income among so many OECD member governments in the 1980s might suggest a conviction that household saving would increase as tax rates were reduced.

Even if one accepts the result of the minority of studies that claim to find a positive saving response to tax cuts, it is clear that abolishing remaining taxes on capital income entirely would have, at best, a modest net effect on aggregate national saving. If this action resulted in loss of tax revenue, it would cause the government budget situation to deteriorate further. However, tax-reducing policies could be justified on alternative grounds. Some consumption tax advocates, for instance, believe that these taxes would be fairer or simpler than an income tax. In a number of countries (most notably the United Kingdom and the United States), it was argued in the 1980s that resources were likely to be more efficiently used in the private than in the public sector. According to this argument, even if the level of saving does not increase, reducing taxes to leave greater post-tax income in the hands of households leads to better allocation of resources. There may be other good reasons for wishing to reduce taxes on certain types of saving. In most countries, pensions and, to a lesser extent, owner-occupied housing, have received and continue to receive favorable tax treatment.

The empirical studies referred to above show that, even if taxes do not affect the overall level of household savings, they do have an important effect on the decisions of households about *how* to save. Where data are available for OECD countries, it appears that pensions and housing dominate household saving. However, in many cases the effective tax rate on pensions is negative. This occurs wherever saving is tax-deductible, the pension is tax-exempt, and the return to pensioners is either not taxed in full or is taxed at lower rates than those at which the contributions were originally deducted. In such cases there is an effective subsidy and so, for a given level of government expenditure, tax rates on the remaining tax base will be higher than they would otherwise be. Also, many tax systems allow gaming by taxpayers who deduct interest on one side of the ledger and exempt income on the other side.

With free movement of capital between countries, domestic saving need not equal domestic investment. Neutrality in international allocation of savings cannot be achieved because of conflicting claims on that allocation. Many OECD countries have given up their domestic and treaty rights to tax at source and do not withhold tax on interest paid to non-residents. This is mainly because savings are geographically mobile and, therefore, easily moved to low-tax jurisdictions. As a result of inadequate exchange of information among countries, much interest income may currently be escaping tax completely.

If tax measures are introduced to encourage saving in particular assets, these measures must be carefully targeted to avoid simply increasing budget deficits. If tax measures to encourage saving in a particular asset are introduced because of perceived risk of that asset, but do not result in a reduction of that risk, the motivation for using tax measures is unclear.

It is inevitable that governments face conflicting objectives of limiting tax distortions in saving, reducing government deficits, and limiting other distortions from taxation. A desire to minimize only the distortionary effect of taxation on saving and investment decisions suggests that zero effective tax rates are appropriate. But implementing zero rates means either the growth of government deficits or lost tax revenue being raised from somewhere else. If the consequence of exempting all capital income from tax is that taxes on labor are higher than they would otherwise be, this result will also raise important concerns over equity and efficiency. In sum, the clearest route to attacking the savings problem created by deficits is to reduce the deficits themselves—not to depend on tax changes to achieve an offsetting increase in private saving.

References

Agell, J., and P.A. Edin. 1990. "Marginal Taxes and the Asset Portfolios of Swedish Households." *Scandinavian Journal of Economics* 92: 47–64.

Auerbach, A.J., and M.A. King. 1983. "Taxation Portfolio Choice and Debt-Equity Ratios: A General Equilibrium Model." *Quarterly Journal of Economics* 98: 587–609.

Barro, R.J. 1992. "World Interest Rates and Investment." *Scandinavian Journal of Economics* 94, 2: 323–34.

Boskin, M.J. 1978. "Taxation, Saving and the Rate of Interest." *Journal of Political Economy* 86, 2: S3–S227.

Dicks-Mireaux, L.D.L., and M.A. King. 1983. "Portfolio Composition and Pension Wealth: An Econometric Study." In *Financial Aspects of the United States Pension System*, eds. Z. Bodie and J.B. Shoven. Chicago, Il: University of Chicago Press.

Feldstein, M.S. 1976. "Personal Taxation and Portfolio Composition: An Econometric Analysis." *Econometrica* 44: 631–50.

Gylfason, T. 1993. "Optimal Saving, Interest Rates and Endogenous Growth." *Scandinavian Journal of Economics* 95, 4: 517–33.

________. 1981. "Interest Rates, Inflation and the Aggregate Consumption Function." *Review of Economics and Statistics* 63, 2: 233–45.

Hall, R.E. 1988. "Intertemporal Substitution in Consumption." *Journal of Political Economy* 96, 2: 339–57.

Heckman, J.J. 1979. "Sample Selection Bias as a Specification Error." *Econometrica* 47: 153–62.

Hubbard, R.G. 1985. "Personal Taxation, Pension Wealth and Portfolio Composition." *Review of Economics and Statistics*: 53–60.

Juster, F.T., and P. Wachtel. 1972. "A Note on Inflation and the Saving Rate." *Brookings Papers on Economic Activity* 3: 765–68.

King, M.A., and D. Fullerton. 1984. *Taxation of Income from Capital: A Comparative Study of the United States, United Kingdom, Sweden and West Germany*. Chicago: University of Chicago Press.

King, M.A., and J.I. Leape. 1984. "Wealth and Portfolio Composition: Theory and Evidence." NBER Working Paper No. 1468. National Bureau of Economic Research, Cambridge, Ma.

Kusko, A.L., J.M. Poterba, and D.W. Wilcox. 1994. "Employee Decisions with Respect to 401(k) Plans: Evidence from Individual-level Data." NBER Working Paper No. 4635, National Bureau of Economic Research, Cambridge, Ma.

Mankiw, N.G., J.J. Rotemberg, and L.H. Summers. 1985. "Intertemporal Substitution in Macroeconomics." *Quarterly Journal of Economics* 99, 1: 225–51.

OECD (Organization for Economic Co-operation and Development). 1994a. *The OECD Jobs Study: Evidence and Explanations*. Paris: OECD.

________. 1994b. *Taxation and Household Saving*. Paris: OECD.

________. 1994c. *The Tax/Benefit Position of Production Workers: Annual Report 1990–1993*. Paris: OECD.

Steuerle, C.E. 1990. "Federal Policy and the Accumulation of Private Debt." In *Debt, Taxes and Restructuring*, eds. J.B. Shoven and J. Waldfogel. Washington, D.C.: The Brookings Institution.

________. 1985. *Taxes, Loans and Inflation*. Washington, D.C.: The Brookings Institution.

Wright, C. 1969. "Saving and the Rate of Interest." In *The Taxation of Income from Capital*, eds. A.C. Harberger and M.J. Bailey. Washington, D.C.: The Brookings Institution.

________. 1967. "Some Evidence on the Interest Elasticity of Consumption." *American Economic Review* 57, 4: 850–54.

Chapter Ten

FISCAL DEFICIT AND PUBLIC DEBT IN INDUSTRIAL COUNTRIES, 1970–1994

Vito Tanzi and Domenico Fanizza

Since the early 1980s much attention has been paid to the fiscal situation, and especially to the fiscal deficit, of industrial countries. The fiscal deficit has been blamed for many economic difficulties including inflation, slow growth, unemployment, low investment, balance of payments disequilibria, and high real interest rates. Some economists, on the other hand, have considered the fiscal deficit a largely irrelevant variable. Not until the mid-1980s did the growth in the share of public debt as a percentage of GDP also gain notice. A 1984 speech by then managing director of the International Monetary Fund, Jacques de Larosière, calling attention to this growth, was widely reported in economic magazines and newspapers.[1]

Much of the focus over the years has been country-specific, dealing frequently with the United States or with countries such as Belgium or Italy, where the fiscal situation was an obvious cause for concern. Difficulty in assembling relevant data has discouraged most experts from attempting to deal with groups of countries such as the G-7 or the industrial countries. However, the fluidity of capital movements, which has made it increasingly possible for deficit countries to finance their fiscal deficits with the savings of other countries, implies that the country-by-country approach can fruitfully be complemented by more aggregative studies.[2]

The aim of this paper is both modest and ambitious: to try to assemble as complete a set of relevant fiscal data—for individual countries and for groups of countries such as the G-7 and most of the industrial countries—for a period long enough to allow trend assess-

The authors are much indebted to Ms. Michelle Katics and Mr. Derek Bills for their first-rate assistance in the preparation of tables and figures. Comments received from participants in the Tokyo conference, especially from Professor Luis Maccini and from Adrienne Cheasty, are much appreciated. The views expressed are strictly those of the authors and should not be interpreted as official positions of the International Monetary Fund.

ment and some econometric tests. The period covered is 1970 to 1994, the longest for which the needed data could be assembled.

FISCAL DEVELOPMENTS

Table 10.1 shows the four different measures of general government budget balance, expressed as shares of GDP. These figures are shown for the 1970–1994 period and for each of 18 industrial countries as well as for two groupings—the G-7 and all industrial countries. Figure 10.1 gives a graphical view of the behavior of these measures for the two groupings. The four measures are:

A. The general government balance, which is the *normal* or conventional definition of the fiscal deficit including local governments;

B. The general government *structural balance*, which attempts to remove the effect of the business cycle on the fiscal balance (this measure is expressed as a share of *potential* GDP);

C. The general government *inflation-adjusted balance*, which corrects the normal measure (A above) for the impact of inflation on the public debt; and

D. The general government *primary balance*, which removes from government expenditure the interest payments made to the holders of the public debt.

The various reasons why these four alternative versions of the government budget balance have come into use have been discussed at length in the literature (Tanzi and Lutz 1993; and Blejer and Cheasty 1993). Each measure is useful for some purpose and none is clearly superior to the others. Jointly, these four measures provide more information, especially about short-term developments, than any one of them does separately. For example, a country undergoing a recession would find it useful to pay some attention to measure B, which corrects the fiscal deficit for the effect of a recession. A nation undergoing significant inflation would find it useful to estimate measure C, which removes from the deficit the implicit amortization of the public debt caused by inflation. It is wrong, however, to claim that any of these measures is superior *for all uses* to the others. Furthermore, important and at times questionable assumptions need to be made to calculate B and C.

What messages are conveyed by table 10.1 and figure 10.1? The first is that a serious deterioration of the fiscal situation of the industrial countries probably started with the oil-shock-induced recession of 1975. This recession came at a time when many policymakers and economists still strongly held Keynesian views about the role of the fiscal deficit as the "balancing factor" in stabilizing aggregate demand, and about the general economic role of the public sector in the economy. Although the voices of dissent were being heard, the skepticism about these views that came to influence policy in the 1980s had still not taken hold. Thus, in orthodox Keynesian fashion, governments tried to fight the recession and the fall in real income caused by the oil shock with a fiscal expansion. Government expenditure increased, revenue fell, and fiscal deficits widened. The figures for the G-7 and for the industrial countries combined eloquently illustrate this trend (table 10.1, bottom).

The second message is that the poor fiscal performance continued until around the mid-1980s. At that time, corrective measures taken by some governments in response to growing concern for the deteriorating fiscal situation, together with the economic boom that characterized many of these countries for the next several years, led to falls in the fiscal deficit in many of them. The combined normal deficits for each of the two groups of countries fell by more than 3 percent of GDP between 1983 (a recession year) and 1989 (a boom year). Of course, the cyclically adjusted or structural measure of the deficit indicates a much smaller reduction of only a little over 1 percent of GDP between these two periods.

The third message is that after 1989 the situation started deteriorating once again, partly for cyclical reasons. Between 1989 and 1993, all four measures of the fiscal deficit deteriorated for the two groups of countries. By 1993, the gains made between 1983 and 1989 were lost. For both groups of countries, 1993 was fiscally among the worst years in the 24-year period covered by table 10.1. Preliminary figures for 1994 show that some improvement took place that year, due in part to the economic recovery, but that the improvement was marginal.

Finally, no country seems to have completely escaped some fiscal deterioration, even though some countries experienced far less than others. Fiscal virtue has not been very popular since 1970. The reasons for this fiscal deterioration, which has not come from a fall in public sector revenue or in these countries' per capita incomes, deserve serious analysis that is beyond the scope of this paper.[3] A disturbing aspect is that the demographic changes such as aging of the population that are expected to impact negatively on the fiscal accounts of most of these countries have not yet started (see Part One of

Table 10.1 MEASURES OF GENERAL GOVERNMENT BUDGET BALANCES OF G−7 AND INDUSTRIAL COUNTRIES, 1970–1994 (PERCENTAGE OF GDP)

		1970	1971	1972	1973	1974	1975	1976	1977	1978	1979	1980	1981	1982
Austria	A	−0.5	0.1	−0.2	−1.6	−1.6	−4.0	−4.7	−2.4	−2.8	−2.4	−1.7	−1.8	−3.4
	B	1.7	2.1	2.2	1.6	0.9	−1.6	−4.0	−3.8	−3.1	−4.0	−3.7	−2.4	−3.5
	C	NA	0.9	0.9	−0.3	0.1	−2.3	−2.8	−0.8	−1.6	−1.1	0.6	0.8	−1.2
	D	0.2	0.7	0.4	−1.1	−1.0	−3.3	−3.6	−1.0	−1.1	−0.6	0.0	0.2	−1.1
Belgium	A	−1.6	−2.8	−4.3	−3.4	−2.2	−4.7	−5.6	−5.9	−6.8	−8.8	−11.5	−16.0	−14.1
	B	−2.0	−2.5	−3.7	−3.8	−3.8	−4.5	−7.2	−6.6	−7.5	−8.4	−11.7	−14.0	−11.6
	C	NA	0.1	−0.7	1.1	5.6	3.0	0.0	−1.4	−3.8	−5.5	−6.2	−9.3	−5.4
	D	−1.6	−2.8	−4.3	−3.4	−2.2	−1.9	−2.6	−2.5	−2.9	−3.1	−3.9	−6.2	−2.9
Canada	A	0.8	0.0	−0.0	0.9	1.9	−2.5	−1.8	−2.5	−3.2	−2.0	−2.8	−1.5	−5.9
	B	1.5	0.7	0.6	0.7	1.5	−2.4	−2.5	−3.2	−4.1	−2.9	−3.0	−2.0	−3.5
	C	NA	1.5	2.5	4.5	6.7	2.1	1.4	0.9	0.9	0.7	1.7	4.1	−0.8
	D	2.2	1.3	1.2	2.0	2.5	−1.8	−0.9	−1.7	−1.5	−0.3	−0.9	0.9	−3.0
Denmark	A	2.4	3.9	3.9	5.3	3.2	−1.4	−0.2	−0.6	−0.3	−1.7	−3.3	−6.9	−9.1
	B	NA	4.5	3.8	4.3	3.4	0.2	−0.9	−1.4	−1.0	−3.4	−3.4	−4.9	−7.4
	C	NA	4.6	4.6	6.2	4.4	−0.4	1.0	1.3	1.7	0.7	0.5	−2.4	−4.2
	D	NA	4.1	4.0	5.2	2.8	−2.0	−0.9	−1.2	−0.8	−1.2	−2.8	−5.1	−6.5
Finland	A	0.9	0.7	1.2	2.9	0.8	−2.2	−0.0	−1.5	−1.8	−2.5	−2.2	−0.9	−2.1
	B	3.1	4.7	3.5	5.2	3.8	2.4	5.6	4.9	5.8	2.8	1.3	2.8	0.9
	C	NA	1.6	2.1	4.1	2.4	−0.7	1.2	−0.3	−0.9	−1.4	−0.5	0.8	−0.6
	D	1.1	0.7	1.3	2.8	0.7	−2.2	−0.1	−1.5	2.9	2.0	1.9	2.5	0.9
France	A	0.9	0.6	0.6	0.6	0.3	−2.4	−0.7	−0.8	−2.1	−0.8	−0.0	−1.9	−2.8
	B	0.6	0.5	0.8	0.7	0.2	−1.5	−0.6	−1.1	−2.7	−1.9	−0.8	−2.2	−3.1
	C	NA	3.4	3.6	3.9	6.1	2.4	3.1	2.8	1.1	2.5	4.1	2.2	1.0
	D	1.3	0.9	0.8	0.7	0.4	−1.9	−0.3	−0.3	−1.5	0.0	0.8	−0.7	−1.6
Germany	A	0.2	−0.2	−0.5	1.2	−1.3	−5.6	−3.4	−2.4	−2.4	−2.6	−2.9	−3.7	−3.3
	B	−0.5	−0.4	−0.8	0.8	−1.0	−3.8	−3.3	−2.8	−3.3	−4.6	−4.3	−4.1	−2.2
	C	NA	0.8	0.5	2.5	0.0	−4.3	−2.3	−1.4	−1.6	−1.3	−1.2	−1.5	−1.3
	D	−0.5	−0.9	−1.1	0.5	−1.0	−5.1	−2.7	−1.5	−1.5	−1.5	−1.6	−2.1	−1.3

Greece	A	−1.7	−1.9	−2.6	−2.3	−3.2	−3.9	−3.8	−3.7	−3.7	−3.6	−3.1	−8.6	−6.8
	B	−0.4	−1.2	−1.0	−2.1	−0.8	−2.5	−2.4	−1.8	−2.3	−3.2	−3.6	−10.3	−7.3
	C	NA	−1.0	−1.4	−0.8	−0.7	−1.2	−1.7	−2.1	−2.5	−2.3	−1.3	−6.3	−3.8
	D	−2.7	−2.6	−3.4	−3.1	−4.4	−4.9	−4.3	−4.2	0.0	−0.4	−0.5	−7.0	−5.0
Ireland	A	−6.3	−5.4	−5.6	−6.2	−11.6	−13.0	−10.5	−9.7	−14.6	−15.5	−16.6	−19.4	−18.4
	B	NA	NA	NA	NA	NA	NA	NA	−7.7	−8.9	−10.8	−12.3	−13.7	−14.0
	C	NA	0.5	0.0	0.7	−1.8	−0.6	1.1	−0.8	−11.8	−6.4	−3.5	−4.2	−4.7
	D	−4.3	−3.6	−4.3	−4.3	−9.7	−10.6	−7.4	−6.7	−5.8	−6.9	−7.8	−7.7	−7.1
Italy	A	−4.8	−6.6	−7.4	−8.3	−7.3	−11.9	−8.5	−7.1	−8.5	−8.3	−8.5	−11.6	−11.3
	B	−4.4	−5.6	−8.0	−8.4	−8.7	−11.7	−9.7	−8.5	−10.4	−11.0	−9.6	−11.9	−10.8
	C	NA	−4.3	−4.3	−2.2	3.0	−2.3	1.4	3.7	−1.3	0.8	4.3	0.1	−0.8
	D	−3.2	−4.7	−5.3	−6.1	−4.8	−8.8	−4.9	−3.3	−6.0	−5.8	−3.9	−6.1	−4.8
Japan	A	1.7	1.2	−0.1	0.5	0.4	−2.8	−3.7	−3.8	−5.5	−4.7	−4.4	−3.8	−3.6
	B	1.2	1.1	−0.9	−0.9	0.9	−1.9	−3.0	−3.5	−5.6	−5.6	−5.1	−4.3	−3.6
	C	NA	2.0	0.6	2.5	4.4	−0.4	−1.3	−1.3	−3.9	−3.1	−0.6	−1.2	−2.0
	D	1.1	0.5	−0.7	−0.1	−0.3	−3.0	−3.6	−3.4	−4.9	−3.9	−3.4	−2.5	−2.1
Netherlands	A	−1.1	−1.2	−0.1	−0.0	−0.0	−2.8	−2.4	−3.0	−3.0	−4.5	−3.9	−5.4	−6.9
	B	−2.8	−2.5	−1.1	0.0	−0.6	−2.2	−3.7	−3.2	−3.9	−5.7	−5.9	−6.0	−5.3
	C	NA	2.5	3.6	3.5	3.9	1.3	1.2	−0.4	−1.4	−2.8	−1.1	−2.2	−3.9
	D	2.4	2.3	3.3	3.3	3.5	0.8	1.3	−0.9	−0.3	−1.4	−1.4	−2.0	−2.8
Norway	A	−3.1	−2.6	−1.5	−0.9	−1.4	−3.2	7.1	5.7	4.8	5.3	9.4	7.9	7.5
	B	−3.2	−4.5	−4.8	−6.4	−5.2	−4.7	−3.3	−2.5	−1.4	−2.1	−1.6	−2.4	−2.6
	C	NA	0.4	1.9	2.7	2.8	1.9	11.3	10.3	9.3	8.2	15.6	14.7	12.6
	D	−1.3	−0.8	0.5	1.1	0.7	−3.6	6.9	5.6	−0.3	1.3	5.9	4.6	4.0
Portugal	A	−1.7	−1.1	−2.4	−1.3	−2.6	−8.4	−11.5	−6.5	−11.8	−10.1	−9.7	−11.8	−11.0
	B	2.9	2.4	0.8	0.8	−2.1	−3.8	−6.1	−4.8	−7.1	−7.4	4.1	−12.4	−9.0
	C	NA	−0.2	−1.3	0.1	−0.3	−5.6	−8.8	−4.2	−10.2	−8.7	−7.6	−3.4	0.0
	D	−1.7	−1.1	−2.4	−1.3	−2.6	−8.4	−11.5	−5.0	−4.2	−3.4	8.6	−5.3	−2.3

continued

Table 10.1 MEASURES OF GENERAL GOVERNMENT BUDGET BALANCES OF G−7 AND INDUSTRIAL COUNTRIES, 1970–1994 (PERCENTAGE OF GDP) (*Continued*)

		1970	1971	1972	1973	1974	1975	1976	1977	1978	1979	1980	1981	1982
Spain	A	−0.7	−1.6	−0.5	−0.3	−1.2	−1.8	−0.9	−2.2	−2.4	−3.5	−2.6	−3.9	−5.6
	B	0.2	−0.1	0.4	1.0	0.2	0.2	−0.9	−1.7	−2.8	−2.3	−2.8	−3.8	−5.8
	C	NA	−0.4	0.7	1.4	0.9	0.2	1.0	1.3	0.6	−1.2	0.1	−0.8	−1.7
	D	−0.7	−1.6	−0.9	−0.6	−1.5	−2.1	−1.3	−2.5	−1.9	−1.6	−1.9	−3.3	−5.0
Sweden	A	−1.7	−1.3	−1.2	−1.4	−3.0	−2.5	−0.3	−1.6	−4.9	−7.1	−4.0	−5.2	−7.0
	B	3.4	5.2	4.8	3.9	1.6	2.6	4.2	2.9	0.0	−4.7	−5.8	−5.7	−6.9
	C	NA	1.1	0.8	0.9	0.1	0.7	2.8	1.4	−1.1	−4.1	1.2	0.6	−2.1
	D	−2.3	−2.1	−2.2	−2.6	−4.2	−3.6	−1.7	−2.9	−1.7	−4.1	−4.4	−4.9	−5.4
U.K.	A	3.0	1.3	−1.3	−2.7	−3.8	−4.5	−4.9	−3.2	−4.4	−3.3	−3.4	−2.6	−2.5
	B	3.6	2.4	−0.3	−3.5	−4.1	−4.1	−5.3	−3.9	−6.3	−6.2	−4.8	−1.9	−1.0
	C	NA	8.9	4.0	3.8	7.0	11.5	5.6	6.6	0.8	3.9	5.8	4.0	2.1
	D	5.1	3.1	0.3	−1.0	−1.8	−2.7	−2.8	−0.8	−1.8	−0.5	−0.3	0.7	0.7
U.S.	A	−1.1	−1.8	−0.3	0.5	−0.3	−4.1	−2.2	−0.9	0.1	0.4	−1.3	−1.0	−3.4
	B	−0.6	−1.2	−0.4	−0.4	−0.4	−3.0	−1.7	−1.1	−1.0	−0.8	−1.6	−0.9	−1.8
	C	NA	0.2	1.2	3.2	4.1	−0.3	0.3	1.9	3.2	4.7	3.8	2.9	−1.0
	D	0.1	−0.6	0.7	1.6	0.8	−2.9	−0.9	0.4	1.2	1.5	−0.1	0.5	−1.8
G−7 Countries														
	A	−0.3	−1.1	−0.8	−0.3	−1.0	−4.4	−3.0	−2.1	−2.2	−1.7	−2.6	−2.7	−4.0
	B	−0.1	−0.6	−0.9	−1.0	−1.1	−3.5	−2.8	−2.4	−3.2	−3.2	−3.2	−2.8	−2.9
	C	NA	1.2	1.1	2.8	4.2	0.4	0.6	1.6	1.0	2.3	2.8	1.7	−0.8
	D	0.5	−0.3	−0.0	0.5	−0.1	−3.4	−1.8	−0.8	−1.0	−0.4	−1.0	−0.7	−1.9
Industrial Countries														
	A	−0.4	−1.1	−0.8	−0.3	−1.0	−4.3	−2.9	−2.2	−2.3	−2.0	−2.7	−3.0	−4.3
	B	−0.1	−0.5	−0.7	−0.9	−1.0	−3.2	−2.7	−2.4	−3.2	−3.3	−3.3	−3.1	−3.3
	C	NA	1.1	1.1	2.7	3.9	0.4	0.6	1.5	0.8	1.9	2.5	1.4	−0.9
	D	NA	−0.3	−0.1	0.4	−0.2	−3.3	−1.8	−0.9	−1.0	−0.6	−1.0	−1.0	−2.1

Table 10.1 MEASURES OF GENERAL GOVERNMENT BUDGET BALANCES OF G – 7 AND INDUSTRIAL COUNTRIES, 1970–1994 (PERCENTAGE OF GDP) (*Continued*)

		1983	1984	1985	1986	1987	1988	1989	1990	1991	1992	1993	Est. 1994
Austria	A	−4.0	−2.6	−2.5	−3.7	−4.3	−3.0	−2.8	−2.2	−2.5	−2.0	−3.3	−3.9
	B	−3.9	−2.0	−2.1	−2.7	−3.0	−2.7	−2.9	−2.9	−3.1	−1.9	−3.0	−3.3
	C	−2.5	0.1	−0.9	−2.8	−3.5	−1.9	−2.3	−0.3	−0.6	0.3	−1.2	−2.2
	D	−1.7	0.2	0.4	−0.8	−1.2	0.2	0.3	1.0	0.9	1.5	−0.8	−1.3
Belgium	A	−14.6	−11.7	−8.9	−11.1	−9.3	−7.8	−6.4	−5.8	−6.6	−6.9	−6.7	−5.3
	B	−11.0	−8.8	−7.6	−7.5	−5.7	−6.8	−7.5	−7.7	−8.5	−8.6	−5.2	−4.0
	C	−6.2	−4.2	−2.9	−9.4	−7.2	−6.2	−2.2	−1.1	−2.2	−3.6	−2.8	−1.6
	D	−3.2	−0.4	0.8	1.1	2.4	2.7	3.3	4.2	2.9	2.7	3.5	4.5
Canada	A	−6.9	−6.5	−6.8	−5.4	−3.8	−2.5	−2.9	−4.1	−6.6	−7.1	−7.1	−5.8
	B	−4.5	−5.5	−6.7	−5.5	−4.4	−4.1	−4.3	−4.1	−4.0	−3.3	−4.5	−4.5
	C	−3.8	−4.0	−4.3	−2.6	−0.7	0.3	0.6	−0.7	−2.4	−5.8	−5.4	−5.7
	D	−4.0	−2.9	−2.8	−1.2	0.4	1.8	1.9	1.2	−1.0	−1.6	−3.7	−1.9
Denmark	A	−7.2	−4.1	−2.0	3.4	2.4	0.6	−0.5	−1.5	−2.1	−2.4	−4.6	−5.1
	B	−5.6	−3.7	−2.8	1.8	1.8	0.5	0.3	−0.3	−0.2	0.0	−1.9	−3.0
	C	−3.2	−0.1	1.0	5.6	4.7	3.2	2.3	0.0	−0.6	−1.1	−3.7	−3.4
	D	−2.9	1.7	4.1	8.5	6.9	4.8	3.3	1.8	1.4	0.0	−0.8	−0.9
Finland	A	−2.9	−1.0	0.1	−0.1	−0.5	1.3	2.9	5.3	−1.5	−4.9	−8.0	−5.8
	B	−0.4	2.1	2.0	2.5	−0.7	1.1	1.5	0.7	−1.6	−2.1	−3.4	−1.7
	C	−1.4	0.3	1.2	0.5	0.3	2.3	4.1	6.3	−0.6	−3.9	−6.9	−5.3
	D	−0.4	2.1	2.1	2.4	0.2	3.2	5.1	3.6	−3.4	−6.9	−7.5	−3.4
France	A	−3.2	−2.8	−2.9	−2.7	−1.9	−1.7	−1.3	−1.6	−2.2	−3.9	−5.8	−5.5
	B	−2.6	−1.6	−1.4	−1.3	−0.3	−1.0	−1.5	−1.8	−1.6	−2.7	−3.7	−3.7
	C	0.2	−0.1	−0.7	−1.7	−0.6	−0.6	0.1	−0.2	−0.9	−2.9	−4.8	−4.5
	D	−1.4	−0.9	−0.8	−0.6	0.3	0.5	0.9	0.8	0.4	−1.1	−3.3	−2.9

continued

Table 10.1 MEASURES OF GENERAL GOVERNMENT BUDGET BALANCES OF G−7 AND INDUSTRIAL COUNTRIES, 1970–1994 (PERCENTAGE OF GDP) (*Continued*)

		1970	1971	1972	1973	1974	1975	1976	1977	1978	1979	1980	1981	1982
Germany	A	−2.6	−1.9	−1.2	−1.3	−1.9	−2.1	0.1	−2.0	−3.4	−2.8	−3.6	−3.5
	B	−1.2	−0.9	−0.1	−0.3	−0.6	−1.6	0.0	−3.6	−5.2	−4.5	−2.7	−2.1
	C	−1.2	−0.9	−0.2	−1.4	−1.8	−1.6	1.3	−0.9	−2.0	−1.1	−1.7	−2.0
	D	−0.3	0.4	1.1	1.0	0.5	0.2	2.3	0.0	−1.0	0.4	−0.7	0.4
Greece	A	−9.2	−13.6	−16.5	−12.3	−13.5	−15.3	−20.0	−15.2	−13.1	−11.4	−13.8	−14.0
	B	−7.6	−9.5	−14.1	−12.5	−10.6	−14.1	−17.9	−17.9	−15.1	−11.3	−12.5	−11.8
	C	−6.2	−10.7	−6.1	1.1	−3.4	−6.2	−9.9	1.6	5.0	4.5	1.4	−1.5
	D	−4.8	−5.5	−8.6	−6.7	−4.5	−5.9	−8.3	−6.1	−2.8	−0.6	−0.7	0.9
Ireland	A	−15.4	−14.5	−13.7	−12.8	−9.8	−3.3	−2.7	−2.5	−2.9	−2.9	−2.9	−2.8
	B	−10.4	−9.6	−10.4	−7.7	−5.9	−2.1	−0.6	−3.4	−2.7	−4.4	−2.3	−2.2
	C	−6.0	−6.0	−8.1	−8.6	−6.2	−0.9	1.7	0.8	0.2	0.1	−1.5	−0.6
	D	−5.1	−2.8	−3.5	−3.3	−1.1	2.6	5.1	4.7	4.3	3.1	2.6	1.7
Italy	A	−10.6	−11.6	−12.5	−12.0	−11.3	−11.2	−10.5	−11.4	−10.7	−10.0	−10.0	−9.6
	B	−9.5	−10.5	−11.5	−10.8	−10.5	−11.0	−10.5	−11.4	−10.1	−8.5	−8.7	−8.9
	C	−0.5	−3.5	−5.2	−6.9	−7.0	−6.5	−4.4	−4.9	−4.2	−4.5	−5.0	−5.1
	D	−3.7	−4.1	−5.2	−3.8	−3.6	−3.1	−1.5	−1.8	−0.5	1.4	2.0	0.8
Japan	A	−3.6	−2.1	−0.8	−0.9	0.5	1.5	2.5	2.9	3.0	1.8	−0.6	−2.7
	B	−3.1	−1.6	−0.6	−0.2	1.3	1.5	2.2	2.3	2.4	2.0	−0.1	−1.0
	C	−2.4	−0.6	0.6	−0.5	0.5	2.0	4.1	5.1	5.2	3.0	0.3	−2.2
	D	−2.0	−0.3	0.9	0.7	1.7	2.5	3.4	3.5	3.3	2.1	−0.8	−2.4
Netherlands	A	−6.2	−6.1	−4.6	−5.9	−5.9	−4.6	−4.7	−5.1	−2.5	−3.5	−2.9	−3.8
	B	−4.1	−4.6	−2.9	−2.9	−3.8	−3.1	−5.0	−6.5	−4.0	−4.5	−1.6	−2.3
	C	−4.6	−4.0	−3.2	−5.7	−6.5	−4.0	−3.9	−3.2	−0.2	−1.0	−0.8	−1.6
	D	−1.7	−1.4	0.8	1.2	−0.2	0.7	−0.3	−0.6	2.2	1.1	2.0	1.8
Norway	A	7.1	6.9	10.3	3.2	2.4	1.0	1.4	2.5	−0.2	−2.3	−2.7	−2.4
	B	−4.3	−2.5	−1.6	−0.3	−1.1	−0.7	−2.2	−3.0	−4.7	−6.6	−8.3	−6.9
	C	10.5	3.5	12.6	6.5	6.5	3.8	3.4	4.2	1.1	−1.4	−1.7	−1.8

Portugal	A	−14.5	−11.6	−9.6	−6.9	−7.9	−6.1	−4.8	−6.5	−6.5	−3.5	−7.3	−6.5
	B	−10.1	−4.9	−5.0	−4.4	−6.3	−4.9	−3.4	−6.4	−6.9	−4.6	−6.9	−5.2
	C	−0.9	5.9	2.9	0.7	−1.4	1.0	4.5	2.8	1.1	2.3	−3.0	−3.0
	D	−4.0	1.2	1.9	3.3	1.5	2.3	4.1	2.8	2.3	4.3	−0.6	−0.7
Spain	A	−4.8	−5.5	−7.0	−6.0	−3.1	−3.3	−2.8	−3.9	−5.0	−4.5	−7.3	−6.7
	B	−4.5	−4.3	−5.8	−4.9	−3.2	−4.3	−4.7	−6.2	−6.8	−5.3	−5.5	−4.7
	C	−0.6	−0.7	−2.8	−1.5	−0.5	−0.9	0.5	−0.7	−2.1	−1.4	−4.7	−4.1
	D	−3.8	−3.8	−4.2	−2.7	−0.3	−0.3	0.3	−0.8	−1.2	−0.5	−2.2	−1.4
Sweden	A	−5.0	−2.9	−3.6	−1.2	4.2	3.5	5.4	4.2	−1.1	−7.4	−13.4	−10.3
	B	−5.0	−4.7	−5.8	−3.7	0.8	−0.4	0.8	−0.3	−3.7	−7.5	−9.9	−8.5
	C	0.7	2.4	1.4	1.6	6.9	6.8	8.7	9.1	3.4	−6.0	−9.9	−8.5
	D	−3.1	−0.5	−0.8	1.0	6.0	4.5	5.7	4.3	−1.0	−7.4	−12.5	−9.4
U.K.	A	−3.3	−3.9	−2.9	−2.4	−1.3	1.0	0.9	−1.2	−2.7	−6.2	−8.5	−6.9
	B	−2.3	−2.8	−2.3	−3.0	−3.2	−2.0	−2.1	−3.2	−2.3	−4.3	−5.0	−4.7
	C	−0.6	−1.5	−0.1	−0.5	0.7	3.1	3.2	1.7	−0.3	−4.4	−7.2	−5.7
	D	−0.2	−0.5	0.5	0.7	1.7	3.6	3.3	1.1	−0.6	−4.3	−5.6	−4.2
U.S.	A	−4.1	−2.9	−3.1	−3.4	−2.5	−2.0	−1.5	−2.5	−3.2	−4.3	−3.4	−2.3
	B	−2.7	−2.6	−3.1	−3.6	−2.8	−2.8	−2.3	−3.1	−3.6	−4.0	−3.2	−2.3
	C	−2.8	−0.9	−1.5	−2.5	−0.6	0.1	1.1	0.4	−0.8	−2.5	−1.5	−0.6
	D	−2.4	−0.9	−1.0	−1.4	−0.5	−0.1	0.5	−0.4	−1.1	−2.3	−1.3	0.3
G−7 Countries													
	A	−4.4	−3.5	−3.4	−3.4	−2.5	−1.9	−1.2	−2.1	−2.8	−3.8	−4.1	−3.7
	B	−3.2	−2.9	−3.0	−3.2	−2.5	−2.5	−2.0	−2.8	−3.0	−3.3	−3.2	−2.9
	C	−2.1	−1.2	−1.3	−2.2	−0.9	−0.0	1.3	0.7	−0.2	−1.9	−2.3	−2.2
	D	−2.1	−0.9	−0.8	−0.7	0.1	0.5	1.1	0.3	−0.4	−1.1	−1.4	−0.5
Industrial Countries													
	A	−4.6	−3.8	−3.6	−3.6	−2.7	−2.0	−1.4	−2.2	−2.9	−3.9	−4.4	−3.9
	B	−3.4	−3.1	−3.2	−3.3	−2.5	−2.6	−2.2	−3.1	−3.3	−3.5	−3.5	−3.1
	C	−2.0	−1.2	−1.3	−2.1	−0.9	−0.1	1.2	0.7	−0.2	−1.8	−2.4	−2.3
	D	−2.1	−0.9	−0.7	−0.6	0.2	0.6	1.1	0.4	−0.4	−1.1	−1.4	−0.5

Sources: OECD 1994; IMF *World Economic Outlook*, various issues; and authors' calculations.
Note: A = General Government Balance; B = General Government Structural Balance (as a percentage of potential GDP); C = General Government Inflation Adjusted Balance; D = General Government Primary Balance; NA = not available.

Figure 10.1 FOUR MEASURES OF GENERAL GOVERNMENT BALANCES, 1970–1994

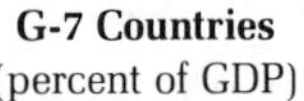

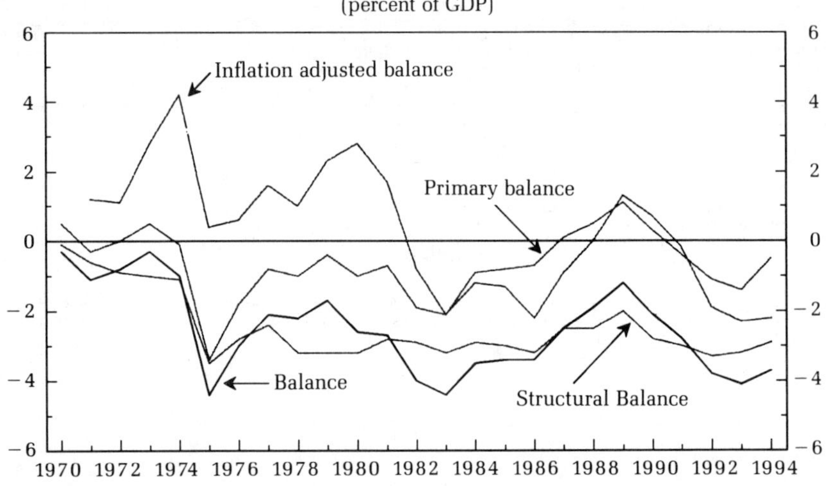

Industrial Countries
(percent of GDP)

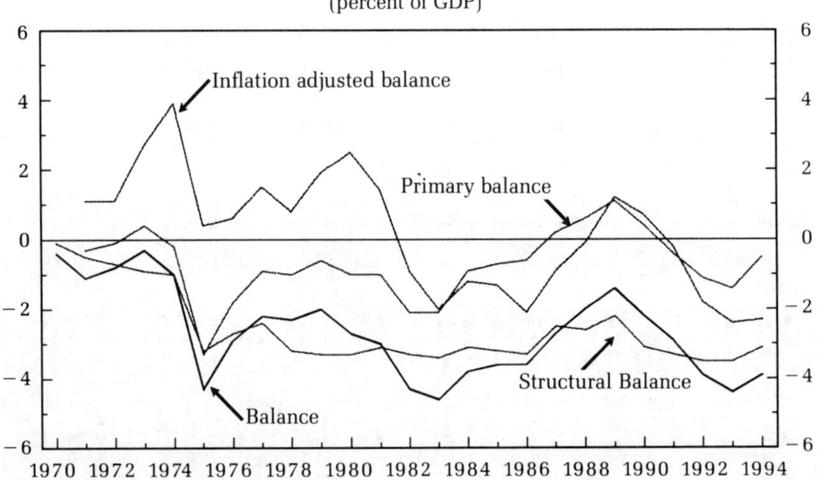

Sources: OECD 1994; IMF *World Economic Outlook*, various issues; and authors' calculations.

this volume). One would hope that by the time they do, countries will be fiscally strong enough to be able to cope successfully with them. However, the data in table 10.1 do not invite optimism.

Table 10.1 also provides information on specific countries. Several nations, including Belgium, Greece, and Italy, have had very large fiscal deficits for much of the period. Belgium has been trying for several years to improve its fiscal situation mainly by cutting its non-interest public spending. Italy has been attempting to reduce its fiscal deficit mainly by increasing its level of taxation, which has risen sharply since 1980. Nonetheless, its fiscal deficit has remained high. Ireland faced a serious fiscal situation in the 1974–1986 period but has made remarkable adjustments since then, showing that adjustments are possible and do not necessarily have the dire effects on output that some economists predict. Canada experienced serious fiscal deterioration in the period up to 1982–1985, made some significant adjustments in the next few years, and has seen its fiscal deficit—measure A—rise again largely as a result of the recession. Spain, Sweden, and the United Kingdom have also experienced sharp fiscal deterioration in recent years. The fiscal accounts of France and Germany also recently deteriorated, while Japan remains the only major country without a large fiscal imbalance. In the United States, the fiscal deficit in 1992–1993 was at its highest level in the whole 1970–1994 period, especially in the cases of measures B, C, and D. Some significant improvement occurred in 1994.

Looking at measure A for the G-7 countries combined, the years in which the deficit was highest were 1975, 1982-1983, and 1993. Similar results are seen for the combined industrial countries. If one takes measure C, the inflation-adjusted measure of the fiscal deficit, 1993 was the worst year for both the G-7 and the industrial countries combined. In fact, the fall in the rate of inflation in most countries since the beginning of the 1980s implies that a conventionally defined fiscal deficit now contributes to a faster debt accumulation than when inflation was higher.

FISCAL DEFICITS AND PRIVATE SAVING RATES

A continuing worry on the part of fiscal commentators has been that fiscal deficits will absorb private savings, thus diverting resources away from potentially more productive private investment toward presumably less productive public sector spending. The optimism of the early 1980s, based on the Ricardian equivalence principle promoted by Robert Barro—that fiscal deficits can be self-financing by inducing more private saving—seems to have evaporated. Economists such as Robert Eisner and, less forcefully, Franco Modigliani, have also argued that a fiscal deficit that finances public investment should not cause concern, because in time the investment will generate enough extra income to finance the additional fiscal obligations created by the deficit. Today, most observers appear unconvinced by this argument. There is no evidence indicating that higher public sector capital accumulation has accompanied a rise in the fiscal deficit.[4] Furthermore, public investment tends to be less productive than private investment. Fiscal deficits have been caused mostly by larger transfers to groups of individuals (the poor, the unemployed, and pensioners) who have relatively high propensities to consume.

Before there was much greater freedom of capital flows across the globe, national economies were relatively closed and fiscal deficits had to be financed by a nation's own savings. Thus, if "crowding out" occurred (whereby higher public debt crowds out private investment by absorbing the private saving that would have financed the latter), it was within a country. However, a country's deficit can now be financed by the savings of other countries. Thus, at least for the short run, crowding out may go international. This implies that a country's interest rate does not need to rise as much as in the past to finance its own deficit. However, collective fiscal deficits may still have an impact on worldwide real interest rates. For this reason, it may be worthwhile to aggregate the fiscal deficits and the private savings of relevant groups of countries to see whether a relationship exists between these factors, and possibly between them and the rate of interest. Table 10.2 shows this relationship for the G-7 countries taken as a group for the 1970–1994 period.

As a share of GDP, gross private saving fluctuated over the period, with a high of over 21 percent of GDP between 1975 and 1979 and a low of 18.7 percent in 1989. Some increase in the share is noticeable for the 1973–1979 period, but this increase is likely to be partly spurious due to the higher inflation rate in those years and the fact that the authorities of the various countries are unlikely to have distinguished between nominal and real interest incomes.[5] The 1973–1979 increase shows up as a higher saving rate because during inflation individuals are likely to save a higher share of the *nominal* than of the real interest incomes that they receive, in order to maintain the real value of their financial wealth. Thus, higher inflation in the 1970s is likely to have led to an overestimate of both genuine interest in-

Table 10.2 AGGREGATED FISCAL DEFICITS AND SAVINGS OF G-7 COUNTRIES, 1970–1994

	General Government Deficit[a]	Gross Private Saving	Net Private Saving[a]	General Government Deficit	General Government Deficit[b]
	As Percentage of G-7 GDP			As Percentage of G-7 Gross Private Saving	As Percentage of G-7 Net Private Saving
1970	0.3%	19.9%	10.7%	1.7%	3.2%
1971	1.1	20.5	10.8	5.2	9.8
1972	0.8	20.2	10.8	3.9	7.4
1973	0.3	21.0	11.6	1.3	2.3
1974	1.0	20.5	10.1	4.7	9.6
1975	4.4	21.8	10.5	20.4	42.2
1976	3.0	21.5	10.3	14.1	29.5
1977	2.1	21.1	10.1	10.0	20.9
1978	2.2	21.8	10.8	9.9	20.0
1979	1.7	21.5	10.2	8.1	17.0
1980	2.6	20.7	10.0	12.4	25.6
1981	2.7	21.2	9.9	12.6	27.0
1982	4.0	21.0	9.6	19.2	42.1
1983	4.4	20.8	9.5	21.0	46.1
1984	3.5	21.3	10.4	16.6	34.2
1985	3.4	20.5	9.7	16.6	35.1
1986	3.4	20.0	9.2	17.2	37.5
1987	2.5	19.2	8.5	13.2	29.9
1988	1.9	19.3	8.8	9.9	21.7
1989	1.2	18.7	8.0	6.5	15.3
1990	2.1	18.8	7.9	11.3	26.7
1991	2.8	19.7	8.1	14.2	34.6
1992	3.8	19.8	8.1	19.0	46.5
1993	4.1	19.6	NA	21.0	NA
1994	3.7	19.6	NA	18.9	NA

Sources: OECD 1994; and IMF *World Economic Outlook*, various issues.
a. Figures are PPP-weighted averages of national figures, as percentage of GDP.
b. Excludes Italy from 1970–1979.

comes and genuine saving rates. Gross private saving and net private saving declined somewhat from the 1970s to the 1990s.

The share of gross private saving absorbed by the general government deficit of the G-7 countries combined rose considerably between the 1970s and the 1980s. This share reached the highest level in 1993, when 21 percent of the G-7 countries' total gross private saving went to finance these countries' fiscal deficits. This resulted in a decrease in the saving available for private investment. Table 10.2 also shows that a much higher share of *net* private saving (than gross private saving) was absorbed by financing the fiscal deficit. This share was particularly high in recession years (1975, 1982–1983, and 1992), when it occasionally reached or exceeded 40 percent. In 1992, almost half of the G-7 countries' net national saving went to finance their fiscal deficits—a figure representing the largest percentage for the entire 1970–1992 period. If figures were available for 1993 they would likely exceed 50 percent. Because net private saving is the most liquid way of financing private investment, its large absorption by the fiscal deficit, if maintained over time, could have serious implications for the growth of G-7 countries as a group.

Similar data can be assembled and similar questions asked in relation to particular countries.[6] For example, between 1970 and 1994 the share of U.S. gross private saving as a percentage of the G-7 countries' total fell from 46 percent to 30 percent. The fall in U.S. net private saving was equally dramatic. Furthermore, by 1989 the United States accounted for 67.2 percent of the G-7 countries' combined fiscal deficit. After that year, the U.S. share fell considerably, due to the increase in the deficits of other countries, dropping to 25.2 percent in 1994. Data also show the sharply increasing contribution of Japan to the aggregate gross private saving and net private saving of the G-7 countries. Japan's increasing share in total saving, and its falling share in total fiscal deficit, may have facilitated the financing of the large and increasing deficits of the other G-7 countries. These trends may also have contributed to keeping down the worldwide interest rate.

THE GROWTH OF PUBLIC DEBT

Up to now we have focused on the yearly deficits as shown in table 10.1. During the 1970–1994 period, fiscal surpluses were rare indeed. Fiscal deficits sustained over time result in public debts. Given the size of the deficits, the level of interest rates, and the rate of growth of these countries' economies, public debts can rise or fall *as shares of GDP*.[7] Table 10.3 shows the data available on the share of gross public debt as a percentage of GDP for general governments of 18 countries and two groups—the G-7 countries and the industrial countries—for the 1970–1994 period.

Focusing on the G-7 countries as a group, table 10.3 shows that there was little change in the ratio of public debt to GDP throughout the 1970s. In 1980 the debt/GDP ratio was roughly the same as in 1970. However, from 1980 to 1987 that ratio grew from 41.9 percent to

57.5 percent. After a pause in the 1987–1990 period, the ratio started increasing again at a rapid pace and by 1994 it had reached the rather high level of 70.6 percent. The behavior of the debt/GDP ratios for the industrial countries was similar, not surprising in light of the weight of the G-7 countries among the industrial nations.

Should one be concerned about the rise of the public debt? It may seem strange to ask this question because we know that governments and financial markets do worry about it. Several books have recently dealt specifically with the various reasons why a high public debt is cause for concern (see, for example, Verbon and Van Winden 1993).

First is the concern that a high and growing public debt will crowd out private investment by absorbing the private saving that would have financed it; we saw from table 10.2 that the rate of absorption can be high. This crowding out may come from different channels. Public debt may raise interest rates by increasing the total demand for credit, and the rise in interest rates may in turn reduce borrowing by private investors. The growth of public debt as a share of GDP may crowd out private debt directly if, as Benjamin Friedman (1987) has argued, there tends to be a more-or-less maximum share of total debt (public plus private) as a percentage of GDP that individuals are willing to hold, and if the share of public debt goes up, the share of private debt must come down. Finally, investment (especially in projects with long maturity) may be discouraged by the expectation that growing public debt may lead to higher taxes in the future.

Second, Edmunds Phelps (1994) has argued that decisions on the part of enterprises about whether or not to hire additional workers are similar to investment decisions and are thus affected by similar considerations. The reason is that firms make an investment in the training of new employees. If public debt raises interest rates and increases the possibility that taxes will go up in the future, it will discourage not just investment but also employment.

Third, under normal circumstances, an increasing debt/GDP ratio will lead to an increase in total public spending, *ceteris paribus*. This will occur because of the higher interest bill that will accompany the increase in the debt ratio. If the increase in spending is financed through borrowing, this may set in motion a debt dynamic that might, under extreme circumstances, lead to a debt explosion. If the increase in interest spending is accommodated at least in part by cuts in other public spending, the most likely candidate for cuts will be capital spending. This, in fact, is what seems to have happened in many industrial countries (Tanzi and Lutz 1993, p. 242). If the expenditure increase that accompanies higher debt is partly accommodated

Table 10.3 GROSS PUBLIC DEBT OF INDUSTRIAL COUNTRIES, 1970–1994 (AS A PERCENTAGE OF GDP)

	1970	1971	1972	1973	1974	1975	1976	1977	1978	1979	1980	1981	1982
Austria	19.4	18.2	17.5	17.5	17.6	23.9	27.4	30.1	33.9	36.0	37.2	39.3	41.6
Belgium	67.5	65.8	65.9	63.7	59.8	61.1	61.2	64.6	70.4	75.2	81.6	95.5	104.7
Canada	51.9	52.9	51.1	45.3	43.2	43.1	41.4	43.4	46.6	43.8	44.6	45.2	50.3
Denmark	11.3	11.4	10.0	7.9	7.4	11.9	14.6	18.1	21.9	27.0	33.5	43.7	53.0
Finland	15.2	13.7	12.4	10.2	8.1	8.6	9.0	10.4	13.5	14.4	14.1	14.4	16.9
France	53.1	49.8	46.7	43.1	40.8	41.1	38.9	38.3	31.0	31.4	30.9	30.1	34.2
Germany	18.4	18.5	18.8	18.6	19.6	25.1	27.1	28.6	30.1	30.8	32.8	36.5	39.6
Greece	21.3	21.9	23.2	19.5	20.3	22.4	22.1	22.4	29.4	27.6	27.7	32.8	36.1
Ireland	67.4	66.7	62.7	59.3	56.3	62.2	66.7	63.7	65.7	71.0	72.5	77.2	83.0
Italy	41.7	49.1	56.6	56.2	52.3	60.4	58.6	57.8	62.4	61.5	59.0	61.1	66.4
Japan	12.1	13.5	17.5	17.1	17.9	22.1	28.0	33.4	41.9	47.0	52.0	56.8	60.9
Netherlands	50.6	48.3	45.2	42.1	40.1	40.1	39.0	38.8	40.2	42.0	45.1	49.5	54.6
Norway	47.0	47.0	47.6	46.1	43.3	44.7	46.7	53.3	60.0	62.9	52.2	47.4	42.2
Portugal	21.8	21.4	20.1	18.5	18.2	26.3	32.1	33.5	37.6	25.7	37.5	47.3	50.7
Spain	14.2	15.2	15.6	13.2	11.8	12.1	13.0	15.3	14.4	16.5	18.3	24.0	30.4
Sweden	30.5	30.9	30.7	30.0	30.4	29.5	27.5	29.9	34.5	39.6	44.3	52.1	61.7
U.K.	81.8	77.9	72.4	67.6	67.8	63.7	62.7	61.3	58.6	54.9	54.1	54.3	52.9
U.S.	45.4	46.2	44.3	41.0	39.8	42.6	42.7	41.1	39.2	37.2	37.7	37.0	41.0
G-7	42.2	42.7	41.9	39.2	36.5	39.1	39.7	39.6	41.6	40.9	41.9	42.7	46.6
Industrial Countries	41.1	41.5	40.6	38.0	37.1	39.6	40.2	40.4	40.7	40.4	41.6	42.9	46.9

	1983	1984	1985	1986	1987	1988	1989	1990	1991	1992	1993	1994
Austria	46.0	47.9	49.6	53.8	57.3	57.6	56.9	56.3	56.9	56.1	57.0	58.3
Belgium	116.0	121.8	126.0	130.7	135.7	136.8	134.2	134.4	137.6	140.2	145.6	145.0
Canada	55.7	59.4	64.9	68.8	69.6	69.2	69.8	72.5	80.0	87.5	92.3	95.7
Denmark	61.6	65.9	64.1	58.3	55.9	58.0	58.5	59.7	60.9	62.4	66.1	68.7
Finland	18.6	17.8	18.9	20.5	20.9	19.6	17.4	16.6	25.3	44.0	51.7	71.1
France	35.3	37.1	38.6	39.3	40.7	40.6	40.6	40.2	41.2	45.5	52.5	55.9
Germany	41.1	41.7	42.5	42.5	43.8	44.4	43.2	44.0	41.7	44.4	48.5	60.4
Greece	41.2	49.5	57.9	58.6	64.5	71.1	76.0	89.0	96.3	104.7	106.1	120.7
Ireland	97.0	101.3	104.3	116.0	117.1	113.0	103.5	96.8	96.6	92.2	90.5	88.1
Italy	72.0	77.4	84.3	88.2	92.6	94.8	97.9	100.5	103.8	108.3	113.9	123.1
Japan	66.6	67.9	68.7	72.3	74.9	72.9	70.6	69.8	67.7	71.1	74.7	78.8
Netherlands	60.9	65.0	68.4	69.9	73.5	76.2	76.3	76.5	76.4	77.1	79.0	79.0
Norway	38.8	38.7	40.7	51.1	42.7	42.5	42.7	39.2	38.5	41.3	44.8	47.0
Portugal	56.5	63.0	66.5	64.3	72.4	75.2	71.7	66.6	67.5	63.3	67.5	61.8
Spain	38.7	45.4	50.8	51.8	51.2	47.4	48.7	48.7	50.0	53.2	59.1	64.1
Sweden	65.5	67.0	67.6	67.1	59.1	53.5	48.4	44.4	53.4	70.1	83.0	92.9
U.K.	52.9	54.4	52.7	51.1	48.6	42.2	36.7	34.6	35.4	40.6	46.5	51.8
U.S.	43.6	44.9	48.1	51.0	52.0	52.7	53.2	55.4	58.9	62.0	63.9	64.5
G-7	49.5	51.2	53.8	56.1	57.5	57.3	56.9	58.1	60.0	63.7	67.2	70.6
Industrial Countries	50.3	52.2	54.8	57.1	58.3	58.1	57.7	58.8	60.8	64.5	68.1	71.6

Sources: OECD 1994; and IMF *World Economic Outlook*, various issues.

through higher taxes, as in fact has happened in many industrial countries, the inefficiencies and distortions connected with higher marginal tax rates will increase. All of these factors will contribute to a reduction in the prospects for economic growth.

Fourth, if domestically financed, higher debt may lead to higher consumption and lower saving. For one, higher debt will lead to higher incomes for the holders of government securities, who tend to be older or retired individuals with lower (remaining) life expectancy and, thus, with a higher propensity to consume. This will, once again, tend to reduce a country's growth potential. If the higher debt has been financed by foreigners, potential balance of payment problems may develop, because a heavily indebted country needs to transfer a growing portion of domestic resources abroad to service its debt. Unless the country keeps borrowing abroad, it will eventually need to run a surplus in its trade balance in order to earn the foreign exchange to make the foreign interest payments. Because this surplus occurs in the private sector, from which the government needs to buy the foreign exchange, the country will need to have a surplus in its domestic fiscal accounts in order to buy the foreign exchange from the private sector in a non-inflationary way. Creating this surplus through higher taxes will create more distortions in the economy (see Reisen 1990 for a discussion of this issue).

Finally, public debt that is both large *and* growing always brings some *potential* or actual financial instability. This may occur because of several reasons including implicit or explicit pressures on the central bank to facilitate the financing of the debt; concerns on the part of those who hold the debt about the ability of the government to keep servicing it or, more likely, about future taxation of the stock of public debt or of the interest on it (which reduces the debt holders' willingness to hold the debt instruments and leads to an interest rate premium); the impact of changes in international interest rates on the cost of financing the debt; and varying psychological attitudes on the part of current or potential bond holders.[8]

Table 10.4 shows the increasing cost of the public debt in terms of gross interest payments. For the G-7 countries combined, that cost has increased from less than 2 percent of GDP in the early 1970s to almost 5 percent in 1994. The percentage increase would be shown to be greater if the fall in the rate of inflation in recent years had been taken into account. This fall, of course, increases the *real* expenditure component of interest payment expenditures.

As seen in tables 10.3 and 10.4, over the 1970–1994 period very large *increases* in the debt/GDP ratio occurred in Austria, Belgium,

Canada, Denmark, Finland, Greece, Italy, Japan, Portugal, Spain, and Sweden. Very high *levels* in the debt/GDP ratio were achieved by Belgium, Italy, Greece, Ireland, Canada, and the Netherlands. Significant reductions in the ratio were registered in Ireland and Norway in recent years. In the most recent period, 1990–1994, large increases took place in Canada, Finland, Greece, Italy, Sweden, and the United Kingdom.

In the United States, the debt/GDP ratio fell from 45.4 percent in 1970 to 37 percent in 1981, in part as a consequence of very low or even negative real interest rates and substantial growth in nominal GDP. Between 1981 and 1994, the ratio grew from 37 percent to 64.5 percent (table 10.3). This latter figure may not look very worrisome when compared to other countries. However, as recently as 1981 only two relatively small countries, Belgium and Ireland, had ratios higher than the United States does today. If unattended, the debt ratio can grow very fast and can constrain fiscal (and monetary) policy in ways that cannot be totally anticipated.

FISCAL DEFICITS, PUBLIC DEBT, AND INTEREST RATES

Figures 10.2 and 10.3 visually summarize some of the information discussed earlier. The upper part of figure 10.2 shows the long-run increase in both public revenue and public expenditure as shares of GDP for both the G-7 countries and all industrial countries. (A table showing expenditure and revenue trends over the 1970–1994 period for each of 18 countries as well as for the G-7 and industrialized countries as a whole is available from the authors.) The lower part of figure 10.2 shows the behavior of general government balances and of net private saving for G-7 countries and of general government balances for the industrialized countries.

The combination of rising fiscal deficits and falling net private saving might be causally linked and is likely to create difficulties for these economies. Figure 10.3 (top sections) shows the movements in net private saving in relation to both interest payments by the government and gross public debt. The lower panels of the figure show the behavior, over 24 years, of long-term real interest rates and the share of public debt to GDP. It is clearly possible, as seen here, that the rise in the aggregate share of public debt as a percentage of aggregate GDP may cause a rise in long-term real interest rates. This possibility has been recognized and investigated in several studies that, with few

Table 10.4 GROSS INTEREST PAYMENTS OF INDUSTRIAL COUNTRIES, 1970–1994 (PERCENTAGE OF GDP)

	1970	1971	1972	1973	1974	1975	1976	1977	1978	1979	1980	1981	1982
Austria	1.1	1.0	1.0	1.0	1.0	1.3	1.7	1.9	2.2	2.3	2.5	2.8	3.1
Belgium	NA	NA	NA	NA	NA	3.6	3.7	4.1	4.5	5.1	6.1	7.7	9.1
Canada	3.6	3.7	3.8	3.8	3.6	3.8	4.1	4.3	4.8	5.0	5.4	6.3	7.2
Denmark	NA	1.4	1.3	1.3	1.2	1.2	1.4	1.9	2.2	3.5	3.9	5.3	6.0
Finland	1.0	1.0	0.9	0.8	0.6	0.6	0.6	0.8	0.8	0.9	1.0	1.1	1.3
France	1.1	1.0	0.8	0.8	0.8	1.2	1.1	1.2	1.3	1.4	1.5	2.0	2.0
Germany	0.4	0.4	0.4	0.4	1.3	1.4	1.6	1.7	1.7	1.7	1.9	2.3	2.8
Greece	0.9	1.0	1.0	1.0	1.3	1.4	1.6	1.5	1.7	2.2	2.4	3.2	2.6
Ireland	3.7	3.6	3.3	3.4	3.6	4.1	4.6	4.9	5.3	5.7	6.2	7.0	8.5
Italy	1.6	1.8	2.1	2.2	2.5	3.0	3.6	3.8	3.6	3.7	5.3	6.0	6.6
Japan	0.4	0.4	0.5	0.6	0.6	1.2	1.5	1.9	2.2	2.6	3.1	3.5	3.8
Netherlands	3.5	3.5	3.4	3.3	3.5	3.7	3.7	3.8	3.9	4.1	4.5	5.4	6.1
Norway	1.8	1.8	2.0	2.0	2.1	1.7	2.1	2.4	2.8	3.2	3.4	3.3	3.2
Portugal	NA	NA	NA	NA	NA	NA	NA	1.7	2.7	2.9	3.1	5.3	5.3
Spain	NA	NA	NA	NA	NA	NA	NA	NA	NA	NA	0.7	0.8	1.0
Sweden	1.8	1.9	1.9	1.8	2.0	2.1	2.1	2.5	2.6	3.0	4.1	5.3	6.8
U.K.	3.9	3.6	3.5	3.6	4.2	3.9	4.2	4.3	4.2	4.4	4.7	5.0	5.0
U.S.	2.2	2.1	2.1	2.2	2.3	2.4	2.5	2.4	2.5	2.8	3.1	3.6	4.1
G-7	1.9	1.8	1.8	1.9	2.1	2.3	2.4	2.5	2.6	2.8	3.3	3.8	4.2

	1983	1984	1985	1986	1987	1988	1989	1990	1991	1992	1993	1994
Austria	3.0	3.4	3.5	3.7	3.9	3.9	4.0	4.1	4.3	4.3	4.4	4.2
Belgium	9.2	9.7	10.5	11.0	10.4	10.0	10.2	10.7	10.4	NA	NA	NA
Canada	7.3	7.8	8.4	8.5	8.3	8.3	9.0	9.5	9.6	9.2	9.1	9.2
Denmark	8.1	9.6	9.9	8.8	8.3	8.0	7.5	7.3	7.4	6.9	7.8	7.3
Finland	1.5	1.6	1.8	1.7	1.7	1.6	1.4	1.4	1.9	2.6	4.8	5.4
France	2.6	2.7	2.9	2.9	2.8	2.7	2.7	2.9	3.1	3.4	3.1	3.3
Germany	3.0	3.0	3.0	3.0	2.9	2.9	2.7	2.7	2.9	3.6	3.6	3.9
Greece	3.7	4.6	5.3	5.7	7.2	7.9	8.2	9.6	10.5	NA	NA	NA
Ireland	9.0	9.5	10.3	9.3	9.3	8.7	7.8	7.8	7.6	7.0	6.7	5.7
Italy	7.3	8.0	8.0	8.5	8.0	8.1	8.9	9.6	10.2	11.4	12.0	10.6
Japan	4.2	4.4	4.4	4.4	4.4	4.2	4.0	3.9	3.8	3.8	3.7	4.3
Netherlands	6.8	7.3	7.5	7.4	6.4	6.3	6.0	6.0	6.2	NA	NA	NA
Norway	3.3	3.3	3.5	4.3	4.3	3.9	4.0	3.9	3.6	3.6	3.7	4.0
Portugal	6.1	8.2	9.3	9.7	8.8	8.2	7.2	8.5	NA	NA	NA	NA
Spain	1.3	2.0	3.5	4.0	3.5	3.4	3.5	3.5	4.0	4.2	5.3	5.4
Sweden	7.2	7.6	8.4	7.4	6.5	5.6	5.4	5.0	5.1	5.7	6.1	6.8
U.K.	4.7	4.8	4.9	4.5	4.2	3.9	3.7	3.4	3.0	2.9	2.9	3.3
U.S.	4.3	4.6	4.8	4.9	4.8	4.7	4.8	4.9	5.0	4.7	4.4	4.7
G-7	4.4	4.7	4.9	4.9	4.7	4.7	4.7	4.8	4.9	4.9	4.8	5.0

Sources: OECD 1994; and *World Economic Outlook*, various issues.

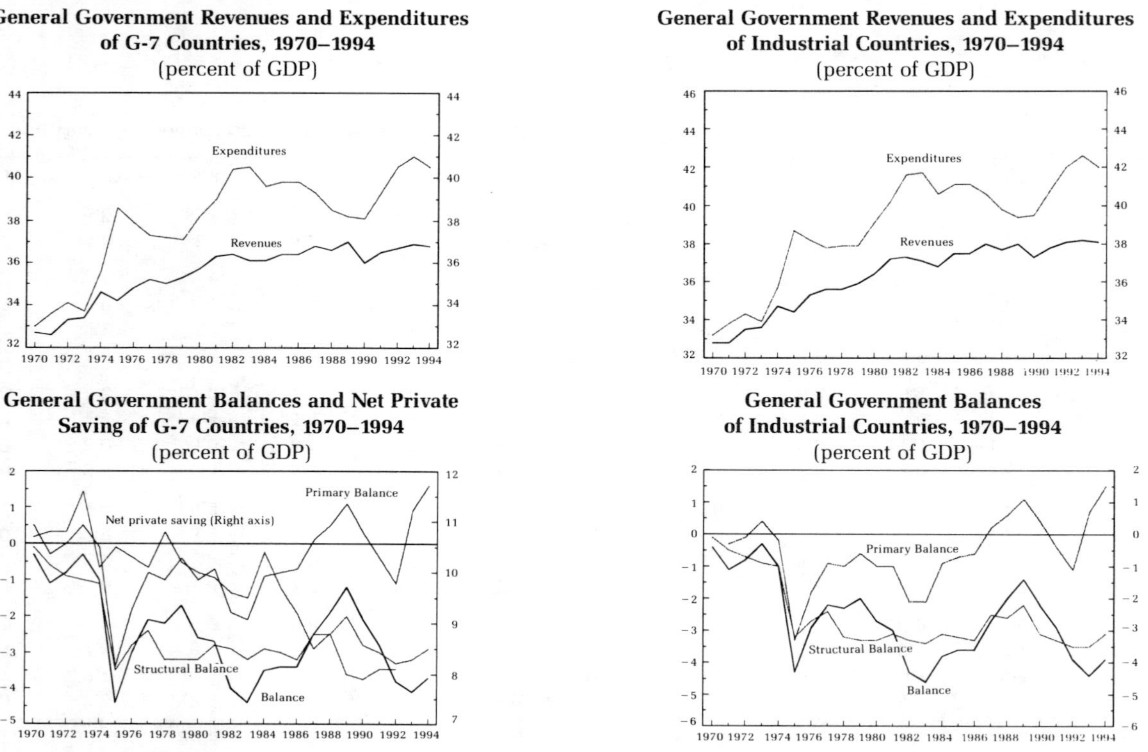

Figure 10.2 GENERAL GOVERNMENT EXPENDITURES, TAXES, AND BALANCES, 1970–1994

Sources: OECD 1994; IMF *World Economic Outlook*, various issues; and authors' calculations.

Figure 10.3 GOVERNMENT INTEREST PAYMENTS AND DEBT, REAL INTEREST RATES, AND NET PRIVATE SAVING, 1970–1994

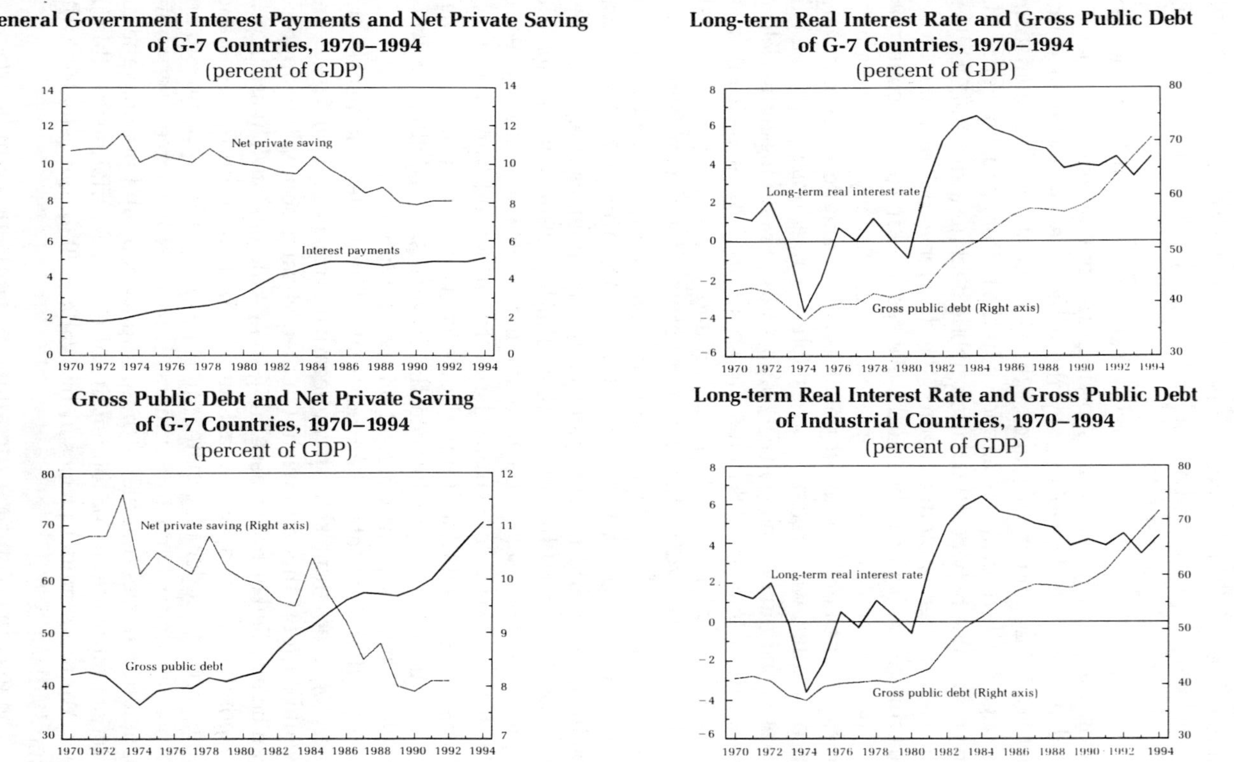

Sources: OECD 1994; IMF *World Economic Outlook*, various issues; and authors' calculations.

exceptions, have generally concerned individual countries (*U.S. Economic Report of the President* 1994). With the exception of the United Kingdom, a high debt/GDP ratio appears to be associated with a high long-term real interest rate.

For Italy (figure 10.4) the relationship appears to be particularly strong, especially when, as shown in the middle panel, the level of real interest rate is replaced by the difference in real interest rates between Italy and the average of the G-7 countries. The relationship strengthens further when, as shown in the bottom panel of figure 10.4, the difference between the Italian public debt (as a share of GDP) and the G-7 average is plotted against the difference between the level of real interest rates in Italy and the average level in the G-7 countries.

The econometric results reported in table 10.5 represent an attempt to assess the effects of fiscal policies on real long-term interest rates. In particular, we attempted to establish a relationship between the level of the public debt-to-GDP ratio and the real long-term yield on government bonds in 18 industrial countries. This exercise is based on the idea that, in essence, monetary and fiscal macropolicies consist of decisions regarding the size of government budgetary deficits and the way in which they should be financed, either by issuing government bonds or by printing base money. Over time, for given private savings, we would expect easier budgetary policies (i.e., larger deficits) accompanied by non-accommodating monetary policies (i.e., equivalent increases in bond financing) to have a positive effect on the real interest rate, because large deficits would translate into increasing demands for funds. However, when the quantity of base money is increased to finance the larger fiscal deficits, we would expect a smaller positive effect on the real interest rate.

A positive correlation between real interest rates and fiscal variables, together with a short-term negative correlation with base money, would support this approach. On theoretical grounds, this approach can be justified either by assuming some kind of sluggishness in price responses, or by applying a finite horizon overlapping generation equilibrium model of consumption behavior. (An appendix to this paper, available from the authors, illustrates a simple overlapping generation model that yields these implications and provides the theoretical foundations for the empirical exercise performed in this paper. We use a model proposed by Wallace 1984, but see also Miller and Wallace 1985.)

The existing empirical literature on the relationship between real interest rates and fiscal variables has reported mixed results.[9] However, using our panel data for 18 industrial countries over the

Figure 10.4 DEBT-TO-GDP RATIOS AND INTEREST RATES: THE CASE OF ITALY

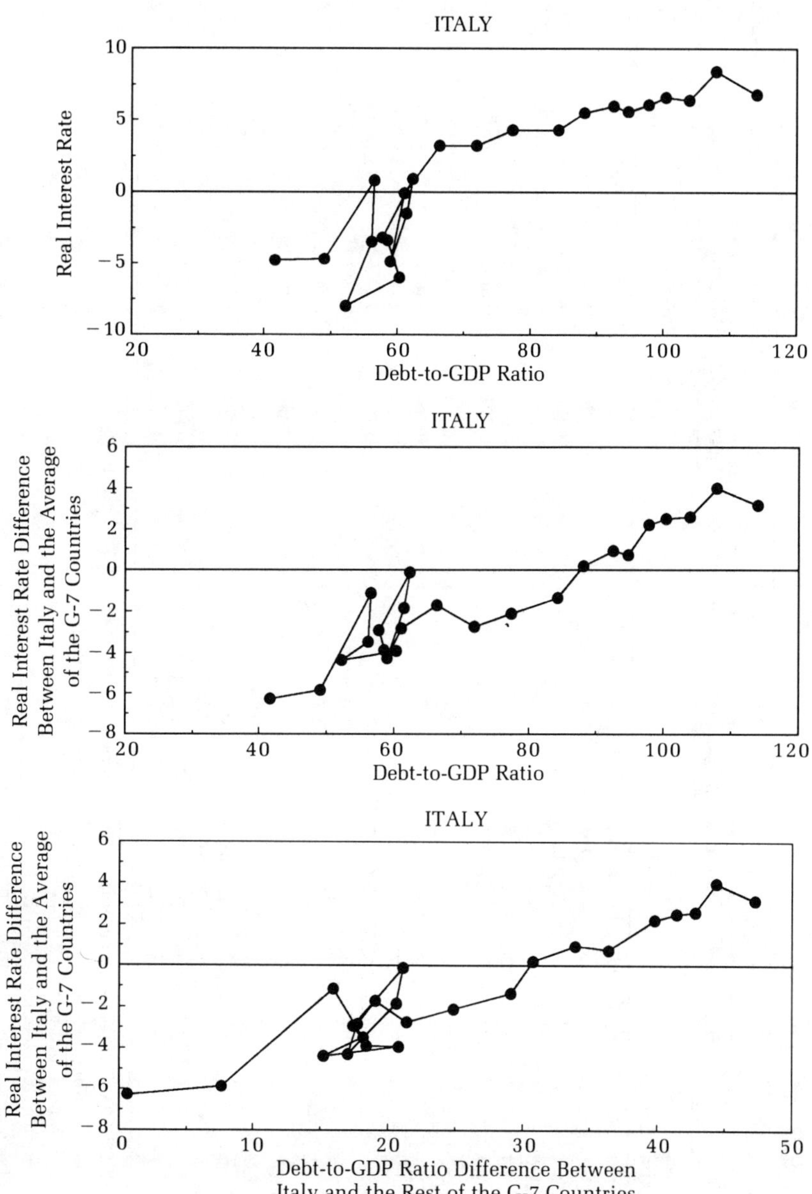

Table 10.5 REGRESSION RESULTS[a]

Countries	Gross Public Debt[b]		Reserve Money[c]		Constant (Fixed Effect)		Constant (Unrestricted)	
	Coefficient	Std. Error	Coefficient	Std. Error	Coefficient	Std. Error	Coefficient	Std. Error
G-18 Countries[d] (Panel Estimation)	0.072	0.002	−0.200	0.019	NA	NA	NA	NA
1. AUSTRIA	0.177	0.014	0.880	0.145	2.760	0.379	−13.427	2.044
2. BELGIUM	0.103	0.015	0.315	0.133	−1.194	0.583	−9.415	2.603
3. CANADA	0.049	0.024	−1.452	0.374	0.336	0.477	8.144	3.017
4. DENMARK	0.088	0.010	0.065	0.111	3.585	0.348	1.699	0.748
5. FINLAND	0.243	0.025	1.006	0.151	2.357	0.923	−5.910	0.854
6. FRANCE	0.410	0.035	−0.760	0.092	0.978	0.588	−9.566	1.611
7. GERMANY	0.058	0.015	−0.486	0.146	3.491	0.318	6.912	1.801
8. GREECE	−0.149	0.027	0.477	0.216	−0.763	1.668	−3.264	4.682
9. IRELAND	0.137	0.030	0.214	0.208	−0.767	0.797	−11.051	4.765
10. ITALY	0.176	0.013	−0.326	0.082	−0.767	0.853	−6.034	1.960
11. JAPAN	0.144	0.016	−1.018	0.341	−0.131	0.694	9.259	3.330
12. NETHERLANDS	0.212	0.027	1.980	0.270	0.393	0.566	−1.364	1.623
13. NORWAY	−0.024	0.063	−1.980	0.472	0.989	1.267	18.878	3.938
14. PORTUGAL	−0.008	0.032	−0.289	0.066	2.407	1.074	8.177	2.593
15. SPAIN	0.222	0.039	0.029	0.101	2.628	1.001	−5.345	1.560
16. SWEDEN	0.191	0.020	0.569	0.323	−0.270	0.539	−11.239	2.738
17. U.K.	0.072	0.040	−1.271	0.282	−0.901	0.823	5.399	1.720
18. USA	0.140	0.042	−1.631	0.349	0.700	0.637	6.765	2.594

Sources: OECD 1994; IMF *World Economic Outlook*, various issues; and authors' estimates.
a. Results from seemingly unrelated regressions (SUR) on panel data.
b. General government gross debt as a percentage of GDP.
c. Reserve money as a percentage of GDP.
d. Restricts the slope coefficients to be equal across countries.

1970–1993 period, we found that *an increase in the gross debt-to-GDP ratio of 1 percent raises the long-term interest rate by around 7 basis points on average*. Thus, the increase in the debt/GDP ratio that took place between 1980 and 1993 would have increased real interest rates by more than 1.5 percentage points. At the same time, we found evidence of a negative (short-term) relationship between the long-term real interest rate and the ratio of reserve money to GDP. A 1 percentage point increase in this ratio (with respect to GDP) would imply a 20 basis point decline in the real rate. It should be noted that in order to increase the ratio of reserve money to GDP by 1 percentage point, money must increase substantially faster than GDP.[10] Thus, the coefficient estimates shown in table 10.5 appear reasonable and, we stress, do *not* imply that monetary policy could be freely used to manipulate real interest rates. These results suggest that the way in which fiscal deficits are financed matters, and that finite horizon equilibrium models fit our data set better than do infinite horizon models, which imply irrelevance of both monetary and fiscal policies for real variables.

These estimates were obtained by allowing a "fixed effect" for each country, that is, a different intercept for each country regression. However, the slope coefficients have been restricted to be equal across countries. This restriction improves substantially the estimation since it allows one to utilize cross-country information, thus increasing efficiency. These restricted estimates could be interpreted as a summary of the single country estimates, which are reported in table 10.5. In addition to the usual time-series interpretation, these estimates contain information on the relation between the level of the debt-to-GDP ratio and the real interest rate within the set of countries we considered.

The restricted estimates are broadly consistent with the unrestricted estimates (which are also reported in table 10.5). For the major countries, the debt coefficient is generally significant and is of the expected sign. Only three small countries (Norway, Portugal, and Greece) show a negative debt coefficient. However, for Norway and Portugal, the coefficient is not significantly different from zero. Given the size of these countries, it is not surprising to find no evidence of a relationship with *domestic* debt, as international variables can be expected to play a major role. Moreover, Greece and Portugal maintained portfolio restrictions in favor of government bonds that, over most of the sample period, limited the extent to which interest rates reflected market conditions. The coefficient estimates for reserve money tend to vary more across countries. Most of the small countries' estimates have a positive sign, whereas the coefficient estimate is negative for all of the G-7 countries.[11]

The estimation procedure assumed a seemingly unrelated structure (SUR) for both the restricted and unrestricted case. In other words, it was assumed that shocks were correlated across countries, instead of being country-specific. While this assumption appears more than reasonable, it improves the estimates' efficiency substantially. Moreover, a Hausmann's specification test failed to reject this assumption at the usual five percent confidence level.

CONCLUSIONS

In this paper we surveyed the fiscal landscape of most of the industrial countries, focusing on the G-7 countries individually and as a group, showing the extent to which fiscal deterioration has occurred and how widespread this deterioration has been. Our findings lend empirical support to the belief that higher debt/GDP ratios lead to higher real, long-term interest rates. Regardless, the fiscal situation has undoubtedly worsened in many countries because the flow problem of large fiscal deficits is now accompanied by the stock problem of large public debts. Furthermore, the countries examined have less flexibility in their adjustment policies because many of them have largely used up the margin they had on the revenue side. When adjustment comes, it will have to come on the expenditure side and will have to deal additionally with demographic changes that increasingly will have a strong impact on public expenditure.

Notes

1. The speech was given at the 40th Congress of the International Institute of Public Finance, Innsbruck, Austria, August 27, 1984 (De Larosière 1984).

2. For an early argument for this aggregative approach and an attempt to follow it, see Tanzi 1985 and Tanzi and Lutz 1993.

3. See Part Two of this volume. For another interesting analysis of some of the reasons for the fiscal deterioration, see Alesina and Perotti 1994.

4. On the contrary, Tanzi and Lutz (1993) found that the rise in fiscal deficits and in interest payments on the public debt had a negative impact on public sector capital accumulation.

5. When the inflation rate becomes high, national accounts authorities are more likely to make that distinction.

6. These data tables for the United States, the United Kingdom, Japan, Italy, Germany, France, and Canada are available from the authors.

7. For a given primary deficit and level of seignorage revenues, the increase in the debt-to-GDP ratio will be higher the larger the gap between the real interest rate and the rate of growth in the economy, and the higher the existing stock of debt. We denote the debt-to-GDP ratio with b, the government primary deficit as a percentage of GDP with d, reserve money as a percentage of GDP with m, the real rate of growth of the economy with n, the real interest rate with r, and the inflation rate with π. If one assumes constant reserve money as a percentage of GDP, the debt-to-GDP ratio will move over time according to the following law of motion:

$$\Delta b = d + b^*(r - n) - m^*(\pi + n)$$

If $r > n$, this expression implies that to stabilize the debt-to-GDP ratio, a country needs to run a primary surplus of a given magnitude unless revenues from seignorage are significant.

8. There is some evidence that countries with high debt have progressively reduced the tax rates that apply to the interest received from those who hold public sector bonds.

9. For an excellent review of this debate, see Seater 1993.

10. If we assume that base money is 6 percent of nominal GDP, and that GDP grows by 10 percent, then base money would need to increase by almost 30 percent to obtain a 1 percent increase in the ratio to GDP. An M1 multiplier of 2.5 would then imply a substantial loosening of monetary conditions.

11. The real interest rates have been obtained by deflating the interest rate on long-term bonds by the actual average annual increase in the Consumer Price Index. In principle, one should use a measure of expected inflation, which is often computed on the basis of an estimated ARIMA process. The relatively short time series sample precluded an efficient use of this procedure. However, for a number of countries, expectations have been computed with an ARIMA, yielding substantially identical results.

References

Alesina, Alberto, and Roberto Perotti. 1994. "The Political Economy of Budget Deficits." IMF Working Papers, WP/94/85, August.

Blejer, Mario I., and Adrienne Cheasty. 1993. "How to Measure the Fiscal Deficit." Washington, D.C.: International Monetary Fund.

De Larosière, J. 1984. "The Growth of Public Debt and the Need for Fiscal Discipline." Washington, D.C.: IMF.

Friedman, Benjamin M. 1987. "New Directions in the Relationship Between Public and Private Debt." Cambridge, Ma.: National Bureau of Economic Research.

Miller, P., and Neil Wallace. 1985. "International Coordination of Macroeconomic Policies: A Welfare Analysis." *Quarterly Review* (Spring), Federal Reserve Bank of Minneapolis.

OECD. 1994. *National Account Statistics 1970–1994*. Paris: OECD.

Phelps, Edmunds. 1994. *Structural Slumps*. Cambridge, Ma.: Harvard University Press.

Reisen, Helmut. 1990. "Interaction between the Exchange Rate and the Public Budget in Major Debtor Developing Countries." In *Fiscal Policy in Open Economies*, edited by Vito Tanzi. Washington, D.C.: IMF.

Seater, John. 1993. "Ricardian Equivalence." *Journal of Economic Literature* 31, 1 (March).

Tanzi, Vito. 1985. "The Deficit Experience in Industrialized Countries." In *Essays in Contemporary Economic Problems: The Economy in Deficit, 1985*, ed. Phillip Cagan. Washington, D.C.: American Enterprise Institute, pp. 81–119.

Tanzi, Vito, and Mark Lutz. 1993. "Interest Rates and Government Debt: Are the Linkages Global Rather Than National?" In *The Political Economy of Government Debt*, eds. Harrie A.A. Verbon and Frans A.A.M. Van Winden, Amsterdam, North-Holland.

U.S. Economic Report of the President. 1994. Washington, D.C., February.

Verbon, H.A.A., and F.A.A.M. Van Winden, eds. 1993. *The Political Economy of Government Debt*. Amsterdam: North-Holland.

Wallace, Neil. 1984. "Some of the Choices for Monetary Policy." *Quarterly Review* (Winter), Federal Reserve Bank of Minneapolis.

COMMENTS ON "FISCAL POLICY AND WORLDWIDE SAVING AND INVESTMENT"

COMMENT BY MARCUS NOLAND

The paper by Professors Kawai and Onitsuka uses relatively long-run data from OECD countries to abstract from cyclical effects and focus on important macroeconomic relationships. The basic implication of the paper is that government is bad: as the authors succinctly state, "Countries with large budget deficits tend to have low private investment, less favorable current account positions, and high rates of inflation and unemployment; and countries with big governments tend to have low economic growth."

The argument that government activities on both the expenditure and taxation side inevitably distorts private incentives and leads to deterioration in economic performance is a plausible one, though even Kawai and Onitsuka would probably admit some minimal role for government in the provision of public goods. Nevertheless, the evidence presented in the paper does not completely hold together: increase in government size (but not the fiscal balance) reduces growth; deterioration in the fiscal balance (but not the size of government) is associated with inflation and unemployment. Moreover, there is reason to believe (on the basis of results reported in an earlier version of the paper) that some of the correlations reported in panel B of table 8.1 might not be robust to changes in the sample period.

Two sorts of extensions might make the evidence more persuasive. First, some analysis of the robustness of the results to changes in the country and period samples would presumably narrow the number of "stylized facts" that could truly be regarded as such, and provide a better anchor for the political economy exploration in the latter half of the paper. Second, some causality analysis on monthly or quarterly data, though a departure from the long-run orientation of the paper, might provide some insights on transmission mechanisms, which again could be used to sharpen the political economy analysis.

Indeed, the striking thing about the data reported in this paper is just how much variability there is. For some of the Scandinavian countries, the government accounts for approximately 60 percent of output, while for the United States and Japan it accounts for about half of that. At the same time, U.S. tax and expenditure shares are relatively flat, while in the case of Japan they drift upward. This does not appear to be consistent with the paper's depiction of the Ministry of Finance as "benign dictator," nor by implication, with the characterization of multi-party political systems as structurally tending toward larger governments. It might also be noted that although government size appears to have a trend upward (figures 8.1 and 8.2), there appears to be little secular trend in the fiscal balances of the OECD countries (figure 8.3).

One is tempted to posit two related alternative explanations for these stylized facts. First, demographic factors (which are analyzed more fully in other papers in this volume) would appear to be very important: Scandinavia has the oldest populations and the largest governments, while the United States and Japan have the youngest populations (during this period) and the smallest governments.

Second, democratic political systems may, in effect, only belatedly spend out of changes in their permanent or long-term national income. Suppose that, as long-run income levels rise, so do secular demands for insurance in the form of transfers. At the same time, government only gradually adjusts to new circumstances: changes in transfers occur more slowly than changes in income. This implies that looking at a cross-section of countries—countries with positive "shocks" or unexpected increases in long-term incomes—should have relatively small but growing governments. This would appear to be consistent with the Japanese data reported in the Kawai and Onitsuka paper and the experience of Japan during the postwar period. Conversely, negative shock countries should exhibit large governments. However, as long as income was rising secularly, the trend in government size would be ambiguous and depend on whether the positive impact of secular demands for redistribution or the negative lagged adjustment to slower growth would predominate. One is tempted to argue that this could explain the outcomes observed in Scandinavia or in Europe as a whole, though the plausibility of divergence between expected and actual income growth would seem less obvious in these cases than in the case of postwar Japan.

COMMENT BY SEIJI SHINPO

Fiscal policy has two roles—as a major tool of short-term macroeconomic stabilization, and as a determinant of long-run capital accumulation and economic growth. If recession continues for a long time, like the one experienced in Japan from 1991 to 1993, the trade-off between the two roles could become serious. In such cases, policymakers may be obliged to sacrifice one of fiscal policy's two roles.

Since the 1980s the focus of fiscal policy discussion seems to be shifting from its short-term to long-term role. This shift is reflected in the economics literature. According to Dr. Tanzi, although the Keynesian view about the short-run role of fiscal policy was strongly held by policymakers and economists in the 1970s, a skepticism about these views came to influence policy in the 1980s. Gregory Mankiw has pointed out that a group of economists called the New Keynesians is gaining power and that these economists are very different from Old Keynesians.* While Old Keynesians were concerned with excessive saving, New Keynesians fear that the U.S. saving rate is inadequate to maintain America's high standard of living.

Another economic change is reflected in global markets. As Barry Bosworth has pointed out, "In a world of increasing capital mobility, fiscal policy is an increasingly ineffectual tool of domestic stabilization and the role of monetary policy has expanded. Fiscal policy is freer in that situation to focus on longer term concerns of capital accumulation."**

In spite of this shift of focus abroad, the main target of discussion about fiscal policy in Japan is how to reduce excessive saving. The reasons are two-fold. First, the influence of monetarism and new classical economics has been very limited; a large majority of Japanese economists are Old Keynesians. Second, there has been strong pressure from overseas for the Japanese government to take an expansionary fiscal policy stance in order to reduce its current surplus.

However, as indicated in Parts One and Two of this volume, on top of Japan's high government debt-to-GDP ratio, growing entitlements and potential liabilities of the public sector are also enormous. Moreover, the chapters by Dr. Tanzi and Professor Kawai clearly show that

*N. Gregory Mankiw. 1991. "The Reincarnation of Keynesian Economics." National Bureau of Economic Research Working Paper no. 3885. October.

**Barry Bosworth. 1994. "United States Budget Developments." Presented at a conference on the U.S. fiscal situation sponsored by the Institute of Fiscal and Monetary Policy, Ministry of Finance, Tokyo, March 30.

growing public debts have serious negative effects on capital formation. Therefore, more attention should be given to the effects of fiscal policy on capital formation and on the supply side of the Japanese economy. Although the cyclical component of Japan's current surplus might be reduced by a fiscal policy aimed at temporarily increasing demand when unemployment is high, it is not at all justifiable for Japan to reduce its high-employment current surplus—that is, its surplus as measured when labor is more fully employed—in view of a worldwide shortage of saving.

COMMENT BY LOUIS J. MACCINI

In my discussion I want to focus on three topics that go beyond the scope of the papers in Part Three: the monetization of deficits, the intertemporal nature of fiscal policy, and the theoretical framework underlying analyses of the effects of fiscal policy on worldwide saving and investment. My purpose is to identify additional work that needs to be done to understand fully the macroeconomic impact of fiscal policy.

Let me first address the issue of the monetization of deficits. Tanzi and Fanizza perform an extremely useful service in compiling the stylized facts on fiscal deficits and movements in public debt for 18 industrialized countries over the period 1970 to 1993. The authors show rather dramatically that for almost all industrialized countries, fiscal budgets began to deteriorate after the first oil-price shock, improved some in the mid-1980s, and began to deteriorate again in the 1990s. In fact, in some countries, deterioration has now reached alarming levels. It is particularly disturbing that for many countries fiscal deficits as a percentage of GDP are now at higher levels than at any time since 1980.

One issue that arises with the current deterioration of structural fiscal deficits is the prospect that the deficits may eventually be monetized, that is, that the central bank will finance the deficits by purchasing the debt and "printing money"—creating the potential that ultimately a serious inflation problem may develop in many countries. It would have been useful to have data for each country on the degree to which deficits in the past have been financed through money creation for seignorage.

Inflation is not now a widespread problem in the industrialized countries, but our purpose is to look at the future consequences of growing deficits. Structural deficits have now become very substantial in relation to GDP and could worsen in the future, since the aging of the population will put upward pressure on expenditures, and resistance to tax increases will make it difficult to raise revenues. Hence, there is a danger that money finance will be more widely used in the future. Whether or not money finance will be used to finance deficits will depend on the independence of the central bank and related features of various economies. It may be necessary for many industrialized countries to make institutional changes to prevent seignorage from being used to finance deficits in the future, and thereby to prevent inflation from developing as a serious problem. This amounts to a recommendation that countries adopt measures that ensure the independence of the central bank.

A second topic I want to discuss is the intertemporal nature of fiscal policy: persistent deficits must be financed in the future by higher income taxes, expenditure cuts, or seignorage. A particularly interesting issue is whether the data on this intertemporal government budget constraint can be constructed. Granted, this requires assumptions to be made about the future, but it would be useful to gain some picture of the seriousness of the problem across industrialized countries. A practical example of such a procedure is the concept of "generational accounts" advocated by Auerbach, Gokhale, and Kotlikoff in many recent writings.* To be sure, generational accounts do not come to grips with all the issues raised by the intertemporal government budget restraint, but they are at least a useful beginning to putting together intertemporal data on fiscal policy. This is especially so in view of the fact that, given current policies, the aging of the population is apt to give rise to increases in social security, health care benefits, and welfare payments that are thought to worsen the deficit picture in many industrialized countries. Because countries have different aging patterns and thus different future deficit developments, countries with roughly the same deficit picture today may have very different future deficit prospects and thus different generational accounts. Broad comparisons of generational accounts across countries could be useful for understanding the intergenerational distribution of the burden of financing deficits.

The final issue I want to raise is the development of a theoretical framework needed to analyze empirically the effects of deficits on the economy and of policies that attempt to reduce them in the future. A theoretical framework is needed to analyze the effects on saving, in-

*See, for example, their article in *The Journal of Economic Perspectives*, Winter 1994.

vestment, the current account balance, interest rates, inflation, and unemployment. The papers in Part Three of this volume, especially those by Tanzi and Fanizza and Kawai and Onitsuka, perform the useful task of undertaking some empirical work to shed light on the effect of fiscal policy on important economic variables, but I believe additional work with a clearer theoretical framework is needed.

Tanzi and Fanizza undertake some innovative work, finding that, contrary to much previous empirical evidence, higher debt measured across countries seems to push up real interest rates. Kawai and Onitsuka take a similar sample of countries and look at the effects of fiscal deficits on saving, investment, and the current account, and examine the effect of government size on macroeconomic variables including growth and output, inflation, and unemployment. They too find some intriguing results, though I must say that I am troubled by regressions that regress endogenous variables on endogenous variables without worrying about the econometric problems, such as simultaneous equations biases, that arise. The results from such empirical studies may be quite fragile.

While regressions of the type reported in these papers are useful first steps to identifying patterns in data, more careful empirical work will require the development of a theoretical framework to evaluate the effects of fiscal policy changes. Unfortunately, existing standard models have some serious flaws, especially in looking at the intertemporal effects of fiscal policy.

I believe that an appropriate theoretical framework should include at least the following elements:

- To highlight capital mobility and the international transmission of the effects of fiscal policy measures from one country to another, a multi-country model needs to be developed with a focus on the world determination of real interest rates.
- To tackle the sustainability of deficits, the intertemporal government budget restraint will need to be incorporated into the framework—indicating whether current deficits will be closed by income taxes or inflation taxes in the future. Further, households and business firms will need to make intertemporal decisions to deal with changes in fiscal policy variables. Anticipation of future fiscal policy changes may affect current economic variables in this framework.
- If "Ricardian equivalence" prevails, current and future deficits will have essentially no effect on the economy because people react now to prepare to pay for the deficits. Hence, if meaningful and insight-

ful results are to be derived, a rationale—e.g., finite lifetimes or liquidity constraints—for the violation of Ricardian equivalence must be imposed.

- The model will need to allow for the possibility of switches in financing methods, in particular switches from bond financing to tax or money financing of deficits in the future.

I suspect that the tendency to monetize deficits is apt to be more and more likely for industrialized countries if the current bond-financed deficits persist and worsen due to the aging of the population. Hence, a theoretical framework will need to draw out consequences of possible future monetization of the deficits for current economic conditions.

COMMENTS ON THE FUTURE

COMMENT BY EISUKE SAKAKIBARA

I'd like to summarize the discussion in this conference and suggest some lingering issues. I think on the broad line we seem to have agreed in each session, not by conspiracy but by the common sense of the people here. The question is not the theoretical framework versus empirical studies, the question is recognition of the reality facing industrial countries. And the reality is very clear. Aging is a major problem that impinges upon the fiscal authorities of each country.

We seem to have agreed that aging does have a major impact on the fiscal balance in the future, provided that current policies are continued. Mr. Scherer indicated that current policies, current fixed coefficients, need not be considered to be fixed, so that there's room for policy changes and the changes of policy regimes. That is true, but I will come back to this issue later. Even Mr. Scherer seems to agree that provided that these coefficients remain relatively fixed, the impact of aging is quite significant on the future position of the fiscal balance and expenditures.

We also seem to have agreed that prior commitments do have a major impact, again on the fiscal expenditures in the future. Various suggestions have been made, but it is my impression that the main thrust of the argument is that major policies should be either reduction of benefits or restriction of eligibility, on the expenditure side, and on the tax side, either higher taxes or pension premiums. Finally, we seem to have agreed that relatively large expenditures, big government, and deficits do have a negative impact on economic performance and on savings, growth rates, investment, and so on.

One impression I get listening to the discussions of the paper providers is that none of them seems to be plainly, intentionally, consciously optimistic with regard to what we can do to rectify this serious situation. I tend to be quite pessimistic. Of course, being economists, we are asked to provide policies to counteract difficult realities. Unfortunately, the political reality in the G-7 countries is that political leadership has become increasingly weakened. Elections all over the world reflect great uncertainty of direction. Another apparent fact is that there is increasing frustration among the middle class or lower middle class and that they are expressing that frustration in the form of somewhat ad hoc election behaviors. The incumbent in any country or the established institutions like the Ministry of Finance in Japan are having a very difficult problem countering populist attacks on the establishment and on political leaders. This is the major problem, in my perspective, that we have not discussed.

Are we in the political situation where we can really make major decisions with regards to reducing benefits, restricting eligibility, or increasing taxes? Reality seems to be that the state of mass democracy in the United States, Europe, and Japan is a public becoming increasingly irrational, increasingly irritated, and increasingly frustrated with the establishment and the political leadership. This interaction of politics and rational economic analysis is something that needs to be analyzed in the future. As a government official who has to confront this kind of problem almost every day, I am increasingly aware of this populist sentiment, which is widespread in Japan, in the United States, and elsewhere.

COMMENT BY ADRIENNE CHEASTY

Ten years ago, Vito Tanzi's work on the globalization of the fiscal deficit led to an influential proposition: the liberalization of world capital markets that had taken place in the 1970s had removed important limits on governments' access to financing for fiscal deficits; governments were no longer constrained by national savings because they could always outbid private borrowers for world capital. Hence, capital market liberalization would lead to higher fiscal deficits, upward pressure on world interest rates, higher interest rates, the crowding out of private investment, and potentially a slowdown in world growth.

The question of capital market effects on fiscal deficits has resurfaced in the 1990s because of a second wave of capital market liberalization that took place between 1989 and 1990. While the liberalization of the 1970s had integrated industrial country capital, this second round mainly affected developing country capital markets, thereby allowing emerging markets to grow. Our concern, in the context of the new world fiscal order, is for the likely fiscal impact of this recent boom. I suggest that fiscal pressures are playing out very differently in the 1990s than in the previous two decades.

In particular, the second round of capital market liberalization did not create the same fiscal pressure as the first, because the fiscal environment and the macroeconomic institutions of the 1990s are qualitatively different from those of the 1970s. One piece of evidence is that real interest rates dropped from around 5 percent in 1987 to about 3.5 percent at the end of 1993, despite the build up in G-7 debt from 58 percent of GDP in 1987 to 67 percent in 1993 (Tanzi and Fanizza, table 10.3). So, then, what is different?

First, fiscal developments in a large bloc of the G-7 countries have been constrained—if not determined—since the late 1980s by the fiscal convergence criteria of the Maastricht Treaty. As you know, these countries' deficits must be below 3 percent of GDP, and public debt below 60 percent of GDP, before they can be admitted to the European Monetary Union, which plans to be fully operational by 1999. Buiter et al. show that the impact of attempts to comply with the criteria by the deadline imply a strong fiscal contraction for European Union countries.* Their analysis is borne out by the calculations in the IMF's *World Economic Outlook*, which indicate that the fiscal impulse for all G-7 countries other than Japan has been contractionary or neutral in all years but one since 1986. Thus, while debt has continued to rise—because deficits have been lowered but not eliminated—pressure on interest rates has been alleviated by the relative withdrawal of government from European Union economies. One must thus conclude that the union-on-the-horizon has fundamentally changed the global fiscal environment of the 1990s.

Second, the private sector has begun to fight back against government competition in the capital market. Since the late 1980s, capital markets have seen a massive shift into securitized borrowing and a mushrooming of foreign direct investment, especially in emerging markets. The newly fashionable forms of private sector capital have more of the characteristics of government debt than did the unsecured bank loans of the 1970s and 1980s: securitization spreads risk; foreign direct investment collateralizes capital. The result has been a large turn-around in the uses of industrial country savings. Mark Robson's table 9.3 gives us a graphic illustration. It shows cross-border direct investment in the United States swinging from a net inflow of around

*Willem Buiter, Giancarlo Corsetti, and Nouriel Roubini. 1993. "Excessive Deficits: Sense and Nonsense in the Treaty of Maastricht." *Economic Policy*, April.

US$ 40 billion in 1989 to a net outflow of US$ 15 billion by 1991. Hence, from now on any analysis of interest rate determinants must take into account the recently enhanced ability of the private sector to compete with government for capital. Of course, one perverse corollary is that the incentive for government to cut its deficit in order to release funds to jump-start private investment is much reduced when a significant share of fiscal savings may well go abroad.

Finally, no analysis of debt and interest rates in the 1990s will be able to avoid adjusting for the cost of financing the transition of planned economies to the market. These economies have larger deficits than in the West, and an urgent need to replace their public infrastructure. Hence, we should expect to see a higher world fiscal deficit, growing public debt, and upward pressure on interest rates throughout the 1990s on account of this adventure in integration. But such effects represent the impact of a one-time stock adjustment and should not be confused with a secular upward shift in deficits. Had capital markets not become more liberal and efficient before the Berlin Wall came down, the drain on savings to finance transition economy deficits would have been more painful.

COMMENT BY MICHAEL DALY

Large deficits do not automatically mean lower saving, investment, and economic growth. Nevertheless, there is widespread agreement that present public debt levels are excessive and could therefore have serious adverse effects on macroeconomic performance. Consequently, most OECD member countries have either announced plans or are currently taking steps to achieve fiscal consolidation.

How might the existing fiscal situation evolve in the near future and to what extent will already implemented or planned consolidation measures redress fiscal imbalances in OECD countries? According to the December 1994 *OECD Economic Outlook* (no. 56), government deficits as a proportion of GDP for member countries as a whole could decline from 4.2 percent in 1993 to 1.8 percent in the year 2000. However, public debt could continue to grow from an average level of 68 percent of GDP in 1993 to close to 75 percent in 1996, before dropping slightly to around 73 percent in the year 2000. It is noteworthy that this stabilization of debt/GDP ratio by 2000 requires primary balances to move from a deficit of roughly 1.7 percent in 1993 to a surplus of around 1 percent in 2000.

Unfortunately, improved fiscal balance is far from assured, in either the medium or the long term. The above are medium-term projections based on the assumptions of a 2.5 to 3 percent average annual growth rate of real GDP and a 3.5 percent real long-term interest rate. If growth falters and/or real interest rates remain high, the projected improvements may not materialize.

In the longer term, some major components of expenditures (such as those associated with public pensions, health care, and transfer payments), and thus the primary deficit are, if anything, perhaps more likely to rise than fall as a result of several factors. One of the most important of these is the aging of populations in most member countries, as discussed in this book.

Countries' fiscal imbalances could also be exacerbated by growing contingent liabilities, particularly those related to unfunded public pension schemes. On the basis of existing demographic trends, the present value of net pension liabilities could be as much as 165 percent of 1990 GDP in the G-7 countries.* In addition, for OECD countries as a whole, total public expenditure on health care as a percentage of GDP rose from 2.5 to 6.4 percent between 1960 and 1992.** The aging population is likely to further increase this share in the future.

Moreover, other transfer payments could continue to remain high—not only if unemployment persists at currently high levels as a result of many countries' failure to address labor market rigidities—but also if, as a result of greater wage flexibility, there is a relative increase in low-wage jobs and thus the proportion of working-poor and single parents in need of income support, child care, and so on. Increased public expenditures on education, training, and retraining are likely to be required in order to improve labor market quality and flexibility. This means that there may be little scope for offsetting increases in expenditures on health and pensions with cuts in expenditures on education as the proportion of the young population relative to the old diminishes. On the other hand, there are a number of factors that lead to a more optimistic assessment. For example, there could be a longer term payoff to such active labor market policies—eventually obviating the need for some income transfers but also expanding the tax base. Another factor that should relieve pressure on the expendi-

*See Paul Van den Noord and Richard Herd. 1993. "Pension Liabilities in the Seven Major Economies." OECD Economics Department Working Paper, no. 142.

**See Howard Oxley and Maitland Macfarlan. 1994. "Health Care Reform—Controlling Spending and Increasing Efficiency." OECD Economics Department Working Paper, no. 149.

ture side is reduced defense spending as a consequence of the end of the cold war. An especially important downward pressure on expenditures in Europe involves likely steps by some European Union members to adhere to two of the Maastricht Treaty convergence criteria, namely those establishing ceilings of 3 and 60 percent, respectively, on deficit/GDP and government debt/GDP ratios.

In general, OECD simulations suggest that fiscal consolidation through higher taxes appears to be more costly in terms of GDP losses, inflation, and unemployment effects than consolidation through expenditure cuts. The reason is that tax increases tend to be inflationary and hence lead to negative effects on real wealth, private demand, and governments' debt servicing.

Although there may still remain some room for achieving fiscal consolidation by broadening the base of existing taxes through the elimination of certain tax expenditures, greater international capital mobility suggests that countries may be forced to restructure their tax systems and rely increasingly on taxes on immobile factors (other than labor) and on consumption. There may also be some scope for the increased use of taxes that pay "double or multiple dividends" by serving several purposes: notably "sin" and eco-taxes, which are designed to correct for market failure by forcing consumers or producers themselves to pay for—and, therefore, reduce—the damages (or externalities) that their consumption or production imposes on others. Also possible are taxes earmarked for specific purposes, since such taxes might be more acceptable to taxpayers.

On the expenditure side, a number of steps may be required:

- Providing more cost-effective public services, notably in health care and education;
- Converting social security systems into a true safety net;
- Removing labor market rigidities and work disincentives that may be embodied in existing transfer programs;
- Increasing retirement age or length of service required for full public pension benefits;
- Increasing contributions (taxes) and reducing benefits;
- Providing adequate capitalization, and encouraging greater reliance on private pension provision on personal saving.

Fiscal consolidation could also be facilitated by greater transparency of current spending as well as future commitments. This would permit closer public scrutiny and evaluation of various expenditure programs, including tax expenditures, thereby contributing to the curtailment of such programs.

A final comment. The manner and extent to which different countries grapple with these problems of fiscal balance and the challenges of aging population could have important repercussions for one another. As one example, insofar as some countries redress their fiscal imbalances more quickly than others and do so by relying on taxes based on consumption rather than income—thus reducing the tax disincentive to save—this could result in their achieving higher savings rates and larger trade surpluses with trading partners who do not consolidate their fiscal positions. Such a scenario would possibly exacerbate international trade friction. As another example, countries might also become increasingly aggressive in their efforts to counteract international tax avoidance, thus provoking disputes between national tax authorities.

COMMENT BY ROBERT D. REISCHAUER

I spend most days warning the Congress of the deteriorating budget situation and the problems that will arise when the baby boom generation begins to retire and the costs of our entitlement programs start to soar. So let me take a break from that role to play Pollyanna, whose voice has been silent at this conference. I will suggest that, with some moderate efforts at reform, the fiscal problems described at this conference may not prove to be as cataclysmic as some of the speakers have suggested.

There are four ways in which we can respond to the commitments we have made to provide benefits to various groups of vulnerable people. The first is to expand the size of the public sector, that is, to raise the taxes necessary to finance these commitments. If this expansion were accomplished through a consumption tax, the consequences for the economy would not be devastating. The consumption of one segment of the population would be supported by a slight reduction in the consumption of the majority. We often look at the future and assume that the constraints that currently shape the political environment will not change. But that is not true. The political environment in which decisions will be made 10 to 20 years from now will be very different from that of today. When faced with the alternatives, the public may be quite willing to pay higher taxes to maintain very popular programs, programs that are of vital importance to their parents and grandparents. If the size of the public sector in the United States or Japan were close to the limits set by the

European democracies, one might consider this to be an improbable scenario. But both countries could probably cover their future commitments through higher taxes and still have public sectors that are smaller relative to GDP than is the case in several European nations today. In other words, neither country would be sailing into uncharted waters.

The second way to respond to the explosion in spending required to meet existing entitlement commitments is to change the composition of public spending to accommodate these commitments. There have been huge shifts in spending in the past. For example, U.S. defense spending, which amounted to 14 to 15 percent of our GDP in 1953-1954, is now under 4 percent. If the deficit could be brought down to $50 billion, debt service outlays would fall by a percentage point or two of GDP, freeing up resources for other uses.

The third way to respond is to scale back our commitments in an implicit or explicit fashion. Most of the discussion at this conference has focused on explicit ways such as means testing benefits or raising the retirement age. These approaches have been and will probably remain non-starters. But it is important to keep in mind that we have had some success with implicit cutbacks. One example of this is the movement to subject benefits to taxation. Unemployment compensation was included in taxable income in the 1970s, and Social Security benefits received by relatively well-off beneficiaries were subjected to tax in the 1980s. The harder task will be to convince middle-class beneficiaries that their Social Security checks should be included in their taxable income. It will require a major education effort to inform the public of the fact that very little of their benefit represents amounts that have been previously subject to tax. That will be a difficult informational and administrative undertaking. One constructive step would be to provide each Social Security beneficiary with an annual statement that showed how much of each individual's benefit represented a return of previous contributions, how much represented a subsidy, and how much represented money that had previously been subject to taxation. There are a number of difficult conceptual problems that would have to be addressed before this type of information could be provided.

A related way to scale back existing commitments in an implicit way is to refine ways in which the tax and the income transfer systems are indexed for inflation. The Consumer Price Index (CPI) probably overestimates changes in the cost of living. Even a half a percentage point reduction in the annual inflation adjustment could make a huge difference in expected revenues and the projected costs of indexed programs. Another means of implicitly reducing our commitments is through major sectoral reform such as health care reform. If we were to adopt the structural reforms some politicians are advocating, we might have a percentage point or two of GDP to devote to other priorities.

The fourth solution to the problem of exploding social commitments is faster economic growth. Since 1973, the United States has experienced relatively slow growth in productivity and per capita income. Some economists expect growth to speed up as computer and communications technologies mature. If this occurs, the pie will be bigger and a larger slice could be devoted to public social commitments.

In the end, all four of these mechanisms are likely to contribute to solving the problem identified by this conference. What we face is a difficult, but not an insurmountable, problem. We shouldn't be too discouraged by the current state of affairs nor too worried about the political constraints that limit the scope of policy responses today. As Paul Posner and Barbara Bovbjerg point out in their paper, democracies do respond to problems, but only when they absolutely have to.

ABOUT THE EDITORS

Masahiro Kawai is a professor of economics at the Institute of Social Science, University of Tokyo. He received his Ph.D. in economics from Stanford University. He has taught at the University of British Columbia and Johns Hopkins University. His most recent publication is "Accumulation of Net External Assets in Japan," in Sato, Levich, and Ramachandran, eds., *Japan and International Financial Markets: Analytical and Empirical Perspectives*, 1993.

C. Eugene Steuerle is a senior fellow at the Urban Institute and author of a column, "Economic Perspective" for *Tax Notes* magazine. He has worked under four different U.S. presidents on a wide variety of social security, health, tax, and other major reforms. His books include *Retooling Social Security for the 21st Century: Right and Wrong Approaches to Reform*, 1994; and *The Tax Decade: How Taxes Came to Dominate the Public Agenda*, 1992—both published by the Urban Institute Press.

ABOUT THE AUTHORS

Barbara Davis Bovbjerg is assistant director of budget issues for the U.S. General Accounting Office. She received her Master's of Regional Planning from Cornell University in 1978. Previously she led the city-wide analysis unit of the District of Columbia's Budget Office; prior to that she was a research associate at the Urban Institute, analyzing state and local fiscal strategies.

Joseph J. Cordes is professor of economics, chair of the Department of Economics, and director of the Ph.D. Program in Public Policy at George Washington University. From 1989–1991 he was Deputy Assistant Director for Tax Analysis at the Congressional Budget Office. He has published widely on tax policy, government regulation, and government spending.

Domenico G. Fanizza is an economist with the Fiscal Affairs Department of the International Monetary Fund. His fields of specialization are macroeconomics and public finance. His current research interests focus on the link between capital taxation and growth, and on the effects of both tax and expenditure policies on the business cycle.

Toshihiro Ihori is professor of economics at the University of Tokyo. His research interests include public economics, fiscal dynamics and growth, and macroeconomics. His book, *Public Finance in an Overlapping Generations Economy*, is forthcoming from Macmillan.

Yusuke Onitsuka is a professor in the Department of Social and International Relations at the University of Tokyo. He holds a Ph.D. in Economics from the University of Chicago. He has been professor and associate professor at Yokohama National University and Osaka University, an economist at the International Monetary Fund, and lecturer at the Illinois Institute of Technology.

Paul Posner is director for budget issues at the U.S. General Accounting Office (GAO). He oversees GAO's work assessing the effects of federal deficits, alternate deficit reduction strategies, and options for restructuring the federal budget process. Previously he directed the federal program review office of New York City's Office of Management and Budget.

Mark H. Robson is principal administrator in the Fiscal Affairs Division, Organisation for Economic Cooperation and Development in Paris. He was also tax manager/senior manager at KPMG Peat Marwick in London; economic adviser to the Board of Inland Revenue, London; and research associate for Financial Markets Group, LSE, London. His most recent articles include "Charity and Consideration" (coauthor), *British Tax Review*, 1993.

Peter Scherer is head of the Social Affairs and Industrial Relations Division of the Organisation for Economic Cooperation and Development. He was previously acting director of the Bureau of Labour Market Research in Canberra, Australia; research fellow at the Centre for Economic Policy Research at the Australian National University; and lecturer in the Department of Industrial Relations at the University of Sydney.

Vito Tanzi is director of the Fiscal Affairs Department at the International Monetary Fund (IMF). Before joining the IMF he was professor and chairman of the Department of Economics at American University. He has worked as a fiscal expert in a large number of countries and has published many books. His major interests are public finance, monetary theory, and macroeconomics.

Naohiro Yashiro is professor of economics at the Institute for International Relations, Sophia University (Tokyo), and senior economist at the Japan Center for Economic Research. He has also been senior economist at Japan's Economic Planning Bureau under the Economic Planning Agency. He received a Ph.D. in economics from the University of Maryland.

ABOUT THE COMMENTATORS

Adrienne Cheasty is senior economist at the International Monetary Fund. She has previously taught at Yale University, John F. Kennedy School of Government at Harvard University, and at the School for Advanced International Studies at Johns Hopkins University. Her recent publications include *Financial Relations Among Countries of the Former Soviet Union* (co-author), IMF, 1994.

Michael Daly is principal administrator in the Economics Department of the Organisation for Economic Cooperation and Development. His main research focuses on taxation and trade. His publications include "Corporate Tax Harmonization and Tax Competition in Federal Countries: Some Lessons for the European Community?" *National Tax Journal*, 1993.

Katsuhiro Hori is professor of law at Sophia University. He graduated from the University of Tokyo and studied social policy and administration at the London School of Economics. He has worked for Japan's Ministry of Health and Welfare. His current research interests include public pensions and long-term care insurance.

Yasushi Iwamoto is an associate professor at Kyoto University's Institute of Economic Research and senior economist at the Ministry of Finance's Institute of Fiscal and Monetary Policy. His research interests are public economics and macroeconomics. His papers include "Effective Tax Rates and Tobin's Q," *Journal of Public Economics*, 1992.

Yutaka Kosai is president of the Japan Center for Economic Research. From 1981–1987 he was a professor at the Tokyo Institute of Technology and prior to that served in many different capacities at Japan's Economic Planning Agency. He received an M.A. in economics from Stanford University.

Louis J. Maccini is professor of economics and chair of the Department of Economics at the Johns Hopkins University. His research is primarily focused on the intertemporal effects of deficits and on theoretical and empirical work on inventory movements. His publications include "Twin Deficits Versus Unpleasant Fiscal Arithmetic in a Small Open Economy," *Journal of Money, Credit & Banking*, August 1995.

Marcus Noland is a senior research fellow at the Institute for International Economics. He has taught at the University of Southern California and at Saitama University (near Tokyo). His most recent works include *Japan in the World Economy* (co-author), and *Pacific Basin Developing Countries: Prospects for the Future*—both published by the Institute for International Economics.

Robert D. Reischauer is a senior fellow at the Brookings Institution. From 1989 to 1995 he was director of the Congressional Budget Office. In 1975, he helped Alice Rivlin set up the Congressional Budget Office and then served as Assistant Director for Human Resources and Community Development and later as Deputy Director. He is an economist who has written extensively on federal budget policy, Congress, social welfare issues, poverty, and state and local fiscal problems.

Stanford G. Ross is a senior partner in the law firm of Arnold & Porter, where he specializes in federal tax law and administrative law. He is also Public Trustee of the Social Security and Medicare Trust Funds. He has dealt extensively with public finance issues while serving in the Treasury Department, on the White House domestic policy staff, and as Commissioner of Social Security. He is the author of many papers on federal taxation and income security subjects.

Eisuke Sakakibara is director general of the International Finance Bureau, Ministry of Finance. He has served in many different positions at that ministry, most recently as president of its Institute of Fiscal and Monetary Policy. He has published numerous books and articles in English and Japanese including *Japan Beyond Capitalism*, Tokyo, 1990 [in Japanese]. He received a Ph.D. in economics from the University of Michigan.

Hiroshi Shibuya is professor of public finance at the Institute of Social Science, University of Tokyo. His books include *U.S. Tax History* (1995) and *Reagan's Budget Deficit and Tax Reforms* (1992), both published in Tokyo.

Seiji Shinpo is deputy director of the General Coordination Bureau, Economic Planning Agency (Japan). From 1993 to 1995 he was vice president of Japan's Institute of Fiscal and Monetary Policy at the Ministry of Finance. His research focuses on macroeconomics.

John B. Shoven is dean of the School of Humanities and Sciences at Stanford University. He previously served as director of the Center for Economic Policy Research. His research has focused on taxation, the inflation process, the impact of comparable worth legislation, the determinants of saving, various aspects of Social Security, pension funding, intellectual property rights and economic growth, and the cost of capital in the U.S., Japan, and Canada.